A FORCE FOR JUSTICE

Also by Michael Clifford

Non-fiction
Love You to Death
Scandal Nation (with Shane Coleman)
Bertie Ahern and the Drumcondra Mafia (with Shane Coleman)

Fiction
Ghost Town
The Deal

A FORCE FOR JUSTICE

The Maurice McCabe Story

Michael Clifford

HACHETTE
BOOKS
IRELAND

First published in 2017 by Hachette Books Ireland

2

Copyright © Michael Clifford, 2017

A CIP catalogue record for this title is available from the British Library.

ISBN 978 1 47365 624 6

Typesetting by redrattledesign.com
Printed and bound in Clays Ltd, St Ives plc

Hachette Books Ireland's policy is to use papers that are natural, renewable and recyclable and made from wood grown in sustainable forests. The logging and manufacturing processes are expected to conform to the environmental regulations of the country of origin.

Hachette Books Ireland
8 Castlecourt Centre
Castleknock
Dublin 15, Ireland
A division of Hachette UK Ltd
Carmelite House, Victoria Embankment,
London EC4Y 0DZ
www.hachettebooksireland.ie

In memory of John Clifford

PROLOGUE

It was early afternoon on 24 January 2014 when John McGuinness pulled into the carpark in Bewley's Hotel on the N7 carriageway out of Dublin. The TD for Carlow-Kilkenny was on the way home after a particularly long week in Leinster House. The previous day, he had chaired a meeting of the Public Accounts Committee, at which the garda commissioner Martin Callinan had been a witness for over five hours.

Then that morning he had received a text from Callinan, looking to meet up for a quick chat. He was surprised. At the conclusion of meeting the day before, he had gone over and had a few words with the commissioner, thanked him for coming, probed that there were no hard feelings about how the members of the committee had questioned him.

And that, he thought, was that. McGuinness had since then focused his energy on the next item on the committee's agenda: a highly controversial scheduled appearance from Sergeant Maurice McCabe, the garda whistleblower who was causing major turbulence in Garda HQ. But now Callinan wanted to see him, something to do with McCabe. McGuinness said they could meet in Bewley's on his way back home to Kilkenny if that suited.

Within a few minutes, he spotted Callinan's car entering the carpark, the commissioner in the passenger seat beside his driver. Callinan saw him, nodded and got out of his vehicle, walked over and got into the passenger side of McGuinness's car.

McGuinness had thought they were to meet in the hotel, but now realised that it would take place here.

According to McGuinness, Callinan got straight to the point. Maurice McCabe was not to be trusted. Did McGuinness realise who exactly he was dealing with? Callinan went on to detail what he said were flaws in McCabe's character.

They spoke for about twenty minutes. Callinan then got out of the car, leaving McGuinness with a few words to the effect of hoping he would do the right thing. Callinan denies this version of the exchange.

Within minutes, McGuinness was on the road to Kilkenny, his head a jumble of thoughts.

That had just been one of the most extraordinary meetings of his long career in politics. On one level, he wasn't surprised at the nature of what Callinan had told him. He'd heard the rumours around Leinster House. McCabe, the rumour machine had spewed out, was a man not to be trusted. Tread warily.

And yet McGuinness had met this sergeant from County Cavan and found him genuine and impressive in the detail of what he wanted to convey. They had been in contact now for over two months. The McCabe he was getting to know was far removed from this figure stalking the rumours.

But how could you dismiss what was effectively a briefing from the commissioner of An Garda Síochána? How could you ignore what he had to say? Martin Callinan was one of the most powerful figures in the state, who knew more about what was going on in law enforcement, crime and security than any other individual, overseeing a force of 13,000 members. If you couldn't believe him, then who could you believe?

Of course that was what it all came down to. Who do you believe? Do you believe the commissioner of An Garda Síochána? Or do you believe this sergeant from a rural outpost, who was now obviously persona non grata within the force and among a large swathe of politicians in Leinster House? Who the hell was the guy who had them all in such a tizzy?

PART I

BEHIND THE BLUE WALL

1

'Good Citizen Praised in Court Hearing' Evening Herald

When Maurice McCabe was twelve, his class was given an exercise to map out their lives from cradle to grave.

Maurice went away and devoured newspaper cuttings to sculpt this fantasy life that he had not yet lived. He cut out photos of babies, and then young boys. For the projected end of his life he got his hands on a photo of an elderly man, whose teeth had gone the way of spent years. Under that photo, he wrote the caption 'Me at 100'.

For his middle ages he cut out a photograph of a police commissioner from Australia, in conversation with another uniformed man. This, Maurice asserted, would be him. He was going to be the head of the Guards one day.

The idea of being a policeman is not uncommon among young boys. The police represent the good guys, and good boys like to pick the right side, chasing after bad guys and putting them behind bars.

The exercise with the essay was to prove prescient in Maurice's life. He would go on to be a policeman, but he would also go on to feature in the public domain, the kind of figure that for a period had his photograph in newspapers, more for being in conflict with the Garda commissioner than for occupying the office himself.

Maurice's fascination with policing and policemen outlived his adolescence. When he was in fifth year in St Oliver Plunkett's in Oldcastle, Co. Meath he went in to have the mandatory chat with the career guidance teacher.

'I want to be a guard,' he told the teacher, who advised that maybe he should get something else behind him before joining up.

Maurice took that on board, but heading into his Leaving Cert he knew there was only one career for him. He would join up and he wouldn't just be a guard, he'd be one of the best of them.

There was no history of policing in the McCabe family. Maurice was born as a twin in 1961 to Michael and Peggy. He and his twin sister Patricia came second last in the family, with older sisters Dominica, Rosemary – who also had a twin who died at age four – and brother Michael. Younger brother Declan arrived a few years later.

The same year that Maurice and Patricia were born, their parents opened a hotel on the banks of Lough Sheelin, a freshwater trout lake that laps up onto counties Cavan, Westmeath and Meath. Michael McCabe had spotted the potential for fishing tourism on the lake, and the Sheelin Shamrock quickly gained a reputation among the fishing fraternity. The family lived in the hotel, and worked hard.

Through the late sixties and into the seventies Michael McCabe demonstrated the kind of drive and resilience in taking on officialdom that his son would ultimately become known for.

Lough Sheelin's reputation as a freshwater lake was slowly being stained with the pollution emanating from up to four dozen piggeries in the region. Michael McCabe led a fight against the piggeries at a time when the agricultural sector had a major foothold in politics. In

1972, Michael McCabe was quoted in a Dáil debate on the pollution problems. Ultimately, the issue had a major impact on the hotel.

In 1991, Peggy McCabe was diagnosed with cancer, and had to step back from the business. Her loss was felt keenly. Not long afterwards, the combination of factors bearing down on the Sheelin Shamrock led to Michael shutting up shop. Soon after, he started up a boat-building business which continues to this day. Peggy McCabe died in 1994.

For Maurice it was an idyllic childhood. Perhaps unusually, he eventually set up home a few miles from where he grew up, within the orbit of his widowed father, and his younger brother, to whom he remains close.

He got involved in sports without being naturally sporty. He wasn't into the GAA, the staple of rural Ireland, but from his teenage years he did develop a fascination with cars. This was something that was handed down to him by his father, and is an interest he has shared with his brother Declan throughout adulthood. When times got tough for Maurice years later, when pressures piled up and the phone wouldn't stop ringing, his refuge from all the stress was to wash or wax one of his cars.

There was some debate at home and among friends as to where to turn following the Leaving Cert. Maurice's dream of being a guard was fast approaching the realisation stage. After much thought, he decided that it might be best to delay entry for a few years. Instead, he opted to check out third-level education to see where it might take him. For a youth with an interest in cars, the best thing on offer was a mechanical engineering course at Dundalk Regional Technical College, as it then was. He applied and was accepted, packed his bags and left home.

Student life was all it promised to be – the social awakening, the sense of camaraderie, the freedom, the socialising that for many takes priority over any course being studied. McCabe threw himself into the whole way of life, including the ability to manage the academic side, despite studying as little as possible.

But through it all, the old itch never left him. Frequently, he found himself wandering down to the Garda station in the town. What lay behind the doors and windows retained for him a child's fascination.

One evening when he was hanging around outside, he fell into conversation with a young plainclothes garda. The latter could hardly have missed Maurice's enthusiasm and invited the student in for a look around.

At the time in question, around 1980, Dundalk was one of the busiest – and, for a raw enthusiast, exciting – stations in the country. The town is located just south of the border with Northern Ireland, and the Northern security forces regarded it as a launching post for the IRA's campaign of violence. To that end it was known as El Paso, a reference to the Texan town synonymous with lawlessness in the late nineteenth century.

Maurice drank in all around him during his station tour. The rooms were crowded and loud, with staff either rushing around or busy with heads bowed into paperwork.

Despite the apparent chaos on one level, he loved the sense of order he could detect, a sergeant here giving directions to one of the rank and file, a pair of plainclothes officers on their way somewhere fast, a member of the public being comforted. Within minutes he felt at home. He was momentarily overwhelmed by impatience. Mechanical engineering was alright for the moment, but it would never be a vocation. This was where he belonged.

On 7 July 1980 Maurice was working in the Sheelin Shamrock when news broke of the killing of two gardaí, shot dead following a bank robbery in Ballaghaderreen, Co. Roscommon.

Three armed men were making their escape outside the town when a car occupied by Garda Henry Byrne and Detective Garda John Morley intercepted them. The gunmen opened fire, fatally wounding the occupants of the Garda car. Within hours, two of the gunmen, Colm O'Shea and Pat McCann, were apprehended. Some weeks later, a third man, Peter Pringle, was arrested in Galway. All three were sentenced to death but this was commuted to life in prison. In 1995, Pringle was released after a court of appeal declared his conviction unsafe. The other two were released in 2013.

The deaths of the two gardaí sent shock waves across the country. Despite the ongoing violence in the North, where the death toll mounted on a weekly, if not daily, basis, there was still revulsion when the violence spilled over into the southern state. (The bank robbers had operated under a republican flag, although this was largely regarded as a convenience for their crimes.)

In contrast to that of many European countries, the Irish public enjoyed a close relationship with its police force, whose membership was drawn largely from the rural heartlands. Now, two of them had been murdered, and both were spoken of in glowing terms across the media. Morley, in particular, had been well known because he had played intercounty football with his native Mayo.

Maurice was fascinated and horrified by the deaths. It brought home to him the dangers of policing, but also the heroism. The respectful tones in which the deceased men were spoken about was indicative of their status as guardians of the public.

Michael McCabe was no less appalled. He was of a generation for whom the gardaí represented unquestionable authority. In a black-and-white Ireland that had eked out a living in the post-independence decades, the local guard was up there with the parish priest and the school teacher as standard-bearers of aspiration and authority. Now guards were being shot dead on the roadside.

In 1980, at the height of the Northern Troubles, the killings instilled fear in the psyche of middle Ireland. Since the advent of the Troubles in the late sixties, the gardaí were seen by many as the last bulwark against the violence spilling over onto the streets of the Republic's cities. John Morley and Henry Byrne were the fifth and sixth members of An Garda Síochána to be killed in the course of the Troubles.

As a businessman, Michael McCabe knew that the gardaí had not descended from the pantheon of angels. He had dealings with some who might have had scant regard for the power and moral authority vested in the uniform. But these were more the exception than the rule. And now when two of their number had fallen, he, in common with thousands of his generation and standing, felt the loss as keenly as if the deceased had been drawn from his own local community.

Sensing his son's interest in the matter, Michael McCabe suggested a very Irish thing – that they travel to pay their respects. They drove the near two-hour journey to Knock, Co. Mayo for the removal of the bodies on the eve of the funeral. The father and son were actually captured on the RTÉ camera recording the event, two figures at the periphery of the gathering outside the church.

The occasion left an indelible mark on nineteen-year-old Maurice, deeply moved by the inexplicable grief that permeated the thousands who felt they had lost one of their own, even though the deceased were not personally known to most of them.

He couldn't help noticing the sense of belonging that bonded processions of guards, turned out impeccably, marching for their fallen comrades. The whole occasion was, for him, proof positive that he was making the right decision. He would one day belong to that band of brothers.

The following year, impatience got the better of Maurice and he quit his course in Dundalk RTC. He returned to the Sheelin Shamrock, where he worked for another two years, awaiting the next opportunity for entry to the force.

In 1983, as is still the case today, the police force was a popular career choice. Typically, the number of applications was a multiple of the places available.

The application process was broken into three parts: written exam, interview and medical. Maurice had no problem with the first two. A few days after completing the medical, however, he received shocking news by post. His application was rejected because he did not make the height requirement of five foot nine inches. He was one-eighth of an inch too short.

He briefly fell into a state of despondency. The door to his future had just been slammed shut, with an accompanying note that he wasn't suitable material.

He had never contemplated a return to college. He didn't mind the work in the Sheelin Shamrock, he got on well with his old man within the context of a family business, but it had always just been a pit stop on the road to the guards. Now that road was closed.

After a few days, however, his despondency was replaced with resolve. There was no way that one-eighth of an inch was going to have an impact on his chosen life. For the following six months, Maurice slept on a board on the floor beside his bed. The objective was to straighten out the smallest kink there might be in his spine, that little twist that in the ordinary course of a life meant very little, but right now meant the world.

He had been given a window in which he would be able to have his medical reassessed. So it was that six months later he returned for the assessment, confident that he was now straightened out and ready to report for training.

But this time it wasn't his height that stood in the way but his weight. In the complicated assessment used by the force, Maurice McCabe was now deemed, at nine stone, to be too light to serve. The sacrifice and discomfort hadn't done the job. Try again next time.

He returned to work in the Sheelin Shamrock, this time convinced that his dream was merely on hold. A new intake was scheduled for the following year, and he was determined that nothing would come between him and entry to the guards.

But though he wasn't yet a member of the force, the guard inside him was bursting to get out. This was evident on a trip to Dublin in 1983. He had driven his mother and sister up for the day to go shopping.

He was sitting in his car on Marlborough Street in the city centre, awaiting the return of the shoppers, when he spotted a man emerging from a public house and taking off at pace. It was obvious to Maurice that the man had just robbed the place. Instinctively, he leaped from the car and gave chase.

After a number of minutes, the fleeing robber turning every now and again to see if this busybody was still on his tail, Maurice caught up with his quarry on Talbot Street, grabbing him and pinning him to the ground. As the crowd gathered, he felt the adrenalin pumping in his veins. He had made a citizen's arrest, or at least that was how it felt. Within minutes the real policemen arrived via a patrol car.

Two members jumped out and arrested the robber, offering congratulations to the energetic citizen. A few months later, during the subsequent prosecution, the presiding judge did likewise, prompting a front-page headline in the *Evening Herald*: 'Good Citizen Praised in Court Hearing'.

An interesting aside from the incident was the identity of the arresting officer who emerged from the patrol car. Some sixteen years later, Maurice would recognise him and approach him on the first day of a promotion course for sergeants that the two men were attending.

The recruitment notices went up again the following year, 1984, and this time Maurice got through the process with more confidence.

When it came to the interview, he marched in with a copy of the *Evening Herald* under his arm. The three-man panel of senior officers was suitably impressed. So was the medical officer with an individual who just about reached the height requirements and who, while he could perhaps have done with a feed of spuds, had made the grade.

At last, the start that he wanted. Maurice McCabe got word that he was accepted, with an instruction to attend at the training college in Templemore. The rest of his life was opening up.

Training for the gardaí was relocated to the town of Templemore in County Tipperary in 1964. Prior to that, training had taken place in Garda HQ in the Phoenix Park. With the expansion of the force in a modernising society, and space being at a premium in HQ, it was decided to move operations to Templemore.

The town had the perfect facilities in McCan Barracks, an old army venue that had been named in honour of Pierce McCan, the first Sinn Féin TD for Mid-Tipperary, who died on hunger strike in 1919.

History has left its mark on the Victorian barracks, which had been built in 1815 and the subject of plans and attacks against the crown all the way up to the War of Independence. Thereafter it was initially a post for the national army, until it was transferred to the Minister for Justice. So it was that on 14 February 1964 recruits and staff left Phoenix Park and marched to Heuston station, where they boarded the 'Templemore Special' as it came to be known, bound for the wilds of Tipperary.

The relocation of training to Templemore was a significant development in the history of An Garda Síochána, although it would take decades for it to be recognised as such.

Templemore is located in the heart of Munster, on the N62 that connects the main Dublin–Cork and Dublin–Limerick roads (now the M8 and M7 respectively). In the 1980s, the population stood at around 2,000.

Into such a provincial outpost came up to 600 personnel, including staff and recruits. Maurice McCabe walked through the gates of the training college in August 1985, one of a class of sixty, exclusively male, recruits.

The training was tough. Every day was crammed with new material to be learned, on procedure and law and dealing with the public. Physically, the trainees were put through their paces in order to ensure that the required level of fitness was reached within the timeframe.

They were billeted three to a room. Life revolved around the centre, with the odd foray into the town, or to Polly's bar, the local near the barracks. There was a curfew of 11pm and the sleeping quarters were frequently policed by staff patrols.

From the off, the concept of discipline was instilled in the trainees. They quickly got to know all about rank, even from the colour of the ranking officers' shirts. Blue sufficed up to inspector, but those of superintendent rank or higher wore white shirts.

Inspections were a daily occurrence. If shoes were not shining, or buttons were missing, a reprimand was inevitable. Beds had to be made neatly. Again, any deviation from the standards merited a mention. For young men – and only the odd woman in the 1980s – many of whom would have been accustomed to 'the mammy' taking care of most of these things, the shock reverberated on a series of different levels.

More than anything, though, Maurice noticed the importance of discipline. Now that he was in the force, he was answerable to higher authority at all times, which instilled in him the notion of responsibility for all his actions.

Years later, he would reflect that one thing there was no emphasis on was the concept of independent thought, or any notion that received wisdom should always be questioned within an organisation as powerful as a police force.

The first weeks were the loneliest. During that period the regular letters he received from his twin sister Patricia were all that kept him going. Gradually, though, as the shock wore off and body and mind adjusted to the tough regime, the idea that he was fulfilling his childhood dream kept him going.

The twenty-two weeks of training flew by. They got home for Christmas, but in a foretaste of the 24/7 nature of the job, they had to be back on campus the day before New Year's Eve. The following month, Maurice McCabe graduated with his class in front of his proud parents.

He got word the week before graduation that his first posting would be to Drogheda, Co. Louth.

2

'I remember thinking that these guys should be going to college with everybody else. They needed to mix with people of their own age who weren't in the guards.' *Lorraine McCabe*

McCabe was sitting in his Opel Manta, looking out on the broad sweep of the River Boyne as it entered the town of Drogheda. He was barely a wet week in the job. That morning he'd been dispatched down the quay to keep an eye out for a vessel that was carrying explosives for a local quarry.

With the violence in the North just twenty miles up the road, there was always a possibility that one of the paramilitary groups might decide to commandeer the cargo. The chances of such a raid were low, so it routinely fell to a new addition to the station to sit out the arrival.

McCabe, eager to make an early impression, volunteered for the task and headed down to the docks in his own car. He didn't see the two balaclava-clad men approaching. One of them pulled open the driver's door and grabbed him by his shirt front. 'Where's your fucking radio?' he shouted.

McCabe was gripped by a low sense of panic. Barely out of Templemore and here he was being thrust into the frontline of policing in a border county. This was his beginning, and somewhere in his head a low voice told him it could be his end, before he'd even got going.

The two men lunged at him and dragged him from the car. There was nobody around to raise the alarm. He lashed out against them, but they kept pulling him towards the pier's edge. He reached for solace in the knowledge that he could swim. Those torturous sessions in the swimming pool in Templemore might save him.

If they just threw him in, without pummelling him beyond consciousness, he might live. As long as they didn't shoot him.

Then, just as the pier's edge loomed into his peripheral vision, he grabbed out at the collar of one of the men beneath the assailant's jumper. His fingers closed around it, pulling the collar away from the jumper and suddenly relief flooded through every strained muscle in his body.

'Get off, ye bastards, come on,' he shouted as the eyes behind the balaclavas began to widen. Their grip on him loosened, hands raised to remove the balaclavas, and the two assailants revealed themselves as colleagues from his own unit. The pair of them began to fall around the place laughing, while McCabe allowed himself a smile through the receding shock.

He had been warned. Every new recruit was subjected to a prank of one form or another, but never would he have expected it to materialise while he was out on what he regarded as important work.

Back in the station, word spread quickly and he was greeted by knowing smiles for the rest of the day. His two colleagues were not as fortunate. The details of the prank found their way to the superintendent, who was not amused.

He understood the rite of passage thing and was prepared to turn a blind eye for the sake of *esprit de corps*. This was different, though. Bombs were going off just up the road in south Armagh, a no-go zone for the British security forces. The prospect of an attempt to steal explosives under the eye of the local gardaí was not at all fanciful. As far as the super was concerned, this was a prank too far.

He called in McCabe and told him he wanted chapter and verse about the whole incident, starting with the names of the two offenders. McCabe refused, saying it was unfair to expect him to do so. It had been a prank and he had no problem with it.

'You give me those names or you're out of a job,' the superintendent told him. Because McCabe was still on probation, the threat was real. A recommendation from the super that he wasn't fit to be a police officer could spell the end of his career before it had even started.

Following further argument, McCabe eventually revealed the names, and the two men were fined and disciplined. It was an early indication to McCabe of what working for a disciplined force entailed. It also gave him an insight into the power that senior officers could wield.

Such wobbles notwithstanding, the job was everything McCabe had dreamed it would be. In his first two years on the force, every day offered something new. Drogheda was a busy station. The town is on the main Belfast–Dublin corridor, and has a population, including its hinterland, of over 40,000. In terms of the broad spread of human activity that requires the presence of a law enforcement agency, it had everything.

McCabe started off on the beat, pounding pavements with a colleague. This ensured he got to know both the intimate geography of the town and its people. It also meant that the people got to know him.

The daily routine might be interrupted by word of a violent incident or a robbery of one sort or another. Road traffic accidents were a constant. Quickly, McCabe got to grips with one of the more difficult tasks of a garda. Attending at a fatal accident was something that few guards ever grow accustomed to, but a professional approach is required in the name of the victims and their loved ones.

McCabe was a stickler for procedure from the word go. Even early on in his career he could see how easy it was for the criminal justice system to fail. An arrest is made at the scene of an incident, whether it be a public order offence or an instance of drink driving, the suspect is detained, details taken, a report written up, and yet when the whole thing gets to court, it can fall on the smallest procedural issue.

In his first few appearances in court, he saw how prosecutions involving other members ran into the sand, or even how a member suffered embarrassment in open court because all his or her ducks were not in a row. To him, it was simply a matter of doing the job the way it was designed, staying concentrated and not looking for any shortcuts. Apart from his own love of the job, he was just deploying the work ethic that had been instilled in him from a young age.

The shiftwork took a bit of getting used to. Each was eight hours, beginning at 6am, 2pm and 10pm. There were four units in the station. Each Garda unit typically is led by a sergeant. In addition, there was a crime unit, regarded by many as a plum posting. This unit concerned itself with any serious crime, such as burglaries, serious assaults and sexual offences.

For a new recruit, Drogheda provided an excellent grounding, being busy but not chaotic, urban but not one of the more difficult districts in a city.

After two years McCabe was transferred to Dundalk. He didn't want to go, but a system of last in, first out operated when it came to transfers. Within a week of making the move, though, he was thrilled. Dundalk was even busier than Drogheda, with plenty to get the young and eager member through the shift.

The move also brought him back to the town where he'd spent time as a student a few years previously. Now he was turning in an entirely different guise, one of those who was actually operating out of the station of which he had been shown around as a green-eyed student.

He spent the best part of two years in Dundalk and one incident during his spell there would stay with him for the rest of his life.

On the morning of 23 July 1988, McCabe was working as controller in the radio room. All communication to the station, from the public, from members out on patrol or members in radio contact with that station, came through the radio room, which was located on the first floor. At the time, in the pre-internet age, the controller was also responsible for sending and receiving urgent telex messages.

The morning in question was sailing along at its usual steady pace when a call came through at 9.30 from a car leaving Dublin on the Belfast road. The communication was to let the station know that two special branch officers were escorting a Northern Ireland high court judge, Eoin Higgins, up to the border. The judge and his wife had flown into Dublin from a holiday and were en route home. The car supplied McCabe with a code word by which it could be identified when it came into the County Louth area.

All this was routine police work at a time when subversives were active on both sides of the border with Northern Ireland. The station also had a special 'red phone' hotline to the RUC – the then police service of Northern Ireland – to be used in times of emergency. McCabe took the details, including the make of the vehicle being escorted, which was a jeep.

About half an hour later, a detective came into the radio room and asked if there was much happening. When McCabe told him about the escort, the detective said he'd take a spin up there, a routine exercise for the times that were in it.

Within half an hour, the red telephone rang. McCabe lifted it to be told by an RUC man that there had been an explosion just over the border in the North. Had the judge come through?

McCabe immediately contacted the escort car. No, they hadn't reached the border yet. Turn around and get back to Dundalk, McCabe told them. The escort car informed the judge that there was a problem.

The problem turned out to be tragic. The detective from Dundalk had gone up to the border and spotted a Shogun jeep. He fell in behind it for a few miles and then broke away as the border loomed into sight.

A spotter for the IRA had seen the car from Dundalk, known it as an unmarked Garda vehicle and mistakenly assumed that the jeep in front was carrying the judge and his wife. The actual occupants of the vehicle were Robin Hanna, his wife Maureen, both 44, and their six-year-old son David. Mr Hanna was a builder, with no direct link to the security forces or to any state agency. Like Higgins and his family, the Hannas were returning home from a holiday abroad.

Just over the border, at the townland of Killeen in south Armagh, a 1000 lb bomb exploded under their vehicle, killing all three instantly. The blast left a crater in the road, and, according to witnesses, bodies and luggage were scattered all across the main Dublin–Belfast route.

Later that morning the IRA issued a statement saying the Hannas were the 'unfortunate victims of mistaken identity', and that the attack was a carefully planned military operation that had ended in 'tragic and unfortunate circumstances'.

The tragedy left McCabe shaken. He couldn't help speculating on his own peripheral role in it. If the detective hadn't walked in on him that morning, if he hadn't said there was a judge en route for the border, would the Hannas have driven on through, ignored by the waiting killers? Equally, would the judge and his wife have instead ended up dead?

Six years later, when the first child was born to Maurice McCabe and his wife Lorraine, they gave her the name Hannah.

In September 1989 it was time to move on again, another posting in the itinerant role that is often the lot of the youngest recruits in the force. McCabe heard that he would be in line to go to Hackballscross, in County Monaghan. That kind of posting would be manna to a cop who wanted to kick back, put his feet up and watch the world go by. Not much happened in Hackballscross. Had McCabe ended up there, he would most likely have questioned his will to live.

So he pushed hard for another posting, and struck lucky. There was an opening in Bailieboro, County Cavan. It ticked all the boxes. In the first instance, it brought him closer to home. During the four years he had worked in Drogheda and Dundalk, he had commuted back to Lough Sheelin, and now a chance had arisen to cut the commute. Bailieboro station was twenty-one miles from his old family home. Garda regulations stipulated that members could not be based in a station less than twenty miles from immediate family members.

Now he had a chance to put down roots. He always wanted to return to Lough Sheelin, and apart from that, Bailieboro was known to be an extremely busy district.

Structurally, An Garda Síochána is divided into regions, divisions and districts. There are six regions: the Dublin Metropolitan, Northern, Western, Eastern, Southern and South-Eastern. Each region is overseen by an assistant commissioner.

Regions are divided into divisions, which are commanded by a chief superintendent. For instance, Bailieboro is in the Cavan/Monaghan division. Divisions are in turn divided into districts, overseen by superintendents, who are also known as district officers. In turn, districts are divided into sub-districts, each of which has a Garda station, often with fewer than half a dozen guards based therein.

Bailieboro is the district headquarters for the Bailieboro district, which has seven sub-districts, each with its own station. These are in the towns of Cootehill, Tullyvin, Kingscourt, Shercock, Virginia, Ballyjamesduff and Mullagh. Bailieboro is the only twenty-four-hour station in the district.

The district covers about 350 square miles, with a total population of around 25,000. All the towns are busy at the weekends, leading to the usual social problems that result from alcohol intake. The combination of these factors meant that Bailieboro was highly attractive for the kind of guard who was eager to work and learn.

As well as being the effective capital of the policing district, the town was also a busy hub in its own right. It is the second largest town in County Cavan – after Cavan itself – and has a population of around 4,000.

Away from the job, Maurice's life began to take shape. In 1989, while still serving in Dundalk, his brother Declan fixed him up with a blind date. Lorraine O'Reilly was from Arva, a town about twenty miles from Maurice's native place. She was working in Dublin at the time, but like many from the area, she returned home most weekends.

The couple began a steady relationship which continued when Maurice relocated to Bailieboro. They set about making plans, including the building of a home near Lough Sheelin, outside the village of Mountnugent.

For Lorraine, going out with a guard was a new experience. There were no guards in her family, and she quickly became aware of what she regarded as an insular culture.

'I didn't like it,' she recalls of her early years when she and Maurice would hook up with his colleagues. 'They were all just so much keeping to themselves. I remember thinking that these guys should be going to college with everybody else. They needed to mix with people of their own age who weren't in the guards, but there wasn't very much of it.

'I never got involved in that culture. I didn't mind being married into the guards, but that clique thing was never for me.'

Lorraine's observation on the socially insular nature of many within the force is not unusual. Many observers have questioned the wisdom of locating the Garda training college in a rural outpost, far from the cities where students from all disciplines and backgrounds are to be found in the main third-level colleges.

The displacement from large groups of their peers may well lead to an enhanced *esprit de corps* that is a requirement for any police or security force. But it could also ensure that a sense of otherness is forged in the formative years of training, which in turn has the potential to elevate loyalty to each other above any higher calling. Such a hierarchy of priorities is a well-known feature of soldiers in wartime. Whether or not it is as justified or even desirable in a police force whose first priority is to serve the public is another matter.

Lorraine got past her reservations about the social confines of Maurice's job. There was, in any event, the odd quirky perk to going out with a guard.

While she was still working in Dublin, Lorraine took the first bus back to the city on Monday mornings. When Maurice was on the early shift, he was his eager beaver self by getting out and conducting the odd early-morning checkpoint on the roads. And, by coincidence, more than once he selected the main Dublin road as a suitable location, offering him the opportunity for a furtive wave to the woman in his life, who typically wouldn't know whether to blush or laugh.

In 1993 the couple married and moved into their new home. Hannah was born the following year, and between then and 2008, the couple had four more children, Niamh, Robert, Alison and Tom.

Life was good for the young couple in the shallows of married life. Children were busy being born, Lorraine immersed herself in making a home fit for nurturing and Maurice was thriving in the job. Only years later would McCabe look back and appreciate just how important Lorraine and the solid family foundations were in supporting him when the going got tougher than he might ever have imagined.

Bailieboro was a different ballgame from Drogheda and Dundalk. Not as busy, the area more dispersed, there were times of great activity and other times you'd have to go hunting for work.

McCabe quickly gained an insight into how different life could be for a guard away from the cities or big towns. The constant pressure was not there. If you wanted to work, there was plenty to do. But if you were disposed towards kicking back, there were many possibilities there also.

He noticed this particularly on the graveyard shift. Some guards automatically ensured that they were out and about policing. Others knew they could get away with hanging out in the station, answering calls, or even sometimes not answering calls. Work could be as busy or as cushy as you wanted it to be.

He found himself in a unit of workers who were eager to get on with the job. As a result he didn't pay much heed to those who took life easy. He also found that the experience garnered in the previous urban postings was now standing to him. In a less intense atmosphere, a looser approach to following procedure can slip in. McCabe, schooled in the strict adherence demanded in a busy station, wouldn't let that happen to him.

One of the major new innovations in An Garda Síochána was bedding down just as McCabe settled in to Bailieboro. In 1999, the force introduced a national computer system, known as PULSE, which centralised all information. The acronym stands for Police Using Leading Systems Effectively, a description that would, in time, prove to be somewhat ironic. Every crime committed, every incident at which gardaí attended, every arrest and charge was recorded on the system. Crucially, it also made provision for tracking the progress of investigations, allowing files to be updated. Intelligence gathered was also stored on PULSE. This information was available to every member of the force. PULSE was a major tool in the fight against crime, and in maintaining law and order. It was also an instrument of awesome power given all the information it stored.

McCabe's decade as a guard in Bailieboro could be summed up as steady progress. At home, his family was growing. He was gaining a reputation, both within the station and among the public, as a good cop. The next obvious step was to apply for promotion.

In 1998 he sat the sergeant's exams but didn't make it through. The following year he did. Now came the next leap. For most who are promoted to sergeant, it's time to fold the tent, pack up the family and move to the next posting. The promotional trail can lead anywhere in the state.

Luck was on McCabe's side. Within the Cavan/Monaghan division at the time it was practice not to allow promoted officers move outside the division's boundaries. McCabe was transferred to Clones, Co. Monaghan. An extra commute for sure, but there was no need for the family to move.

In ordinary times, Clones is a relatively quiet place, but in 2000 it was hopping. BSE, known as mad cow disease, had the organs of state in a fluster. It was already rampant in the UK, and known to be present in Northern Ireland. The big fear south of the border was that it would leak across, having an enormous impact on the major beef export business.

So it was that every extra Garda resource that could be mustered was sent north to patrol the border in search of mad cows. Clones was one of the hubs from where the boys in blue panned out across the frontier to keep the country sane. The station was charged with manning seven border crossings around the clock, requiring a huge amount of manpower.

The town was full of activity, with members arriving from as far away as Cork and Kerry to pull in the huge chunks of overtime on offer. For McCabe, his first posting into this frantic atmosphere was full of excitement.

After a few months, the BSE scare dissipated and things settled back into a normal routine. He found himself in charge of a unit of four guards with whom he got on well. The transition wasn't anything huge, but he quickly grew accustomed to his new responsibilities.

He also quickly made an impression because within two years he was promoted to sergeant-in-charge in Clones. This new job moved him from the frontline to the administrative side, a further rung up the career ladder.

The sergeant-in-charge occupies a central role, effectively running the station. He (or she) is in charge of all the administration, records, accommodation, and works required. He is the go-to guy for any problems that arise. If he is doing the job properly, that would mean keeping an eye on the overall operation, checking that court files are in order, monitoring PULSE to ensure that there is nothing outstanding. In terms of the career ladder, anybody interested in moving up to inspector would be well advised to do a stint as sergeant-in-charge.

McCabe took to the role with gusto. It appealed to his sense of order, and gave him the opportunity to get to know every facet of the job. Again, Clones was an ideal learning post, not being too big, but big enough to be busy.

After two years, McCabe spotted on the bulletin board that there was a vacancy for the job of sergeant-in-charge in his old stomping ground of Bailieboro. The posting was tempting. He would be closer to home, he knew the terrain. Sure, he could envisage some problems with a transient management culture, but that was a challenge he would relish.

McCabe's initial musings were boosted when a senior officer asked him in passing whether he was applying for the post. The question would not have been asked casually. Quite obviously his name was in the frame.

He applied and was told within days that he'd got the job. Clones had been good to him and good for him. He'd learned a lot in what was a very suitable first posting as a sergeant. The sergeant-in-charge job was also ideal in that it wasn't too hectic a station to begin with. Now, though, things were likely to heat up.

On one of his last days in the job, his contribution was acknowledged in Clones District Court. The local *Northern Standard* paper reported that solicitor Brian Morgan had told the court that all the legal profession had enjoyed a very good working relationship with Sergeant McCabe and were sorry to see him go.

Garda Inspector Pat McMorrow said that Sergeant McCabe was a 'very professional and competent officer who had contributed to the well-being of Clones and its people'.

From the bench, Judge Cormac Dunne described the departing sergeant as 'a pastoral police officer'. He said he had known Sergeant McCabe for nearly twenty years and at all times, while based in the town, he had shown great concern for the people of Clones, particularly the young in the community. He had great skills, Judge Dunne said, and Clones' loss would be Bailieboro's gain.

McCabe was chuffed at the praise, but it wasn't going to go to his head. He knew that a pat on the back was just six inches away from a kick in the rear end, and a garda doing his job properly had to be constantly on his toes.

3

'We brought him into the house and placed him on a rug in the living room.' *Maurice McCabe*

Lorraine was against the move, but she relented in the end. If Maurice really wanted this challenge, then she'd go along with it. Of course it would be easier when he was based much closer to home. And she knew that her husband had to feel occupied, useful, busy in order to be fulfilled. But her intuition told her there could be trouble ahead.

When he had been a guard during his previous stint in Bailieboro, she had been appalled at some of the stories he'd told her about what went on there. OK, he had been lucky to be on a unit of workers. But occasionally he had told her about some of the laziness he'd witnessed, and even drinking on the job, and she couldn't believe it. And why? Because they knew they could get away with it.

'I was worried about how the other guards might take to him,' Lorraine said. 'He had been an ordinary guard, gone away and become a sergeant and now he was coming back to run the station. Would some of them think he was getting ahead of himself? And would that mean that they'd make his life difficult? I wasn't sure about it at all, but Maurice was set on it and I went along because the job meant so much to him.'

Lorraine's concerns were largely intuitive, but well-grounded. Bailieboro had a loose culture. The district officers tended to be absent for protracted periods, engaged in other garda-related work. As such, all problems were likely to congregate at the door of the sergeant-in-charge.

McCabe's work ethic ensured that he focused on a can-do attitude. He got down to the job, and for a while he was happy, occupied with the kind of policing matters that were his bread and butter.

Not that it was easy. The station itself was the first issue. When he'd served as a guard, McCabe had tried as best he could to ignore the physical state of the building. Now, with his whole day revolving around the place, that was no longer possible.

Bailieboro Garda station was a kip. There is no other word for it. Converted from a domestic residence, the two-storey building was old, decaying and completely unfit as a place of business. Superintendent Liam Hogan, who served as district officer the year after McCabe returned to Bailieboro, later set out the working conditions for an inquiry into Bailiboro in stark terms. 'There were health risks in relation to the constant stench from the ground-floor toilets. And there are no fire escapes on the first floor. The offices are cramped. There are no storage facilities. The only exit from the first floor is a wooden stairs with no fire retardant. There were no secure facilities for processing prisoners and the processing took place in full view of the public.'

During McCabe's time there, efforts were made to give the station a makeover, but these ran into the sand. One report to the head of the Cavan/Monaghan division in 2006 made the case that the issue was at crisis point.

'The conditions that members are expected to provide a

professional service in can only be described as appalling. It is embarrassing to hold multi-agency meetings with HSE (the Health Service Executive), county engineers etc. ... the station clearly reflects the ambivalence of transient district officers over a protracted period.'

That report was buried. In line with other, more serious, issues within the gardaí, the attitude seems to have been to say nothing for fear that it might cause grief for those higher up the chain of command.

McCabe, like everybody else who came through the station, just got on with it. But when the starting point for a busy district is a headquarters unfit for purpose, it doesn't bode well for the prospect of efficient policing.

There was also a much bigger problem at Bailieboro. In the accommodation report above, reference is made to 'transient district officers over a protracted period'. There simply was no continuity of management.

Superintendents didn't hang around. In McCabe's three and a half years as sergeant-in-charge, he served under five different superintendents. Ideally, a district officer should be at least two years in a posting in order to familiarise himself with the area and provide continuity.

In 2004, as McCabe was taking up his new role, the Morris Tribunal into garda corruption in County Donegal had already been sitting for two years. It was examining a series of incidents in the north-west county, including officers planting explosives – to be later 'discovered' – and the framing and harassment of a family for a murder that never occurred. The tribunal would find that a key problem had been the lack of continuity of senior officers.

Invariably, newly promoted superintendents drew the short straw and were sent north to Donegal. They suffered their tenure up until the first chance to get the hell out of there. In such a milieu, a disciplined force finds room for some of its members to engage in plenty of ill-discipline, and so it turned out in Donegal. The problems there dated from the late 1990s.

By 2004 this was being recognised in the Morris Tribunal, and should have been obvious to anybody with the slightest interest in policing. Yet Bailieboro was another example of a staging post.

Nearly all the superintendents who had passed through the district were newly promoted. With few exceptions, they had come from the greater Dublin area, and had continued to live in the city. In that regard, Bailieboro was an excellent staging post, a large district to staple to one's CV, and less than two hours from the capital.

Who in their right mind would move lock, stock and barrel to Cavan when the objective was to put down the time and get out of there with the least amount of fuss? Either that, or the succession of transient superintendents didn't like the Cavan weather.

The situation would be bad enough if the load could be shared with a middle management figure in the form of an inspector. But Bailieboro was not allocated an inspector. The requirement for an inspector in the district was laid out in blunt terms by Chief Superintendent Colm Rooney, who oversaw the Cavan/Monaghan division. He made a strong case in 2006 for an inspector to be allocated to Bailieboro: 'It has been part and parcel of the placement of newly promoted superintendents in the Bailieboro district that they complete their superintendent's development course and many of them have engaged in degree courses during their tenure,' he wrote to HQ. 'In conjunction with annual leave requirements, this inevitably results in extended absences of superintendents from the district.' This, he pointed out, meant that 'inspectors were frequently [brought] in to act as district officers'. Despite the plea, no inspector was allocated to Bailieboro.

All this meant that a huge responsibility fell back on the sergeant-in-charge. One could even surmise that the person occupying that role was performing duties way beyond his or her pay grade or rank. Maybe that was why McCabe was successful in his bid for the job. He was known as a worker, and all the reports from Clones were that he was well capable of running a station.

He threw himself into the job. He had a good sense of order, a prerequisite for overseeing a busy station. He was always prepared to go beyond the stated parameters of his own brief. He processed all the court files for the local Bailieboro court, but he also kept an eye on the investigation files from across the district. In addition, he was available 24/7 to deal with any issues that arose within the station, particularly when it was short-staffed.

Problems concerning discipline were not infrequent. One such incident arose soon after five o'clock one morning in 2005. There had been a fatal traffic accident in Virginia. McCabe was contacted at home and he directed that a patrol car attend the scene.

At 6.15am he phoned one of the guards, a young member, for a progress report. He told McCabe that he wouldn't go to the scene because the member who drove there was drunk

As with other such transgressions, McCabe followed up on it and referred it to the superintendent. Disciplinary action followed. This was typical of a number of such incidents. Bailieboro was not unique in that regard, but discipline would inevitably be looser where there was a succession of transient district officers.

The other problem that McCabe encountered on a regular basis was the number of probationary guards based in the station. At one stage in 2006, there were nine sergeants and fifty guards in the district, along with eleven probationers. That's a lot of probationers, requiring a high degree of supervision, which simply wasn't available.

Later, Superintendent Liam Hogan, who had served in Bailieboro in 2005, told an inquiry that at one stage there had been 18 probationers in the district: 'My impression is that there were too many and they were constantly changing, with no hope of developing a strong team to meet the needs of professional policing in the area.'

McCabe ploughed on through the difficulties. When problems arose, he brought them to the superintendent of the day, and generally they were dealt with. But he was still carrying the burden of managing way beyond the brief of sergeant-in-charge. Holding the responsibility without the corresponding rank provided him with some problems. Any of the members at the station who considered it their right to doss and even drink on the job would resent a mere sergeant who was effectively minding the shop.

As will be seen later, McCabe was highly regarded as the sergeant-in-charge in Bailieboro by both those he reported to and the general public. But what about the guards? Attempts to canvass opinion directly from some of those who had served with him in the 2004–08 period met with little success. Much of this can be attributed to all the fallout from the Maurice McCabe story over the following decade.

Two phrases did crop up in conversations with other members who were familiar with Bailieboro. McCabe was regarded in some quarters as 'a stickler', someone who insists on doing things by the book, irrespective of circumstances. Yet that would be to suggest that McCabe didn't exercise any discretion when dealing with the public. The description of him in Clones District Court as a 'pastoral policeman' defies that notion. And there were examples in Bailieboro where he exercised sensible and compassionate discretion in the best traditions of policing.

The term 'stickler' might just as well apply to the standards that he expected of his colleagues working out of the station; for example, refusing to turn a blind eye to a member drinking during the night shift.

The other phrase that cropped up in relation to McCabe was that he wasn't 'clubbable'. It may well have been the case that he wasn't the kind of guard whose social life revolved around the force. All his closest friends were guards, but he had plenty of outside interests. He certainly wasn't afraid to socialise and nobody would have described him as, for instance, a loner. But the culture within the force ensures that some believe that to venture outside the clique at all is to be singled out for suspicion of less than total loyalty to one another.

Through all of that, McCabe managed to run the station, keep his calm, and juggle a busy home life with work. Then, in early 2006, an incident occurred that in time was to have a profound effect on his job, his family and his life.

McCabe was at home watching television when he got a call from the station around 11pm on 11 January 2006.

The guard on the line related that there had been another tragedy of the type that is all too common in rural Ireland. A young man, well known in the Bailieboro area, had taken his own life. The 19-year-old had hanged himself in a shed at the rear of his family's home. There were two young guards at the scene, but there was no sergeant on duty.

McCabe would have been perfectly entitled to refer the matter to the acting district officer, or attempt to have one of the unit sergeants contacted. But he offered to take up the slack. He dressed for work and swung by Bailieboro to pick up another member.

When they arrived at the house, on the outskirts of town, McCabe noticed that, apart from the two on-duty members, there were three other off-duty gardaí there. The three were next to the shed, 'literally on top of the crime scene', McCabe would later report. As far as he could see, the trio had drink taken. He established that they had been attending a funeral when word came through about the death and they had travelled out to comfort the young man's family.

McCabe then went about one of the deeply unsettling aspects of the job: 'I cut the rope from around his neck. We brought him into the house and placed him on a rug in the living room. His family then gathered around him. I contacted the coroner and outlined the incident to her and she gave permission to move the body. Because some family members were not present, we decided to wait for them to return before we moved the body.'

While waiting, he got another call from the station. There had been a burglary at an address in the town and a crew was needed out there. McCabe told the caller to get the unmarked patrol car and go to the scene.

The guard said there was a problem. Some time earlier he had noticed three off-duty members emerge from the pub across the road from the station, pop over and commandeer the patrol car. As far as the guard on duty could see, the trio all appeared drunk. These were the off-duty members at the scene of the suicide.

Just as he was getting this information on his mobile phone, McCabe looked up and saw the trio get into the patrol car – which he hadn't noticed there before then – and drive off.

He was fuming. More police work that fell far short of required standards. Another example of the public going unserved. Was there a police force this side of the developed world which would put up with such carry-on?

Once the family were properly attended to and the body removed, McCabe and his colleagues left. They repaired to the home of one of the younger members and discussed what had unfolded. As far as McCabe was concerned, he would have no choice but to report the incident. He didn't receive any objection from his colleagues.

The following day he duly reported what had happened. The acting-superintendent dealt with the matter and disciplined the three members involved. One was moved from his current position in the crime unit to a less senior role, to which he had been recently promoted. To make matters worse, this man had applied for the job of sergeant-in-charge eighteen months earlier when McCabe was appointed.

McCabe took no pleasure in what he'd had to do, but for him the greater crime would have been to ignore it. He'd known the men involved for a considerable time, and guessed that from their perspective there may well be a bitter aftertaste to the whole affair. On such actions, in order to properly serve the job, some members get a reputation for being sticklers.

That was in January. The year passed much the same as the ones that preceded it: busy at work, busy at home, frustrated at work, basking in the glow of a young family growing up at home.

Later that year Maurice and Lorraine would be hurled into a nightmare scenario that was as deeply disturbing to them as it was unexpected. It would also have an impact long into the future. It involved an allegation of sexual impropriety against McCabe made by the daughter of one of the colleagues mentioned above. This related to an alleged incident of inappropriate contact some years previously.

The matter was investigated and dealt with immediately, following appropriate protocol within the force. The file was passed to the local state solicitor, Rory Hayden, who forwarded it to the DPP with the following recommendation.

"A number of inconsistencies arise on the file and the alleged victim's credibility is strained in all of these circumstances. Ultimately, even the allegation itself is unclear and even on the alleged victim's own account amounts to horseplay and no more. This allegedly took place in a house full of children with four adults present in close proximity. I do not think any case arises for prosecution."

The DPP agreed and added that even if there was substance to the allegation it would not have constituted a criminal offence.

For McCabe the whole thing was deeply unsettling, even though he had the support and sympathy of most of his colleagues who were aware of it. As anybody who has been the subject of a false accusation of impropriety involving a child knows, it leaves a chilling and lasting impact.

Due process had been followed, but McCabe was unhappy with some aspects of the manner in which the whole matter was handled. Despite being fully vindicated, he felt that given the invidious circumstances in which he had found himself, he should have been given greater support in dealing with the issue.

Some within the force believe that what McCabe was put through during this period coloured his attitude to An Garda Siochana and contributed to sending him down the road on which he would soon embark.

The fall-out from this period will be dealt with in a later chapter, at a time when it re-enters the Maurice McCabe story.

Meanwhile, things weren't getting any better in the Bailieboro district. In 2007 there were a number of serious incidents that would later achieve national prominence. These involved crimes ranging from criminal damage to serious assault, and, indirectly, murder.

What would set these crimes apart was the manner in which they were investigated and, in some cases, prosecuted. All featured in the claims that McCabe would later make about serious deficiencies in policing. Together they illustrate the kind of crime that can occur in provincial or rural Ireland.

The next two chapters deal with the most serious of these incidents.

4

'He stood back and started kicking me into my stomach on my right-hand side. He was shouting at me all the time.' *Mary Lynch*

On 30 April 2007, Maurice McCabe had a major issue on his mind that had nothing to do with work. Lorraine was about to give birth to their fifth child. Later that day a baby boy, Tom, was born. While the McCabes were engrossed in this life-affirming exercise, life carried on at Bailieboro station in the absence of the sergeant-in-charge.

The day brought the usual fare of crime and law enforcement, but one case, which had its origins early that morning, would reverberate throughout the country and into the lives of many others, some with devastating consequences.

At 2.15am Mary Lynch, a 52-year-old taxi driver based in Kells, Co. Meath, picked up a fare. The man had emerged from the Headford Arms Hotel after a Sunday night disco. He wanted to go to Virginia, around 20km away, which would give Mary time to return to Kells before things got too quiet.

As they set out, Mary opened up a conversation with the man.

His name was Jerry McGrath and he said he was from Dundrum in County Tipperary but was staying with his sister in Virginia. He was 23 years old.

She asked whether he'd had a good night, but he didn't say much on that score. Instead, he began a monologue on things that had gone wrong in his life. His girlfriend had lost a baby. Nobody was giving him sympathy. He related how various members of his family had health issues.

In Virginia he gave her directions that led down a dark cul-de-sac. He didn't seem to know which house was his sister's, even though he had been staying there for some time. Mary stopped outside a random house, and told him the fare was €32.

'I thought he was going to run away,' she said in a statement. 'I could see him walking around the back of the car … I let down the window and he opened the car door and said he had no money. I told him I would have to report this to the guards.

'I tried to drive off and he took the keys out of the ignition. When he took the keys out he started pulling my hair and telling me to get out of the car. I knew if he could get me out of the car, I was in very bad danger.'

Mary resisted being dragged from the car.

'He pulled lumps of hair out of my head. He kept telling me to lean forward and I could see that his zip was open. He stood back and started kicking me into my stomach on my right-hand side. He was shouting at me all the time. At some stage during this I grabbed my mobile phone and pressed the green button which I knew would call the last dialled number.'

That number belonged to her husband George, who was at home in Kells. She kept screaming for help, and George, on the line, could hear her. He rang the gardaí and immediately set out for Virginia.

'I kept trying to say where I was,' Mary later related, about how she was trying to drop hints to her husband on the phone. 'He

[McGrath] leaned across and unbuckled my seat belt. At this point I leaned over to my left and reached into the glove box and grabbed a tin of deodorant. He started biting me on my right shoulder. He had pulled at my t-shirt and was biting my shoulder in the flesh.'

She tried to spray the deodorant on McGrath, and he reared back, rubbing his eyes. She pleaded with him to take the money and let her go.

'He started saying that nobody was listening to him. I said that I was listening to him and I would get him help if he gave me my keys back.'

In the end, McGrath calmed down. Mary, petrified that he might attack her again, out there where nobody would hear her, agreed to drive him into the town. By then, her husband and the gardaí were out looking for her. On Main Street in Virginia, they found her, George arriving first, quickly followed by a squad car, dispatched from Bailieboro station.

McGrath was arrested under section 3 of the Non-fatal Offences against the Person Act.

Mary was in a hysterical state, believing that she had just escaped from what could have been a violent death. George drove her to Navan hospital, where she was seen at around 4.30am. After a few hours in the hospital, she and George returned home to Kells.

At Bailieboro station, McGrath was detained and interviewed. At first he said he had only verbally abused Mary Lynch, but in a subsequent interview he admitted the assault.

'I lost it,' he told the gardaí. 'I grabbed the taxi driver by the hair. I don't know why I did this. There are a lot of things going on in my life at the moment ... I remember kicking the taxi driver on her side. I don't know what came over me ... I remember the taxi driver was roaring at me "go away, I'll give you the money", I think I kicked her three or four times, I don't recollect if I punched her.'

McGrath was charged under section 2 of the Non-fatal Offences against the Person Act, the lesser of two possible assault charges. He was released on station bail of his own bond of €300 at 1.15pm, some ten hours or so after the assault.

Within half an hour of his release, Mary Lynch walked into Bailieboro to give her statement, as requested when she had been rescued early that morning. Much of the detail of the ordeal she had been subjected to echoed what McGrath had confessed. She asked where he was being held and was told about his release. She couldn't believe it. It was explained to her that the gardaí had no option but to do so. Mary just shook her head. It was the first time in the case she would find her confidence in law enforcement badly damaged.

McCabe was back on duty a few days later, but he knew nothing about what had unfolded. The record of the assault charge was relatively unremarkable. The details of the case were the responsibility of the investigating guard and his or her supervisor.

Jerry McGrath appeared in court on 17 May to be formally charged. He appeared again on 21 June and 20 September. During that time, Mary Lynch rang Bailieboro a number of times to ask how her case was progressing. The assault had left her shaken. For a time, she couldn't face returning to work, dealing with the public, not knowing if the next fare would, like McGrath, suddenly turn on her. She wanted this man dealt with as soon as possible.

Her calls didn't receive much attention. On each occasion, she was told that the man she wanted was the officer dealing with the case, who wasn't on duty at the time and to call back. No detective was appointed to investigate, as might be expected for such a serious assault.

Once or twice, a voice on the end of the phone told her that the gardaí were waiting to hear back from the DPP.

In fact, the file didn't go to the DPP until 17 October, nearly six months after the assault. The investigating garda compiled a file and forwarded it to his superior officer. The report stated that the section 2 charge against McGrath was preferred 'on the direction of the office of the Director of Public Prosecutions'. This was not the case. The DPP had not been contacted about the case.

After being examined by the unit sergeant and Superintendent Michael Clancy, a decision was made to upgrade the charge to a section 3. No mention was made of the delay in compiling the file when the superintendent forwarded it to the DPP on 17 October. Superintendent Clancy recommended that the case be dealt with by the district court.

The DPP's office partially agreed. It gave directions that the section 3 charge was more appropriate because of 'the savagery of the attack' but that it should be dealt with by the district court only if a guilty plea was entered. Otherwise it should go before a judge and jury at the circuit court, where, if the accused was found guilty, a considerable prison sentence might be imposed.

But before these changes could be made, Jerry McGrath would strike again.

On 9 October at around 3.30am, McGrath broke into a house in Dundrum, Co. Tipperary, entering through the rear door, which was unlocked. He was carrying a hurley, stolen from the house next door.

McGrath crept into the bedroom of the couple's five-year-old daughter. He applied pressure to her neck, lifted her out of the bed, and carried her down the stairs.

The girl's mother woke up and saw him. She shouted out, bringing her husband from the bedroom to intercept McGrath. The husband restrained him, while his wife rang the local Garda station in Tipperary town. Somebody in the station who knew the area rang a neighbour of the family's, Garda John Ivers, and asked him to go to the house until his on-duty colleagues arrived. Garda Ivers came quickly and helped restrain McGrath until the squad car from Tipperary arrived.

The little girl was taken to South Tipperary General Hospital where she was treated for bruising to her neck and petechial spots around her eye. The whole family was traumatised at the ordeal and the thought of what might have occurred had McGrath not been intercepted.

McGrath was questioned at Tipperary town Garda station and admitted the main thrust of what had happened. He was charged, on direction from the DPP, with burglary, and a section 3 assault.

The PULSE entry for the offence included McGrath's history. 'He has previous history on PULSE for minor assault, public order, criminal damage,' the posting read. At that point, the delay in processing the Mary Lynch incident meant that the PULSE entry still classified the assault on her as a section 2, which could be read as a 'minor assault'.

McGrath was remanded in custody. Three weeks later, on 30 October, his solicitor applied for bail at Limerick District Court. The gardaí objected. The Detective Sergeant, who had overseen the case, put forward seven different grounds for objection. These included the seriousness of the charge, the possibility that McGrath might commit further crimes, the prospect of more serious charges being directed over the incident, and the length of sentence if McGrath was convicted.

There was no objection on the basis that he was already on bail for a serious assault some six months earlier in Cavan. When asked later why he didn't introduce the Cavan incident, the details of which were available on the PULSE system, the detective said he thought it was a minor assault. 'I believed there were seven very strong grounds to object to bail and I thought, if I was asked, "What is he on bail for?" and I was going to say a dispute with a taxi driver. I don't believe it would have greatly furthered my case.'

The detective was not cross-examined by McGrath's solicitor over the bail objections. Despite that, the judge decided to release the defendant on bail. This was not a controversial decision. Without a compelling reason to deny it, and with no serious evidence heard that McGrath was likely to reoffend, the judge's hands were to some extent tied. He would have known that if he denied bail, a higher court would in time overturn his decision.

McGrath was released on strict conditions. His father had to put up €2,000 as surety. He had to sign on daily at Cashel Garda station, observe a curfew between 9pm and 8am and not go within two miles of the house where the incident had occurred.

While McGrath had been in custody in Limerick prison, the assault case on Mary Lynch had come before the court in Virginia on 18 October. When the court was informed that McGrath was in custody over a separate incident, his bail for the Lynch assault was continued.

On 3 December McGrath was back in Virginia for the upgrading of the original charge on the Lynch case from a section 2 to a section 3 assault. If, five weeks earlier, when he was granted bail in Limerick, he had been charged with the more serious assault, it may have been used to object to his bail application in Tipperary.

Four days after the Virginia appearance, McGrath was drinking in Limerick city. Earlier that day, Sylvia Roche Kelly, a separated mother of two, left her home in Sixmilebridge, Co. Clare to go into Limerick to celebrate her 33rd birthday with her sister and friends.

That evening in Ted's nightclub in the city, she met McGrath. Later, she accompanied him back to the Clarion Hotel in the city centre, where he was staying. In the early hours of 7 December McGrath murdered Ms Roche Kelly in a vicious assault.

Around noon the following day, staff at the hotel entered the bedroom and found Ms Roche Kelly's body face down in the bath. There were bloodstained towels around her head and shoulders. McGrath had left the hotel.

That morning he had travelled home by taxi. He stopped off at Cashel Garda station to sign in at around 12.40pm. He then continued on to Waterford and boarded a bus for London. From there he later travelled north to Edinburgh.

It didn't take the gardaí long to focus on a murder suspect. Word was put out to the media that a 23-year-old man was being sought in connection with the suspected murder.

In Kells Mary Lynch and George were watching the *Nine O'Clock News* when the item was mentioned. Mary felt a chill shoot through her body. She turned to her husband.

'Whatever way it was said [on the television], George and me just looked at each other and we knew. I said, "That's McGrath, it has to be."'

Mary rang a garda she knew in Munster. He told her he couldn't say anything because the matter was too sensitive and a suspect was at large. A few days later he phoned back, apologised for his earlier reticence and confirmed that yes, it was Jerry McGrath and he was now in custody.

The suspect had returned on 10 December, at the urging of some people close to him. He made himself available to gardaí in Limerick and was questioned. He admitted that he had hit Ms Roche Kelly in the face, pulled her hair and put his hands around her neck and strangled her. He said he may have kicked her with some force as well. He was charged with murder.

By then Mary Lynch was beside herself with fear and anger. 'I rang Bailieboro [station] and spoke to the superintendent, and I said McGrath has just murdered somebody and you told me I was safe. He said they were sending me a liaison guard,' she said. 'If I was to get a liaison guard, assigned to me, I would have thought it should have happened after the assault and not then. Anyway, he came the following week and said he'd keep me informed and made an appointment to see me the next time. I never saw him again.'

Mary Lynch's main concern was the disposal of her case, and finally it was conveyed to her that a date for the trial had been set. It was to go ahead at Virginia District Court on 7 January 2008. She perpared herself for the occasion. She would have to face McGrath again, which would be traumatic, but she was determined to have her day in court, that her story would be told. Justice had to be done. In the days leading up to the court date, she considered how she might compile a victim impact statement.

Two days before the court was to sit, George Lynch took a call at home from the liaison guard. He said that there was no need for Mary to appear in court the following Monday because the case was not going ahead. The next thing Mary Lynch knew about the case was a call she received on the Monday evening from a senior garda. 'Your man got nine months,' the officer said.

'When I asked who, he stated that Jerry McGrath had got nine months. I told him that I was told the case was not going ahead and he said he knew nothing about that. I told him I was informed I would be given the opportunity to make a victim impact statement to the court. He said he did not know anything about that and he was only handed the case file that morning and told to go into the court.

'He also told me that if I wanted to see Jerry McGrath, he was still in Virginia Garda station. I said I did not want to see Jerry McGrath in a Garda station. I wanted to see him in court.'

After hanging up, Mary Lynch became highly emotional. She had been denied her day in court, a chance to effect some closure. She had emphasised to the gardaí that she wanted to see McGrath in the secure environment of a court, but she found the offer to see him in the Garda station as little short of surreal.

The outcome didn't bring the desired closure for Mary Lynch. She felt she had been ill-served by the gardaí, and would go on to make a complaint to the Garda ombudsman. She had suffered what the judge in the case described as 'the worst aggravated assault' he had dealt with. If she hadn't the presence of mind, or the bravery, to tackle McGrath at the time, her fate may have been much worse.

Nearly one year later, on 12 January 2009, McGrath pleaded guilty at the Central Criminal Court to the murder of Sylvia Roche Kelly. He was handed down the mandatory life sentence. On 11 February he pleaded guilty before Clonmel Circuit Court to six counts, including burglary, assault and false imprisonment for the Tipperary offence. Two days later he was sentenced to ten years' imprisonment.

For years after 2007 a number of questions hung over the handling of the crimes of Jerry McGrath, but none more so than this: could the murder of Sylvia Roche Kelly have been avoided? On the face of it, McGrath should not have been at large to take the life of that young woman who was enjoying a night out to celebrate her birthday.

And if the seriousness of the assault on Mary Lynch had been known to the court in Tipperary dealing with the attempted abduction charge, would McGrath have got bail? Equally, it could be asked why, when McGrath was up for remand in Virginia on 3 December 2007 – after the Tipperary incident and four days before the murder – the court had not been informed of the Tipperary charge.

Many of the problems around the whole affair stem from how the assault on Mary Lynch was dealt with. The garda who investigated the matter was inexperienced, and did not receive any supervision for such a serious case. The original charge – section 2 as opposed to the more serious section 3 – was not appropriate. This had repercussions during the bail application on the Tipperary charge. If the more serious charge had been entered on PULSE, it may have prompted the Tipperary detective to examine it closer in preparing his objection to bail.

The failure to re-examine the bail situation on 3 December in Virginia was another oversight. And the long delay in preparing a file for the DPP meant a consequent delay in having the charge upgraded to a more serious one.

Questions arise also over the failure to inform Mary Lynch that the McGrath case was being dealt with. There is no evidence to suggest that this was done to keep her out of court, but it is undoubtedly the case that Ms Lynch's presence in court that day, and what she might say about the gardaí's handling of the case, could have been highly embarrassing for the force. It is also the case that it was open to the prosecuting garda on the day to request an adjournment on the basis that the victim was not in court through no fault of her own. This course of action was not taken.

All these matters would be raked over in a series of inquiries, conducted by the gardaí, the Garda Síochána Ombudsman Commission (GSOC) and the O'Higgins Commission. Sylvia Roche Kelly's husband, Lorcan, also initiated a civil action on the basis that McGrath should not have been free on bail when he murdered Sylvia, but this was eventually struck out by a court.

Maurice McCabe would be drawn into the affair. During the various inquiries, attempts would be made to blame him for playing a central role in some of the cock-ups. By then, he would be persona non grata among large sections of the force owing to his status as a whistleblower.

Maybe these later attempts to blame him for the kind of shoddy police work that he had complained about were just coincidences. Maybe.

5

Minibus Assault

'He basically said to me, well, in a nice way, you haven't got much of a case.' *Lorraine Browne*

It was going on 3.30am when Lorraine Browne picked up her fares outside the Roma chipper in Carrickmacross, Co. Monaghan. Ms Browne ran a minibus taxi service out of Kingscourt in County Cavan. About ten people boarded her minibus. The mood was good, but finely balanced, in the early hours of 25 February 2007.

She told everybody that she was going to Kingscourt, which is 13km from Carrickmacross. Among the group on the bus were four men whom she didn't know. Later she would estimate that they were in their late twenties, or maybe early thirties. One of the four was a big lad, another shorter. The third was bald and asleep for most of the journey, and the fourth sat behind the driver.

'The minute I pulled off, the verbal abuse from the biggest lad started,' she told gardaí. 'He started verbally abusing the lady passengers that I had on board. Putting women down, saying filthy talk, and talking about their privates. He was trying to start a row with their partners by saying stuff to them. His mates, one of them, the smallest lad, kept laughing and egging him on. The bald lad was asleep in the bus and the last lad was sitting behind me telling them to stop.'

About 6km along the road, Ms Browne pulled up to let a couple disembark. 'When the girl was getting off, the biggest lad grabbed her arse. Her boyfriend turned around and said, "How dare you, mate." The big lad laughed in his face. The couple then left.'

For the remainder of the journey, one of the four kept shouting abuse at the other passengers. At Kingscourt, Ms Browne told the men this was the last stop, and asked the four of them to get off. She still had about six passengers aboard, whom she knew and often dropped to their homes. The men refused to get off. One of them kept shouting that he wanted to be brought to Ardee in County Louth, about 15km away. The abuse continued for up to half an hour while the bus was stationary.

Presently, the other passengers began to disembark. 'When the passengers were getting off, the biggest lad groped another girl.' By then, there was just one other woman left on the bus. Ms Browne's statement went on,

> At this stage I was terrified so I told them I wasn't taking them anywhere but I'd ring them another taxi. I then got off the bus and walked to the middle of the road so they couldn't hear me and rang Bailieborough Garda Station.
>
> The minute I got off the phone I heard the girl on the bus screaming. I ran around to the side door and saw the big lad had a grip of the girl, holding her by her clothes at the front. She then broke free of him and ran up the town screaming. The girl kept running away. I didn't manage to catch up with her. I then turned and went back towards the bus.

They were all on the bus still shouting very loud. I then saw the big, rowdy fella step off the bus shouting, 'Where the fuck has she gone?' At this stage I turned and ran towards Kingscourt Garda station and hid at the corner of the road so that I could still see them. They all got off the bus and walked up towards where I was, so I ran further up towards the Garda station. I then heard the voices were getting faded so I walked back down towards the corner and saw that they were going back towards the bus still looking for me.

Kingscourt Garda station was closed at that hour of the morning. Lorraine Browne could now see the men from up the street. They hung around the bus, and then drifted over towards the Europa chipper:

A fare that I was to pick up in Bailieboro started ringing me at this stage and knew I was in trouble, in a distressed state. They then got another taxi and when they got to Kingscourt rang me to see where I was and picked me up. They then brought me down to the bus and the gardaí landed at the same time.

The men had left by that stage. Ms Browne felt thoroughly shaken. She gave a statement to the gardaí, concluding with an observation: 'I was working with CIÉ as a bus driver, working on route 77 which is the worst one in Dublin, which is the Tallaght one, for five years. Previous to this I was a taxi driver around Dublin for four to five years. This was the worst I have ever encountered in all my years driving.'

The investigating garda was a probationary member. He took a statement from Ms Browne and would have been expected to be fully supervised in investigating the whole matter and preparing a file. The entry to the PULSE system just read, 'Three males caused disturbance on mini bus on Main Street, Kingscourt. To proceed by summons.'

No investigation file was created. A report compiled later suggested that charges could have included public order offences, sexual assault, false imprisonment, and assault.

Lorraine Browne indicated that she would try and identify and locate the girl who had been assaulted on the bus. Precious little was done by the gardaí to look into it. Nobody was formally interviewed. The investigating guard did not make a statement himself about arriving at the scene.

Some weeks after the incident, Lorraine Browne received a call from the garda who had taken her statement.

'He basically said he to me, well, in a nice way, you haven't got much of a case. He went on to say I would have to find the witnesses that were on the bus, find names, go to court, face these guys in court and he said then that they might just get off with a caution. So basically it was like he was saying you're wasting our time, you know.'

The investigating garda traced one of the suspects to Dundalk. He travelled to the town, met the man and had a chat with him. The suspect said he wanted to apologise to Ms Browne and to 'sort her out for her loss of earnings and wanted to give her a meal voucher', according to the garda.

The garda didn't regard the suspect's offer as a sign of probable guilt of the offence. He didn't take a statement from the suspect, or attempt to find out the identity of the other suspects who had accompanied this man on the night in question. Neither did he arrest the suspect.

He contacted Ms Browne to convey the offer of an apology and the meal voucher. He asked her to estimate her loss of earnings on the night, which she put at €150. He told her she would have to withdraw her statement of complaint if she was accepting the offer. He claimed that the issue of compensation was brought up by Ms Browne, but she vehemently denies this.

In the end, Ms Browne came to Bailieboro station and agreed to withdraw her complaint.

Later, GSOC agreed to investigate the incident but later ruled it was beyond the allowable time limit.

Overall, the investigation of a suspected serious crime was pretty awful. The garda who did the work was on probation and should have been supervised. He didn't take statements, he didn't pursue witnesses and he gave the impression to Lorraine Browne that she would be better off forgetting the whole thing. Having located a suspect who was apparently willing to admit guilt, he didn't pursue a prosecution. The unorthodox manner in which he negotiated compensation was contrary to all police practice. And he didn't record the transaction in any official manner, not even making a mention of it on PULSE which he updated by noting that the matter had been 'settled amicably'.

Lakeside Manor Assault

'There is CCTV footage which shows you striking Charles. What do you say to that?' *Investigating garda*

Charles McMahon never saw the blow coming. He had stepped out from the nightclub in the Lakeside Manor Hotel in Virginia, County Cavan. It was about 2.15am on the morning of 14 April 2007.

'I heard some shouting, something about a girlfriend. Then I felt a bang on the side of my head,' he later told gardaí. 'I don't remember anything after that. The next thing I remember was talking to my sister, who was going frantic.'

McMahon was in a bad way, lying on the ground. There is some suggestion that he was also kicked after being felled by the first blow. An ambulance was called and he was taken to Cavan General Hospital. The medical report compiled on him noted that there was a possibility that he had lost consciousness. There was a graze on his right ear, as well as swelling and bruising of the right eye area. More swelling was detected on his right cheek and the upper and lower lip, with abrasions on the left side of his face. By any stretch it was a serious assault, the kind that in different circumstances has seen victims sustain even worse, occasionally permanent, injuries.

Once what had happened became clear, the guards in Bailieboro were called. Three members arrived at 2.55am. By then, Charles McMahon was sitting in the ambulance. One of the guards went and spoke to him.

'I can't say who hit me as I did not see who hit me,' he said.

Following brief inquiries with some of Charles McMahon's friends at the venue, a suspect, who will be referred to here as Mr B, was identified. The guards went looking for him at his father's house but were told he wasn't home.

A few days later, the investigating guard viewed CCTV footage from the hotel. He didn't note the date in his notebook, which was an oversight. Around that time, Charles McMahon went to Bailieboro station and gave a full statement. And that was the end of that for nearly two months.

On 11 July Mr B was arrested and brought to Bailieboro. He was interviewed twice and late that evening was charged with a section 3 assault causing harm, the more serious of the two assault charges most frequently used. In a short report on the case written at the time, the investigating guard noted that 'there are a number of other suspected offenders to be questioned in relation to this incident'.

The following day, Virginia District Court remanded Mr B on bail until a September sitting, to see whether the judge would take the case or deem it serious enough to pass up to the circuit court, where it would be heard by a jury and, if there was a conviction, could attract a much greater prison sentence.

It would be another two months before a second suspect was

arrested. On 19 September, Mr C was brought to Bailieboro station and interviewed.

'Did you throw any punching [*sic*] or kick Charles McMahon at any stage?' he was asked.

'No,' he replied.

Then he was informed. 'There is CCTV footage which shows you striking Charles. What do you say to that?'

'I didn't strike him.'

The only problem with that exchange was that the CCTV footage did not show Mr C striking anybody. Worse still, the guard did not even have possession of the footage. The interviewing had attempted a ruse to elicit something more, possibly a confession, from Mr C. This type of investigation technique is sometimes the stuff of cop shows, but in the real world it's not on. Garda procedure and standards specify that tactics aimed at obtaining a confession by use of a false pretence or a trick should be avoided at all times. Once Mr C was falsely led, the whole investigation was heading for grave danger.

Much later, the guard would admit that he'd messed up. 'In hindsight and with experience now I realise I should never have asked him that question. The reason I asked him that question was because I wanted to know if he had been involved in assaulting him [Mr McMahon],' he told an inquiry.

The investigation dragged on at a torturous pace. A trial date was set for 15 November, after the district court judge said in the September hearing that he would accept jurisdiction rather than passing it up to the higher court.

The big problem was that there was no sign of the CCTV footage, which was vital, even more so now that it had been referenced in the course of an interview with a suspect. A problem had arisen which meant that it couldn't be retrieved.

As station sergeant in Bailieboro, Maurice McCabe reviewed the investigation file two days before the court hearing. He was thrown by what he saw as the case's major shortcomings. He prepared a report for his superintendent in which he outlined ten problems with the investigation. These included: 'Video footage: During questioning of the suspects the video footage was referred to. It must be produced and where is it?'

He also pointed out that seven different people should be interviewed, mainly as witnesses. And that 'The bouncers referred to on file, especially the one referred to as [name], must be interviewed, as requested by the suspect during interview.'

McCabe also asked: 'Has [Mr C's] mother been interviewed in relation to events after the disco? Has it been verified that the defendant did in fact ring Bailieboro Garda station on the morning in question as he states?'

Two days later the case was adjourned for another month. McCabe wrote to his superintendent once more that 'it is lucky that we were not embarrassed in court', pointing out: 'The lack of investigation carried out in the case can only be one of two things: Neglect of duty or Inexperienced. Forwarded for your view please.'

The case was heard on 17 January 2008. The judge heard evidence and submissions and declared that he simply could not convict Mr B. The only evidence against him was evidence from Mr C, which the judge was not happy with.

He also pointed out that the problem over the CCTV footage was unsatisfactory, and that such footage should be made available for six months after an incident, in the public interest.

He said that if the evidence had been there to convict, he would have handed down a sentence of twelve months in prison, such was the seriousness of the assault.

All in all, the case was an embarrassment for the gardaí and totally unsatisfactory for Mr McMahon, an innocent man who had been viciously assaulted and found that there would be no justice for him in the system.

Incident in Cafolla's Restaurant

'The colour of vinegar in the bottle was a urine colour.' *Majella Cafolla*

On 5 August 2007 soon after 3pm three men walked into Cafolla's fast food restaurant in Bailieboro. They ordered their food and sat down.

One of them then took a vinegar bottle from a nearby table, emptied its contents onto the floor and passed it to his pal. He in turn put the bottle into his pocket and headed for the toilet. A few minutes later, he emerged from the toilet with the bottle full of urine and sat back down at the table.

He took the bottle from his pocket and placed it behind the menu, shielding it. He took a quick look around and, satisfied that nobody was watching, placed the bottle of urine back on the nearby table.

The three men were having a great laugh. Behind the counter, Majella Cafolla was on her laptop. The men began to engage with her, shouting jokes, including lines like 'Are you pissed off?' and 'You're taking the piss.'

Majella didn't pay them much heed initially. When they had finished their meal, they went to pay, and by this stage they were in hysterics.

'So I got up to check what they were laughing at,' Majella said. 'They had done something. I knew there wasn't anything missing from the table, but there was liquid spilt on the ground which turned out to be vinegar.'

Two customers, a man and a boy, entered Cafolla's and sat at the table where the vinegar had been replaced with urine. The three men were by then outside looking back in. When they saw the two customers sit down, their hysterics reached a new level.

'So it was very obvious they had done something to the man's table. I looked at the vinegar bottle on the table, and my vinegar is clear. The colour of the vinegar in the bottle was a urine colour. I asked the gentleman and his child to move to another table and told him I had a spillage.'

At that point Majella went to consult the CCTV cameras she had on the premises. The footage confirmed what had happened and identified which of the men had gone into the toilet.

'When I see what happened on the camera I took the bottle and followed the three men to the Benjamin's pub, cause I know they drink there. I walked up to the bar and I put the bottle up in front of him and told him he was a dirty despicable bastard urinating in a vinegar bottle in my restaurant.'

Majella Cafolla left the pub and went down to Bailieboro Garda station. She was met there by two gardaí. One of the pair was a probationary garda but would take the role of investigating officer in the case.

According to Majella Cafolla, the two gardaí thought the whole thing was funny. They denied this, but Majella would have had no reason to manufacture such a story. She was well disposed towards the gardaí.

The two gardaí went with her down to Benjamin's pub. She pointed out the culprits to them, told them these were the so-called gentlemen they were looking for, and returned to her restaurant, leaving the matter in the hands of the law. Some minutes later the two gardaí appeared at the restaurant with the culprit, who, the gardaí said, wanted to apologise to her.

Majella was horrified that the guards would bring the culprit back to, as she saw it, the scene of the crime. They had 'brought the problem back to me', she felt and she 'found it intimidating'.

The gardaí would later deny bringing the culprit to Cafolla's. They claimed that the culprit followed them from the pub. However, an inquiry would accept Majella Cafolla's evidence over that of the gardaí.

A few days later, the investigating garda turned up at the restaurant and requested the CCTV footage, saying that he would call back in a day or two.

He didn't call back, so Majella Cafolla went to the Garda station with the downloaded footage. There she was told that the garda dealing with the matter was 'off sick'.

The guard claimed that he did return to Cafolla's but was told that the footage wasn't yet downloaded. He also claimed that he went back again and was told that Ms Cafolla was off work, at which point he drove out to her home outside the town.

He didn't retain any notes about any of this and, when asked, could not recall where exactly Ms Cafolla lived. The O'Higgins Commission eight years later accepted Ms Cafolla's evidence over the guard's on this matter also.

When nothing happened for a few weeks, Majella Cafolla went once again to Bailieboro Garda station, where the garda on duty told her that a different garda was dealing with the matter, but he couldn't give her this garda's name. When she asked about the CCTV footage she had brought on the previous occasion, she was told it wasn't there. No garda contacted her thereafter about the matter.

A few weeks later she met the second guard who had been on the scene on the day of the incident, at the hatch in her restaurant. She asked what was happening and he assured her that 'it's gone to the DPP and they have to make a decision on it'.

This was at least some assurance. 'I was like, okay, fair enough, that's grand. I was happy enough with that because it didn't mean anything to me except that I thought it was being dealt with.'

Still nothing happened. Soon after that, she went to Bailieboro station to check on progress. She asked to see the investigating guard but was told he was on sick leave. Some weeks later she contacted the station again, and this time was told that the station sergeant would be in touch with her.

The following day Maurice McCabe phoned Ms Cafolla. He told her the matter had now been brought to his attention and he apologised for how it had been handled. When she said she had been told it had gone to the DPP, Sergeant McCabe informed her that that wasn't true and added that she could make a complaint about the handling of the case.

Finally, she had made contact with somebody who was taking her seriously.

The culprits were contacted in the following week and agreed to make statements under caution. A file was then compiled, ensuring that the matter could proceed to summons stage just within the six-month timeframe, after which the case would be statute-barred.

On 21 January 2008 Sergeant McCabe furnished the full report to Superintendent Michael Clancy with a note: 'Ms Cafolla is very disappointed with the Garda investigation and how she was treated and I would agree with her. I am carrying out a full investigation into this incident as the file submitted to me on the 21st December 2007 needs major attention.'

All three men pleaded guilty before Bailieboro District Court on 6 June 2008. The two main culprits were given three-month suspended prison sentences, the third given the benefit of the Probation Act. The judge instructed all three to each pay €500 compensation to Ms Cafolla, but she asked that the money instead be given to the Garda Benevolent Fund.

Years later, Ms Cafolla reflected on what the incident had highlighted for her.

'I am not being the criminal but I am the victim and it has a knock-on effect and people need to know they need to do things properly. That is why it is in place so that things like this don't happen to people and that's for my children and I wouldn't let them disrespect the gardaí ever even because there is as far as I'm concerned the only person who helped me was the man that I met that day Mr McCabe and another gentleman who came from the station and interviewed me were very nice as well. But the thing about it is it doesn't happen to other people that is all.'

Cootehill Assault

'This is a poor investigation into a serious incident'
Inspector Noel Cunningham

On the night of 1 September 2007, Kate (not her real name) was out socialising at the Ivy Bar in Bridge Street, Cootehill, County Cavan. Afterwards, the seventeen-year-old continued partying with some friends. At the end of the night, she and two male friends headed for home. They went their separate ways at the edge of town and bade each other goodnight.

Kate kept walking towards her own home. It was now going on for 6am. As she approached the entrance to her estate, she noticed a man coming towards her. He was small for a man, had a tight haircut and was dressed from head to toe in black.

Kate knew him from around the town. He was a foreign guy; she had seen him at her school a few times, maybe picking up kids. He was stumbling now as he approached her, mumbled something like 'sorry' as they passed each other. But Kate sensed something and turned around. He was now following her. She picked up pace, but he seemed to be drawing closer, so she started to run.

Next thing she knew, he was grabbing her by the shoulder. He put his hand over her mouth. She tried to scream. She fell to the ground and got up. Panicked now, she ran again but soon realised she was running away from her estate and back towards the town. It didn't matter. She just had to get away.

Presently, she turned and saw that her attacker was gone. She made her way back home, her every step accompanied by caution. By the time she arrived home she was shaking. Anything could have happened out there in the cold, lonely dawn.

A few hours later two guards from Bailieboro received a call directing them to go to Kate's home in Cootehill. The local station in Cootehill is open only during the day and Bailieboro is the 24-hour station in the district.

They went to the house, met Kate and her parents and took a statement from the victim.

After that the investigation got underway. The case was brought up at a management meeting in Bailieboro three days later. There was a decision to have a 'photofit' of the suspect compiled. It didn't happen.

There was also a resolution to set up a checkpoint in the relevant area between 5am and 6am in order to 'gather information on the crime'. There is no record of any checkpoint being set up.

Within ten days, the suspect had been identified. A Cootehill garda who had got involved reckoned it was a foreign national he had arrested for a public order offence the previous November. This man was identified on the basis of the victim's description of her attacker.

Meanwhile, Kate saw her attacker twice in the coming weeks around the town. On the first occasion, her father called the gardaí. They telephoned back to say they'd 'done the check and they couldn't spot him or they didn't spot him'.

The second time she saw the man in the local supermarket. Again her father alerted the gardaí. Again he was told 'there was no sighting of him'. The garda who answered the phone made no mention of checking the CCTV in the supermarket. These calls were not noted by any gardaí in Cootehill.

The investigating garda, a female member who had attended at the scene on the morning of the incident, said she kept in contact with the victim, but Kate has no recollection of such liaisons, and there is no record of it on the file.

No formal identification parade was organised. Despite, as one garda put it, the incident being 'the talk of the town', it doesn't appear to have ignited the local constabulary into frenzied action.

Eventually, on 21 January 2008, nearly five months after the incident, the investigating guard arrested the suspect. He was brought to Bailieboro Garda station and interviewed through an interpreter. The interview began at 12.14pm and concluded at 12.36pm. After a five-month investigation in which the suspect was identified early on, he was interviewed for just 22 minutes. Seven minutes after the interview was completed, he was released.

Later there would be attempts to blame Maurice McCabe for releasing him, but it would be shown that McCabe had nothing to do with letting the man leave.

A few weeks after the release, a collection of photos of Eastern European men was brought to Kate's home. She was shown twelve photos, one of which was the suspect. She didn't identify any of them as her assailant. Despite this, the man who had been arrested continued to be the main suspect for the investigating gardaí.

On 8 February, the unit sergeant sent Sergeant McCabe a report on what he described as a 'considerable investigation'. McCabe reported on the matter to the superintendent, noting that the suspect was 'only interviewed for 31 minutes and was then released' (in fact the interview had been only 22 minutes; the suspect was released seven minutes later) and that 'the injured party's statement describes this incident as possibly an attempted rape but the Garda Investigation does not reflect this'.

Later that month Inspector Noel Cunningham reviewed the file on behalf of the superintendent, noting that 'this is a poor investigation into a serious incident and reflects as much on the supervision as the investigation'.

No further progress was made with the investigation. Over three years later, the PULSE entry on the assault was updated: 'i/p [injured party] looked at photos id parade could not identify the s/o [suspected offender]. Insufficient evidence to prosecute.'

So ended another investigation into a serious crime in the Bailieboro district.

Dangerous Driving at Lakeside Manor Hotel

'The matter requires immediate attention and investigation.'
Instruction to Virginia Garda Station

The four, three men and a woman, were thrown out of the Lakeside Manor at 2.30am. Things had got messy inside, the usual stuff involving drink. The four people left with a sense of grievance. They got into a BMW which was parked near the entrance of the hotel.

By now, as would be normal for this time of the night, there were a number of patrons milling around the entrance, some maybe out for a smoke, others preparing to head for the hills.

The BMW started up. Then it began to manoeuvre slowly in an arc. Suddenly it reversed towards the entrance at high speed. Those standing about reacted in horror. There were screams. Three individuals didn't manage to dodge out of the car's way before it screeched to a halt and then took off into the night. It was two days after Christmas 2007.

For those at the entrance, it was a traumatic experience. The three who had been hit sustained relatively minor injuries, but the atmosphere was shot through with shock and anger.

Shortly after the BMW left the scene, a patrol car arrived from Bailieboro station. After talking to the doormen and getting details of the car's registration, the gardaí set off in pursuit. However, the car had disappeared into the night. The guards returned to the Lakeside Manor and viewed footage of the incident which had been captured in its entirety on CCTV. Unfortunately, it was not possible to download the footage onto a disc at the time.

The guards came off their shift at 4am, but later that day they contacted Virginia station and told the garda on duty that 'the matter required immediate attention and investigation by members there'.

Not much happened after that. On New Year's Eve, four members travelled to Laytown, Co. Meath where they had been led to believe one of the suspects could be found, but nothing came of that.

The following day, one of those members, couldn't find anybody to go with him to chase up another lead in Skerries, Co. Dublin. He rang Maurice McCabe in Bailieboro to check if there was anybody at the station who might be up for it. McCabe was off, but as he was unable to find anybody to go, he volunteered to accompany the guard himself.

Nothing came of that inquiry, and later in the day the pair viewed CCTV footage and made another call, this time to Navan, but again it turned out to be futile.

In due course there would be attempts to portray McCabe as being in charge of the investigation, but all the evidence suggests that he was merely giving the garda from Virginia a hand because there was nobody else available. In this, it could well be argued that McCabe was going above and beyond what his job demanded of him.

In mid-January 2009, the district officer, Superintendent Clancy, instructed the station sergeant in Virginia to get cracking on the investigation. This sergeant would, eight months later, be deployed to Kosovo, and for most of that year was engaged in various training courses for his deployment. Still, that didn't excuse the fact that practically nothing was done to chase down the culprits of what had been a dangerous driving incident.

In fact, nothing more was done for fourteen months. In March

2009, as a result of a complaint McCabe had made, the investigation was reactivated.

Three months later – and eighteen months after the incident – statements were taken from the victims and security staff at the hotel. One passenger in the car was identified and interviewed.

It would be more than another year before the driver was arrested in Dublin. He was interviewed at Harcourt Street station where he admitted driving the BMW, but claimed that the car had gone into reverse accidentally.

By that stage, it didn't matter. The time limit for prosecuting had passed and eventually, on 4 January 2011, the DPP's office concluded that that was the end of the matter.

It should have been a routine investigation delivering an excellent chance of prosecution and a sense of closure for the victims. Instead, it was another shambles.

6

'I was aware that he worked hard and long hours displaying absolute loyalty and commitment to An Garda Síochána, to the management team in the district, to his colleagues and to the people of Bailieboro.'
Retired Superintendent Liam Hogan

Towards the back end of 2007, Bailieboro was getting in on the sergeant-in-charge of the station. McCabe noticed the problems mounting up. In his routine perusal of investigation files, he saw that little progress was being made on a number of cases.

He was fielding calls at the station from Majella Cafolla, who wanted to know what was happening over the incident in her restaurant. Another case, involving the seizure of stolen illegal DVD equipment at a house in the town in July 2007, had not been advanced. There was also a backlog of other cases, with little sign of progress.

Internally, things were no better. The number of probationary guards at the station had increased from eleven to eighteen. There simply was not the capacity to ensure that they were properly supervised.

Another lingering problem concerned fall-out from the allegation made against McCabe by a colleague's daughter in December 2006. In late 2007, there had been an attempt to make the DPP's emphatic direction in favour of McCabe available to the girl's family in order to clear up any tension in the district between the two colleagues. It now looked unlikely that this would be possible.

Then there was the case of sexual harassment. In late 2007, a female guard came to McCabe and alleged that she was being harassed by a male member on her unit. In normal circumstances, the best course of action would have been to investigate the matter and interview the man in question. Instead, McCabe simply lifted the phone and told the unit sergeant that the man in question was to be transferred to another unit immediately.

The action brought an end to the female member's problems, but the man in question was making noises about his treatment. (The female member eventually made 27 allegations of harassment, of which twelve were upheld.)

Superintendent Michael Clancy had been appointed as district officer to Bailieboro the previous August. Personally, he and McCabe got on well from the start. There was, however, a major difference of opinion between them on the division of responsibilities, and what constituted an acceptable level of standards.

No internal review or external report, body or court has ever made any criticism of Clancy for how he ran Bailieboro during the eight months he was in situ. A major internal Garda investigation found that he bore no culpability for any issues at the station. He would go on to be promoted to chief superintendent. Yet McCabe claimed that many of his issues in Bailieboro arose from a major difference of opinion between himself and Clancy; the tension between the men was subsequently referred to in the O'Higgins Commission which looked at the issues that arose in Baileboro.

The issues that were getting in on McCabe could hardly be

removed with the prevailing culture and atmosphere, along with the transcient procession of district officers who were often absent from the station, engaged in other work or training. As sergeant-in-charge, a huge amount of work and responsibility was vested in McCabe without even the supportive presence of an inspector at the station.

In another member, that kind of pressure might have led to slackening standards, but that was not an option for somebody of McCabe's disposition and professional pride. He knew of only one way to do the job.

In early January 2008, he put together a memo for Superintendent Clancy with a view to meeting him.

Re: Issues at Bailieboro Garda Station
I list a number of issues that need to be addressed at Bailieboro Garda Station:
  – Members not turning up for duty on time
  – Members not turning up for duty at all
  – Members not signing on or off in diary
  – Members not doing foot patrol
  – Investigation files not being done
  – Investigation files very poor
  – Incidents not being investigated
  – Members constantly hanging around the station
  – Public officers reading paper and watching television
      on duty
  – Calls not attended to
  – Garda members making out duty detail
  – Members not performing the duty they
      are detailed for
  – Summonses not being followed up

- Warrants not being executed
- No briefings
- No supervision on 24 hour basis
- Crime unit not performing public order duty
  at weekends
- No guidance to junior members
- Members' non performance
- Clique forming
- Coffee/tea breaks constantly
- Very unprofessional approach to incidents by P/
  gardaí [probationary gardaí]
- Reported incidents to gardaí not created on PULSE

The above are some of the issues and are quire [*sic*] serious and I can stand by anything I have mentioned. I have tried and attempted to address all the issues but I am failing, through no fault of my own. The above seems to be the acceptable standard in Bailieboro and I am receiving no help addressing the same.

I cannot put up with the situation any longer and under the Health and Safety Act I request an hour meeting with you at your convenience to discuss the matters and to see what process you can put in place to deal with the issues. It is unfair on probationers that these low standards are being accepted and not being dealt with and that they are being trained into this system of low standards.

Forward for your information and attention please.

Superintendent Clancy and Sergeant McCabe met in the super's office on 28 January. There are hugely different versions of what occurred and even concerning the duration of the meeting. One apparent resolution reached was that there would be a meeting called of all the sergeants to discuss the issues, but, for one reason or another, such a meeting never took place.

Feeling no more assured in his concerns following the summit with Clancy, McCabe's gloom worsened over the next few weeks. He was particularly bothered by the progress of one case.

This case concerned a serious assault in Crossan's pub in Bailieboro on 23 May 2007. Mr R – who has not been publicly identified – was punched in the face and head and had to be helped from the premises. According to Mr R, the men who had beaten him up 'were not the type of boys to be messed with'.

A day after the assault, Mr R's wife went to Bailieboro station and made a complaint. A few days later Mr R gave a statement describing the assault and who was involved.

The investigation, after a fashion at the time, was slipshod and was led by a probationary guard. Stretched resources meant that this young man had little benefit of supervision, despite the seriousness of the case.

There was a problem with the CCTV in the pub, which didn't help the investigation. Then there was a change of district officer. In August, Maura Lernihan, who had attended a case conference on the matter, was replaced by Michael Clancy.

In the following months McCabe noticed that little was being done to advance the investigation. He informed his super in November, who in turn prioritised the case. At least nine reminders were sent to the probationer to get cracking.

Later that month Mr R was visited by the probationary guard, who told Mr R that he would be better off withdrawing his statement of complaint.

According to Mr R, the guard arrived and 'he says the matter is basically closed, there is insufficient evidence. It is not going to happen. You know you want to finish it off.'

The guard disputed this, but a later inquiry accepted Mr R's version.

The reality was that there was a relatively good case to be made.

In the middle of February 2008, McCabe was informed of the withdrawal of Mr R's statement. He was highly suspicious. He had kept an eye on the case, kept the super informed, sent out reminders about it, and then suddenly it's all over.

On 25 February he arranged to call up to the home of Mr and Mrs R and find out what had happened. They related that, contrary to the official version being peddled at the station, the decision to withdraw the statement was effectively pushed on them. McCabe would later describe it as a case where the couple were 'forced' to withdraw the statement. In reality, they were encouraged to do so and were misled by the probationer as to the strength of the case.

Mr and Mrs R were seriously upset at this outcome. The husband had decided to pursue justice despite knowing that his assailants were boys not to be messed with. He had made the statement against his better instincts, went along with the investigation and kept looking over his shoulder. And now he was being told that things had not turned out all that well and that he'd have been better off sucking it up from day one, accepting that the law didn't apply to some, enduring the physical and emotional pain because justice was not a priority in Bailieboro.

The meeting shocked McCabe. How many more cases were to end up like this? How many more members of the public were to be ill-served in this manner?

He went home and discussed it with Lorraine. By now, he had formed the view that his authority within the station was shot. Those who were disposed to do as little as possible knew that they could get away with it. The probationers were not going to rock any boats. And the members who just got on with the job as best they could now appeared to hold out little hope that the sergeant-in-charge might be able to steady the ship.

What if he told management that he was jacking in? What if he put it up to them? They knew how hard he worked, his role in keeping everything on an even keel. Would the threat of resignation not jolt them into action? McCabe knew they would have to look far and wide to draw in a sergeant-in-charge with his dedication and appetite for hard work.

In any event, he needed some reassurance that things would get better. Hand in a letter of resignation and let them chew on that? He would tell them he was resigning from his position as sergeant-in-charge to return to an ordinary sergeant running a unit. He wasn't going to be associated any longer with what he saw as systemic failures. He would do his own job, mould a unit with a few good workers, and leave the rest of the station in the hands of somebody else.

On 3 March McCabe met with Superintendent Clancy and indicated that he wanted to resign from his position. Clancy said he would need to have McCabe's decision in writing. (Clancy also took on board what had apparently occurred with Mr and Mrs R and he acted promptly to find out the exact details.)

With that, Maurice McCabe's turbulent tenure as sergeant-in-charge of Bailieboro Garda station came to an end.

Date 04.03.2008
Superintendent
Bailieboro
Re: Sergeant in charge, Bailieboro Garda Station, County Cavan

I wish to make an application to return to mainstream

policing and vacate my positon of Sergeant in Charge of Bailieboro Garda Station. I am doing this solely for reasons that you are aware of as discussed at our meeting on 28.01.2008 and in relation to

– Lack of management support

– Lack of standards

– Lack of accountability

– Lack of duty to the public.

I have discussed the move with my family and would request an immediate return to mainstream policing.

Forwarded for your attention, please,

Maurice McCabe 24261F

Nobody came running. Nobody grabbed McCabe by the sleeve and told him to cop on to himself. Nobody asked him to reconsider.

Management had called his bluff. He wanted to go back on a unit? Then let him go.

The failure to hang on to the sergeant-in-charge, the refusal to attempt to change his mind, to tell him that he was valued and his concerns were being listened to, speaks volumes for the culture of the force in the local area.

McCabe had been doing a commendable job since he had taken up the reins. Four of the supers whom he worked under were effusive in their praise of his work. All relied heavily on him.

So why not make an effort to get him to stay? Maybe he had become more trouble than he was worth. Unlike the district officers to whom he reported, McCabe wasn't just passing through. He wasn't biding time in Bailieboro. If he had been en route to somewhere else, maybe he would have managed to care less about standards, and service to the public.

His capacity for the job was summed up in a subsequent

investigation by some of those under whom he served. Here is chief superintendent Gabriel McIntyre, who was district officer for Bailieboro when McCabe began as sergeant-in-charge: 'I found Sergeant McCabe to be positive and energetic in his position. He displayed a strong work ethic with a strong emphasis in community policing and providing a high standard of policing to the community.'

McIntyre was succeeded by Superintendent Eugene Corcoran, whose opinion of McCabe differed only in emphasis: 'I found Sergeant McCabe to be capable and enthusiastic in his approach to his duties. At all times I found him to be efficient …. I would assess his performance very positively. In my experience he was hard-working and efficient. He understood the need to keep the district officer advised of all matters requiring attention at Superintendent level …. I found him to be very interested in his work and in ensuring that matters were attended to promptly.'

The next district officer to pass through Bailieboro was Superintendent Liam Hogan. This was his verdict of the sergeant-in-charge: 'I considered Sergeant McCabe to be an excellent sergeant and member of An Garda Síochána. He offered 200 per cent commitment and was one of my most reliable members in the district. I relied on him, I trusted him implicitly and I listened to his advice …. He was full of enthusiasm with a very positive attitude. I was aware that he worked hard and long hours displaying absolute loyalty and commitment to An Garda Síochána, to the management team in the district, to his colleagues and to the people of Bailieboro. He took particular interest in the work progress and welfare of junior members in the district HQ.'

The last district officer before Michael Clancy was Superintendent Maura Lernihan. She also was appreciative of McCabe's virtues: 'I found [Sergeant McCabe] to be efficient, flexible and committed.

He was diligent in the performance of his duties. He encouraged and directed those under his supervision and had a good working relationship with the other sergeants.'

Despite these opinions – largely shared by younger members in the station – McCabe was now being allowed to vacate the bridge and return to manning the deck.

He was, by his own admission, surprised. He had thought that the threat of resignation might be enough to spur his superior officers to some action. Now he was being politely asked to shut the door on his way out.

Surprise soon gave way to anger. As far as McCabe was concerned, he had been shafted, and forced, through working conditions, to leave his position. There was no doubt but that he loved doing what he did. Being a guard had been all he had ever wanted since he was a boy. Taking control of a station had given him the kind of responsibility he thrived on. And now he was stepping back down the career ladder on a matter of principle. The question rumbling around his head was the ancient one familiar to sundered lovers. Was it him or was it them? Was he demanding too much, or was the force, through its culture, its focus, the agency he had always imagined it to be?

Through the anger and confusion, one thought remained constant. He wanted his job back, but only on his own terms.

Within a fortnight the merry-go-round of district officers cranked into life once more. On 18 March Michael Clancy was transferred out of Bailieboro. He had been there for just eight months. His role was taken up by Noel Cunningham, who was promoted to superintendent on assuming his new office. At least Cunningham had the advantage of having served as acting district officer for prolonged periods over the preceding years when the various superintendents had been absent. Cunningham had also been the officer who had investigated the allegation concerning McCabe's colleague's daughter.

This was a chance for McCabe to start again. Word was sent to him that there might be a possibility that he could be reinstated in his old job. The catch was that he would have to apply for it in writing.

That he simply could not do. To acquiesce to such a proposal, in his mind, would be to negate the issues he had highlighted. It would be to discount the victims of crime whom he had encountered, and, in a couple of cases, counselled. It would be to admit that things were fine in Bailieboro and he had just been experiencing a hissy fit. Everything in his character would kick against being party to such a deception. He would love to take up his previous duties, but only if he was to be taken seriously.

The official call to return did not materialise. McCabe transferred to working on a unit in Bailieboro, but the sense of grievance did not leave him. He felt he was entitled, within the confines of the job, to have his case examined. He was entitled to have the force determine whether this particular employee had been hounded from the job he loved.

Seán Costello is a Dublin-based solicitor who has served for a long time as counsel to many within the Association of Garda Sergeants and Inspectors. He was an obvious port of call for a sergeant with a grievance.

McCabe visited Costello in Dublin and relayed his concerns. He had vacated his job as sergeant-in-charge because he felt that he had been bullied and harassed into doing so by the conditions at the station. He wanted to use the grievance procedure to get his job back.

A grievance procedure is common in all large organisations and the public service. It involves a review of decisions and conduct within the organisation to see if an employee had been treated fairly. In a case like McCabe's, one possible outcome is a recommendation that he be returned to his old job. Another is that a conclusion is reached that he was treated fairly.

Costello examined the evidence McCabe had assembled. After further discussion, both came to the conclusion that what was at issue in industrial relations terms was not a grievance, but a complaint.

This observation upped the stakes immediately. A grievance might be an issue involving one individual's treatment of a subordinate. A complaint was a different matter.

This was taking on the management as a whole, taking on a culture, taking on his colleagues at sergeant level, the rank and file members. It was bringing to the fore the whole manner in which policing had been conducted in Bailieboro, highlighting it as the main exhibit in McCabe's decision to leave his job. Did he have the stomach for that?

Grievance procedures happened all the time. More often than not, it was between two individuals. The procedure would be dealt with under bullying rules and legislation.

A complaint on the scale of what McCabe was alleging was entirely different. Within An Garda Síochána it was, at the time, practically unheard of.

McCabe knew there were some in Bailieboro who wouldn't hold it against him. He wasn't alone in the frustration he had felt at how the district had developed over time. But there was a difference between others feeling his pain, and coming to his aid. An Garda Síochána was a closed organisation. You didn't break ranks over something like this. You put the head down and just got on with things. A loyalty was forged from the first drops of sweat and tears in Templemore that permeated the whole organisation. Fidelity to each other was more important than anything else, including the badge, the oath, the public. Nobody spelt that out, certainly nobody in the upper echelons ever articulated it, but it was there, as obvious as the uniform.

Now McCabe had been placed in a position where he would be taking that on. He hadn't wanted it. All he wanted was to be a guard, to serve, but his aspiration and his experience were now in major conflict.

He could go back on a unit, put his head down and concentrate on his own little patch, just as others before him, faced with the same dilemmas, had done. But that wasn't for him. To do that would be to live a lie, to pretend that things were not as they were, to forego any hope that there might be change.

He would do what was required and live with his decision.

After thinking it over for a few days, he got back in touch with Costello and said that he wanted to make a complaint.

Within weeks, a process was put in place to examine McCabe's complaints of malpractice in Bailieboro. There was also another issue, though. The female member at the station who had complained of sexual harassment also wanted her complaint examined. The two matters would be dealt with in a single investigation.

The assistant commissioner for the area, Derek Byrne, appointed Chief Superintendent Terry McGinn to investigate the two issues. McGinn was based in Donegal and was one of the highest-ranking female members in the force. She set about her task immediately.

In Bailieboro, McCabe got back to work on a unit while a colleague temporarily filled in as sergeant-in-charge. It didn't take long for word to get around that Maurice McCabe had made a complaint.

Some raised eyebrows. Others reacted angrily, and a number among the station's detail probably issued wry smiles, having known McCabe, known what he had put up with, and known that it was high time something was done about the merry-go-round of district officers and the proliferation of probationers.

McCabe didn't let it bother him. He was left to his own devices. There was no phone call from HQ, offering support for somebody who was highlighting potential issues. There was precious little contact from anybody in management in the whole Cavan/Monaghan division. It became obvious to him from early on that he was now on his own, cast outside the jagged notion of what was considered to be loyalty to the badge.

None of that fazed him. He had made a decision after considered thought. The road he was embarking on would not be easy but it was the correct one, as he saw it, for himself and for the standards the public were entitled to expect from their police service.

By that summer it was obvious that there would be difficulty with McCabe continuing at the station while the internal investigation was underway. There was too much potential for conflict. Some of those with whom McCabe was serving were now under investigation on foot of his complaint.

His staff association (gardaí are not allowed to belong to a trade union, and are represented instead by staff associations. McCabe, as a sergeant was a member of the Association of Sergeants and Inspectors) attempted to ease things by getting him a transfer. Initially he was offered a post in a small station in County Westmeath, which he had never heard of. Then something came up in Mullingar – the traffic unit needed a sergeant.

He discussed it with Lorraine. He had to go somewhere, certainly for the time being. There was no way he could continue working in what was developing into a poisonous atmosphere in Bailieboro. Mullingar was an extra twenty minutes or so of a commute, but it sounded like a busy station, and he would be able to concentrate on the job again and not have to keep one eye looking over his shoulder.

He moved in July 2008. Meanwhile, his interaction with the McGinn investigation began. He was required to produce a full statement, and it was obvious from passages in it that his stance had hardened in the months since he had left his old post.

> Since I vacated the position of Sergeant-in-charge at Bailiboro Garda Station on the 19th of March 2008 no garda officer has contacted me at all and I have been

left totally isolated and victimised. I have been ignored, snubbed and ridiculed by a number of members in the station because they know that I have failed in my bid for proper standards and accountability and that I have failed in my efforts to put procedures in place in the station for proper control.... Article 10 of the Professional and Ethical Standards states that 'individuals or group behaviour of loyalties, which serve to facilitate, encourage or conceal illegal, unethical or unprofessional actions, undermines professional policing and it is the professional duty of each member of An Garda Síochána to actively challenge, oppose and expose such activities for the common good'. I abided by Article 10 and have been punished, penalised, discriminated, bullied, harassed and victimised by garda management for doing so.

Maurice McCabe might have thought things were bad then, but they were about to get a lost worse. He had opened a Pandora's box with his complaint, and there was no precedent as to what might now emerge. There was no precedent either for An Garda Síochána having to deal with a member who was determined not to be cowed, but to be resolute in his conviction that he was offering full loyalty to the state he had sworn to serve.

7

'The whistleblower, like the referee from whom he gets his name, is seen as someone who is not on the team' *Seán Guerin*

The darts began shooting across his chest just outside Castlepollard, County Westmeath. For a few seconds McCabe saw his life flash before him. All day his chest had been at him, but he had relegated any such worries to some recess of his mind. It was one of those days when he had plenty of concerns to be getting on with. The pain wasn't the only thing. He put his hand to his brow and felt the dampness.

It was late September 2008, soon after midnight on the road home from another shift on traffic in Mullingar. The pain had been a dull presence for most of the day, but now it was as if it had really come to life, out here on the lonely road.

Or maybe it was just a delayed reaction. Maybe his subconscious had managed to keep it all under control at work, dealing with more correspondence from Bailieboro, more stuff around the internal investigation under way into his complaints, more of those blank looks from members, who may or may not have him fingered as somebody who was no longer part of the team.

What if this was it? What if his heart was about to give in to the stress that had been piling up now for over a year.

Headlights came at him as he moved onto the far side of Castlepollard. Still the darts kept stabbing at his chest. Twenty-two years on the job had familiarised him with the scene flashing through his mind.

A car in the ditch, the driver's door half-open, a body inside, drained of life in an instant, loved ones as yet oblivious of the emotional carnage about to be visited on them, a huge void, wasted life. Was he to be the latest statistic on the road, the cause of death being determined only much later?

Through the pain, all McCabe could really focus on was Lorraine and the kids. Whenever he fell into physical or psychological turbulence, it was the thought of them which hauled him back from self-pity.

The pain eased a bit within minutes, but maybe, he thought, it was just taking a break, gearing up to return with greater vengeance. He kept going, but turned off before reaching his own neighbourhood, heading instead for Cavan town and the general hospital. He parked and walked in, one of the nurses approaching him immediately when she spotted the uniform. Guards were often in the place at this hour, usually conveying broken bodies or even the recently deceased. But this one wasn't here accompanying patients.

'Could you get somebody to take a look at me?' he asked her, explaining that he was worried about the chest pains.

McCabe thought he'd be in the hospital for an hour or two. As it turned out, it was four days before he got back home. They kept him in on surveillance because his symptoms were sufficient to raise concerns. On the third day, he was transferred to the Mater Hospital for further tests. Only when the results came back, giving him the all-clear, was the medical team happy to allow him home.

It had been a brief interlude, a few days of respite from the storm that was blowing through his life.

By September 2008 McCabe had been through transformative change in a few short months. He was working out of Mullingar, back on a unit, but that was no big deal. At least he could concentrate on his own work. As with all the various posts he'd held in his career, he was equipped to make the most of this.

Mullingar, while not much farther from his home than Bailieboro – due south instead of north – was in a different division. This removed him somewhat from the eye of the storm in Bailieboro.

Regularly he got a call from various friendly members in Cavan/Monaghan passing on the gossip they had heard about him. One friend told him that word was going around that his marriage was over. This, he had been told, was being spread by a particular member of the station, who was telling people that McCabe had left his wife and children.

He was shocked that this was the kind of thing to which some were stooping. As it would turn out, within a few weeks of hearing that, he ran into the member in a town in Cavan. The two knew each other. McCabe was passing in his own vehicle and the other man was on duty, sitting in a squad car. McCabe rolled down his window and leaned across. The other man did likewise, his face lighting up when he saw McCabe, old colleagues on a chance encounter.

'I haven't left my wife and kids, you know,' McCabe said. The other man feigned ignorance, but some of the colour drained from his face.

Word came through from another friend of McCabe's that he was said to be romantically linked to the female member who had brought her complaint of sexual harassment, by a member of the force, to him.

The only connection between the pair was that McCabe had dealt with the problem efficiently, and now both their complaints were being examined by the one inquiry. But none of that mattered. The objective of the rumour was to damage McCabe.

Each of these rumours delivered its own little blow, opening up another wound.

He was now persona non grata among a large cohort of former colleagues in the Cavan/Monaghan division, and the rumours had done their work by deepening the sense of isolation he was feeling.

While Maurice had to cope directly with the fallout, Lorraine had her own battles: 'Maurice would leave for work and head off to Mullingar,' she says. 'I'd have to deal with things locally. I was the one going to football matches, school concerts, all these gatherings where I could and did run into the wives of guards who knew what was going on. Some of them didn't even want to look me in the eye. It was a time full of stress. I'd watch Maurice going off to work, sometimes with the whole thing weighing him down, and I'd wonder would he ever be coming back. I used to be terrified if I rang and he didn't answer the phone. They were terrible years.'

Anecdotes were drifting back to McCabe about how word was going around among old friends that it was best to refrain from showing him any open support. His name now meant trouble in various quarters of management in the Cavan/Monaghan division and among some of the rank and file. As one friendly voice told him during a call, 'Watch your back.'

Mullingar was a relief. Most colleagues there just took him as they found him, and that was fine because he had always been equipped to get on with people.

But there had been one small incident. He'd got word that a member was urging an inspector at the station to set up a roadblock in order to do McCabe for not having a proper NCT.

McCabe's love of cars meant he had two vehicles at the time, a Ford Galaxy and a Jaguar. The latter had failed the NCT, and he was awaiting a re-test. But quite obviously one member saw the car and decided it would be a good way to get at him.

No roadblock was set up. McCabe left a note for the member in his locker, pointing out that his vehicles were in order. That was the end of that.

Despite words of support from some colleagues, Maurice McCabe now knew he was largely on his own. Quickly, he became aware of what his changed circumstances meant for him. He knew the power of the force. The greenest member out of Templemore was handed huge powers – of arrest, of detention, of privileged access to people's lives in times of trouble. It was a power he had often thought of as awesome and for that reason he respected it, and used it as intended.

He knew, though, that that power could be directed against anybody who was deemed a threat to the force. And there was no doubt in his mind that some saw him precisely in that light. Where once he'd been an asset, now he was viewed in some quarters as a liability.

With that in mind, McCabe decided to take precautions to protect himself. The first thing he did was to ensure that he had a record of any conversations he had regarding his complaints. This could be done only by recording things said at meetings.

Practically all such meetings were with officers of a higher rank. In the event of any dispute over what had transpired at a meeting, the senior man or woman would be believed. That's just the way it was in the force.

So since the problems had begun the previous March, McCabe had recorded any meetings he thought might end up being a cause for concern.

There had only been a couple by that stage, the most prominent being a meeting with Superintendent Noel Cunningham, district officer in Bailieboro, who had travelled to Mullingar in August 2008 to interview him about some of the fallout from Bailieboro.

Cunningham had been accompanied by a female sergeant and the meeting had been amicable. The sergeant had taken notes, and at the end of the meeting the three of them had agreed on the notes taken.

Throughout the meeting, McCabe's phone, in his breast pocket, had been on record, as a precaution.

McCabe had taken the recording and stored it at his home, just in case. He largely forgot about that meeting, considering it relatively insignificant. Seven years later, however, he would find himself rooting around in the attic looking for the recording because it would take on major significance in defence of his actions.

Throughout this time McCabe felt insecure about what he had embarked upon. Would any investigation really get to the heart of what he had reported about Bailieboro? Would it want to? Or would it end up running into a convenient sandbank?

He needed some reassurance that at least the issues would be dealt with, and for that he turned to the law. Following the Morris Tribunal into Garda corruption in Donegal, a new system had come into law to facilitate gardaí who wished to report wrong-doing.

The Garda Síochána Act made provision for a so-called whistleblower to go to a third party outside the force, known as the Confidential Recipient. This person would record the details, keep the name of the officer confidential and bring the complaint to the Garda Commissioner to have it investigated.

Once that was complete, the commissioner would report back to the confidential recipient, and he or she would inform the whistleblower of the outcome. By following this path, the whistleblower could be assured of anonymity, thereby negating any fears among any garda member about reporting misconduct in the force.

That was the theory, but in practice the system was fatally flawed. Firstly, it assumed that the commissioner would enthusiastically root out any problems. Perhaps that would be so, but it certainly wasn't something that should be taken for granted.

For instance, if wrong-doing within the force was discovered and could be isolated to a single member or two without repercussions further up the chain of command, then discipline would be applied. If there was a chance that a stain may spread up the ranks, or reflect on the force as a whole … well, the Garda's record in rigorous self-examination was no better than that of the Catholic Church.

The other problem with the Confidential Recipient system was that the officeholders had practically no power. To all intents and purposes, they were simply messengers, passing on complaints, rather than having any say into how the complaints might be resolved.

The first person appointed as a Confidential Recipient under the act was Brian McCarthy, a former senior civil servant, who had acted as secretary general to President Mary McAleese.

McCabe got in touch with him in September 2008 and arranged a meeting at McCarthy's office in Harcourt Square, Dublin. McCarthy listened to McCabe, accepted copies of his complaints and asked a few pertinent questions. He said he would be in touch.

McCabe was happy with the meeting. McCarthy was receptive and appeared to be efficient. Passing the complaint on to him would ensure, at the very least, that an outside agent was aware of it, which would provide some modicum of security for McCabe. Whatever happened, nobody could suggest that this whole business was a figment of his imagination.

The other strand to McCabe's busy life at the time was engagement with the internal investigation. Originally, Terry McGinn, the chief super from Donegal, had been investigating the complaints from McCabe and the female garda.

In late May, McCabe had met McGinn in the Farnham Arms Hotel in Cavan for an interview. That had lasted for over ten hours, all the way past midnight. Through it, McCabe had become emotional at times over the extent of the problems he had raised and where it had all led him. Consequently the interview had had to be adjourned at a few junctures.

McCabe also made further allegations of malpractice. One implicated Chief Superintendent Colm Rooney, who oversaw the Cavan/Monaghan division. (The inquiry would, in time, clear Rooney of any malpractice.)

That put McGinn in a difficult position. She and Rooney were the same rank in the force, so technically at least she could not investigate him.

This matter was referred to HQ and it was decided that an assistant commissioner (AC) would be appointed to the team. This was Derek Byrne, AC for the northern division. From then on, the investigation became known as the Byrne/McGinn inquiry. By the end of 2008, word was drifting out to the media that something big was going on in Bailieboro.

Report from *Anglo-Celt* newspaper, 31 December 2008.

Bailieboro gardaí in malpractice inquiry: Investigation ongoing by Chief Superintendent.

Alleged malpractice by members of the Garda Síochána in the Bailieboro District of the Cavan/Monaghan Division is the focus of a major internal garda inquiry since last April, it has emerged. Two officers are understood to have been transferred amid allegations that they were bullied by some fellow gardaí when they attempted to expose incidents of malpractice. One is a female officer who gained the top marks in all her exams and the other is a more senior officer, both of whom were described as 'exemplary officers' by a well-placed Garda source this week. It appears that the female officer threatened to resign at one stage and eventually accepted a transfer after being on sick leave for a time. The Bailieboro Garda District covers the areas of Bailieboro, Ballyjamesduff, Cootehill, Kingscourt, Mullagh, Shercock, Tullyvin and Virginia. When contacted this week, the Garda Press Office would neither confirm nor deny that the investigation is ongoing. A spokesperson said: 'This office does not comment on internal disciplinary matters.'

However, senior Garda sources told The Anglo-Celt that some of the alleged malpractice incidents are very 'disturbing', with some young gardaí said to be 'out of control'. Despite the allegations, nobody has faced disciplinary action to date. Our source stressed that many of the gardaí in the Bailieboro District are 'brilliant' and the allegations being investigated only relate to some members. The internal inquiry into the alleged activities in the Division is being headed by the current Chief Superintendent in Donegal, Terry McGinn. Her investigation team includes a Detective Superintendent, two Inspectors and two Sergeants.

The source said that the allegations feature a large number of serious breaches of discipline, dereliction of duty and other behaviour of a potentially criminal nature. The senior officer, who was transferred after producing a lengthy list of alleged incidents of misconduct by gardaí, also alleged that two serious offences were not investigated. In one of the alleged cases, the investigation failed to lead to charges, despite the culprits being quickly identified. In the other case, the gardaí allegedly failed to obtain CCTV footage until it was too late. The source said:

'It is just a culture, they expect to get a week's wage for doing nothing. Tell them the DPP said there was not enough evidence to proceed. Stop an odd person for no tax or speeding or drunken driving and have a nice quiet life.' There are also allegations in relation to drinking on duty and the assault of prisoners.

The publication of the story in the local paper cranked up the intensity of feeling within the division. McCabe's phone was constantly on the go, Terry McGinn calling about some aspect of the investigation, friends letting him know the latest rumour, representatives from the Association of Garda Sergeants and Inspectors (AGSI) getting in touch, and calls from Bailieboro about matters still outstanding. All this added to the stress that was now a constant weight on McCabe's shoulders.

In early 2009, a member whom he'd known for nearly a decade arranged to meet McCabe in Navan. Over the course of the conversation it was conveyed to him that his phone was being tapped.

Such an allegation is not unusual for anybody dealing with the security services. (The author of this book was informed a number of times by different people that his phone was tapped as a result of his involvement in this story.) While such information is usually conveyed in good faith and with the best of intentions, questions always remain as to how a third party would have become aware of it.

If some element within the gardaí had taken it upon themselves to tap a phone, it must be assumed that such information would not be passed around carelessly in conversation.

The other issue around surveillance is that, in the modern world, it is possible for phones to be tapped without leaving much trace behind. The days of tape recordings surviving any such operation are long gone. (Although McCabe's own recordings did, thankfully for him, involve digital recordings which he could later access.)

Being told by a source with some authority, whom you respect, that you're under surveillance has the potential to deliver a chill. From then on, McCabe assumed that his phone was being tapped, with the effect that any intimate or private conversations were eliminated from phone calls, to his wife, his extended family, colleagues or his solicitor. It was another reminder that there were people who regarded him as an enemy.

Early in 2009 McCabe was to experience the first of what would become many attempts to frame him for malpractice of one sort or another.

One evening back in 2007, while he had still been operating as sergeant-in-charge in Bailieboro, he was putting on his jacket to go home when he popped his head into the public office, as he routinely did on his way out the door.

A local woman was at the counter, explaining to a guard that she had a big problem. There had been a warrant out for her arrest for failing to pay a fine for a minor conviction. She simply wasn't in a position to pay. Both her children were sick with verifiable long-term conditions and she needed to get particular drugs for them. Her finances were stretched. It was either pay the outstanding fine or take care of her children's immediate needs.

McCabe witnessed the exchange between the woman and the guard on duty and intervened. 'Go home and take care of your children. You can sort this out later,' he said. The grateful woman left. McCabe's intervention was humanitarian and uncontroversial.

Less than two years later, that innocuous incident was cast in a different light. In early 2009, McCabe got word from a neighbour of the woman's that two plain-clothes guards had been up to her house asking about the warrant and how McCabe had dealt with it.

McCabe rang Terry McGinn to ask what was going on. She told him that there had been a complaint from a member in Bailieboro that McCabe had actually 'fixed' the fine for the woman, giving the impression that he had intervened because she was known to him and he was doing her a favour.

A complaint about how McCabe had dealt with the matter had been sent in writing and Terry McGinn was obliged to follow up on it. She had instructed the two guards to interview the woman in question.

A few weeks later, Assistant Commissioner Derek Byrne told

McCabe that it had been established that he had done nothing wrong in the case, but had acted entirely appropriately.

The incident ratcheted up the pressure for McCabe. Was every decision he had made when sergeant-in-charge going to be retrospectively examined? Was this merely an attempt to twist his actions to look as if he was as culpable of malpractice as the others he was pointing the finger at? Once more, he resolved that he would have to take every precaution necessary to protect himself.

While his new status instilled animus in some, it attracted others with a different agenda. Members who quietly remained friends – and the odd one who still braved a social pint or two with McCabe in public houses – saw him now as a form of father confessor to whom they could relay incidents of ill-discipline or malpractice witnessed within the force.

These members knew that he was engaging with Byrne/McGinn and that their concerns would be passed on without ever having to raise their own heads above the parapet.

McCabe had no problem with that. He passed on to Byrne/McGinn various instances about which he'd been informed. Some of these were investigated, others ran into the sand, through no fault of the investigation.

McCabe's willingness to bring these incidents to the attention of senior management – through Byrne/McGinn – could to some eyes have the appearance of a person who was out to root out malpractice wherever he saw it. In reality, McCabe's position was that he had no choice. If members brought issues to him, he couldn't ignore it, after what he had embarked upon himself. Neither was it his place to filter out what should be pursued and what did not merit attention. He would leave that up to Byrne/McGinn.

Members of the force were not the only ones who saw McCabe as a conduit for concerns. When he had served as sergeant-in-charge in Bailieboro – and previously in Clones – he had developed a good reputation among the public. Now, with word going around that he had left the station under a cloud, a number of people contacted him to see what the story was. Among them was a woman involved in a public service job in Bailieboro – an inquiry would describe her under the pseudonym Mrs Brown because she wanted to keep her identity secret for reasons that became obvious.

She met McCabe in Virginia, sympathised with his current predicament, and related that she'd had some problems with members of the force in Bailieboro. In particular, she said, one garda had threatened her and others had treated her shabbily.

McCabe advised her to go to the Garda ombudsman, but she said she already had. He related the complaint to Terry McGinn as another that Byrne/McGinn should investigate. Two sergeants were dispatched to interview the woman in Bailieboro on 17 September 2009. According to their report, Mrs Brown spoke in a 'frank and open manner but was unwilling to make a statement'. She told them that she had gone to McCabe because she had known him as a local guard for years and had developed a trust and respect for him. She related that she'd had problems with some members in Bailieboro, one of whom told her 'her paperwork better be correct', which she took as an attempt to intimidate her. She also said she had been threatened by 'a small black-haired garda'.

She told the pair of sergeants that there was a feeling in Bailieboro that 'the guards do what they like, even when they're off-duty'. The situation was such that there was a general belief that guards didn't respond to calls and therefore some people always rang 999 to ensure that their calls would be recorded. Mrs Brown also felt that one of her sons, who had been in some trouble with the gardaí, 'now felt harassed'.

One of the interviewing sergeants reported of the encounter with Mrs Brown that it was 'very unusual that a [person of Mrs Brown's occupation] would have such a poor relationship with the gardaí. In my opinion she has a grievance which she would not expand on. However, she appears to be an honest and sincere person and her allegations must be treated seriously and are not without foundation.'

Byrne/McGinn had further interviews with the woman, but she remained reluctant to make an official complaint, although she did relate other incidents, including one in which she alleged that she had been verbally abused by a garda.

Her reluctance to officially complain was understandable. Anybody who had to engage with the gardaí on an ongoing basis – particularly with their work – knew that Byrne/McGinn would soon leave town, and they would be left to face at least one local member who might harbour resentment about any complaint that had been made. Mrs Brown related this to the investigation team, noting that she was afraid that she and her family would be 'targeted' if a complaint was made.

Chief Superintendent McGinn, on compiling a report on the matter, noted that it was 'unacceptable that any member would verbally assault a [person in Mrs Brown's occupation] if the facts are as outlined by Mrs Brown. It is further unacceptable that a [person performing her work] should feel intimidated by members of An Garda Síochána.'

McGinn went on to say that the complaints from this woman, along with others, pointed towards 'a breakdown in community engagement in Bailieboro and may well be symptomatic of a deeper malaise'.

Another incident that McCabe brought to Byrne/McGinn was that which came to be known as 'The Rat'. He had received a phone call from a sympathetic female colleague who told him that she was shocked at what had occurred at a gathering in May 2009.

A garda wedding was taking place in County Mayo, which was attended by a large contingent of members from Cavan/Monaghan.

At a pub near the wedding venue, a number of these gardaí had gathered. There was a rubber rat on display in the pub from some event or other.

The guards in the pub took a number of photos of the rubber rat, with a member in each photo, some making rude gestures, one with his finger stuck up the rat's rear end. Eleven photos were uploaded onto the Bebo website, all of which referred to the rat as 'Maurice'. Another label on some of them was 'Cheese-eating rat bastard'.

It was obvious to anybody in the division to whom they were referring.

McCabe felt humiliated by the whole thing and brought it to the attention of Byrne/McGinn during an interview in the Longford Arms Hotel. The matter was investigated and a file sent to the DPP, who decided not to pursue the case.

The perpetrators may have considered it to be a prank, but it conveyed a sinister message. McCabe, the former sergeant-in-charge, was now considered to be a rat, an informer, the type of individual who would betray his colleagues. It is ironic that the most common use of the word 'rat' in this context is among criminal organisations describing a member who had 'ratted' to the law on his associates.

Eventually, the pressure that was mounting for McCabe got the better of him. After a particularly stressful day, in which he began to feel helpless, he visited his GP, who suggested that perhaps he might benefit from a stay in a psychiatric facility.

On 22 April 2010, Lorraine drove him to Dublin with a view to attending the St John of God facility in Stillorgan. The journey was sombre, almost funereal, as if they were travelling towards the end of something.

Lorraine left him there and returned home to the family more unsure than ever of what the future might hold.

Fortunately, McCabe's stay was brief. After one night he realised that, while he had some major problems, he wasn't going to let anybody think he had opted to hide away rather than face the whole thing head on.

Through it all he and Lorraine tried to retain some hope. The Byrne/McGinn investigation was examining his complaints, and from some small hints he could discern whenever he was interviewed by the team, they were making progress.

Maybe the investigation would vindicate him. Maybe they would get to the heart of the malpractice, which to McCabe's mind amounted to corruption, acknowledge that proper standards were not adhered to, and restore his reputation within the force.

They might even come to the conclusion that he should be returned to Bailieboro as sergeant-in-charge, although the atmosphere was such that he was no longer sure he would even want his old job back. Maybe the force would surprise him and take a good look at itself.

Maybe.

8

'I cannot share the view that all matters were fully enquired into.'
Seán Guerin

The internal garda investigation into Maurice McCabe's complaints held the key to everything for which he had fought. If the investigation was conducted in a manner that McCabe regarded as thorough and fair, he would have achieved his aim, and he could get back to the job he loved.

Even if the inquiry ultimately decided that it was in the best interests of everybody concerned that McCabe not return to Bailieboro as sergeant-in-charge, the whole struggle would have been worth it. His campaign for acceptable standards of service to the public would be vindicated.

A police force that was confident enough to address its faults would value a member like McCabe, and he in turn would have complete faith in the body he had sworn to serve.

But things didn't work out that way.

The first problem was one of perception. Assistant Commissioner

Derek Byrne, who was overseeing the investigation, was a well-regarded police officer. During the period being investigated he was in charge of the northern region, which took in Cavan/Monaghan. As such, he could be seen as having a conflict of interest in an investigation into those who reported directly to him. If there were issues in Cavan/Monaghan, and accountability went up the line, then criticism could arrive at the door of the very man who was investigating the problem.

Byrne's colleague in human resources in the Phoenix Park HQ, AC Nóirín O'Sullivan, saw the potential for a conflict of interest. When the investigation team was being put together, she noted in a memo in October 2008, just weeks after Derek Byrne had transferred out of the northern region: 'Having read this file & the serious allegations contained within and in particular the contents of the statement made by Sgt. McCabe on 15th October 2008 alleging a formal complaint against Chief Supt. Rooney, I am of the view that given A/C Byrne's previous involvement, it may be appropriate that an Assistant Commissioner with no previous connection to the Northern Region & Cavan/Monaghan Division should be appointed to investigate this matter.'

But despite O'Sullivan airing this concern, Byrne was selected to oversee the investigation.

The Byrne/McGinn investigation was based in Ballyshannon, Co. Donegal and took nearly two years to complete. It contained a high-powered team of a detective superintendent, two inspectors and two sergeants, as well as Assistant Commissioner Byrne and Chief Superintendent McGinn. Yet the quality of some of the investigation would in time be exposed as less than rigorous.

The most serious case investigated by Byrne/McGinn was that of Lorraine Browne, the minibus driver who, along with her passengers, had been subjected to a frightening ordeal at the hands of three drunken men. The outcome had been an intervention from a probationary guard with one of the suspects in which an arrangement for each to pay €50 to Ms Browne was negotiated.

The investigation did not obtain Ms Browne's original statement. Three times Terry McGinn wrote to the Cavan/Monaghan division requesting the original investigation file. Each time she was told there was no file available. This was a case that involved allegations of sexual assault, false imprisonment and assault, yet there was no file.

McGinn knew that a statement had been taken from Lorraine Browne, but because she was told that there was no file, she presumed it was no longer available. Neither did anybody approach Ms Browne to re-take a statement, or check whether she might have a copy of it, or just to interview her again.

Instead, the Byrne/McGinn investigation largely just reviewed an internal investigation into the incident that had taken place within the division. That investigation concluded that no breach of discipline had occurred. Byrne/McGinn rubberstamped the recommendation, noting only that the matter had been dealt with in a 'shabby' manner.

The Byrne/McGinn report also stated: 'Sergeant McCabe's original assertion that the incident involved false imprisonment and sexual assault is a gross exaggeration of the facts and bears little resemblance to the available evidence.'

This conclusion was reached without reference to Lorraine Browne's original statement which included the line, 'And when the girl was getting off, the biggest lad grabbed her arse', which suggests prima facie evidence of a sexual assault.

If Byrne/McGinn had seen the original file on the matter, they would have noticed that a colleague of McCabe's had categorised Lorraine Browne's statement as containing a number of alleged offences, including 'public order, sexual assault, false imprisonment and assault'.

Yet despite being in the dark about the file, Byrne/McGinn felt confident in accusing McCabe of 'gross exaggeration'.

The Byrne/McGinn investigation into the Lakeside Manor assault on Charles McMahon was also curious. This was the case in which a suspect was told in interview that there was CCTV evidence of him striking Mr McMahon. It wasn't true, and no conviction was ever secured for the assault. McCabe had outlined the various shortcomings of the investigation as he saw them.

The high-powered investigation team interviewed superintendents Noel Cunningham, Michael Clancy and Maura Lernihan, as well as McCabe. Yet for some strange reason they didn't interview the garda who had investigated the Lakeside Manor incident, an inexperienced cop who was entitled to greater supervision. He had been central to the cock-ups in the case. Yet nobody went to hear what he had to say.

Byrne/McGinn concluded that the 'original investigation was not carried out in a timely and professional manner'.

The most serious issue was the interview where the suspect was falsely told there was evidence of him striking the victim. This was entirely false, and McCabe characterised it as 'appalling'. Yet Byrne/McGinn did not address the matter at all. At a later inquiry, Terry McGinn would say that there was a misunderstanding about what McCabe was referring to when he used the word 'appalling'. She thought it was the fact that the CCTV footage was not available at the time of the interview.

If that was the case, it wouldn't have taken much to lift the phone and ask the complaining sergeant to what exactly he had been referring. That was not done, and the central complaint in relation to malpractice in this assault case was not addressed in the Byrne/McGinn report.

In the urine in the vinegar case in Cafolla's restaurant, Byrne/McGinn upheld practically all McCabe's complaints, yet their report also included this passage: 'While Sergeant McCabe was aware that the investigating gardaí behaved inappropriately towards the injured party, he did not take any immediate action himself or bring this matter to the attention of the District Officer.'

As the O'Higgins Commission would bear out, McCabe was the one who acted most promptly once he became aware of it. The very next day he visited Majella Cafolla and apologised for the conduct of some of his colleagues and informed her of her right to complain. He also apprised his district officer of the matter.

Byrne/McGinn effectively upheld everything McCabe had alleged in the Cafolla incident, yet the report felt it necessary to criticise him unjustifiably.

There were other aspects to the Byrne/McGinn investigation that were even more curious. The case of the assault in Crossan's public house was the one that had finally prompted McCabe to take the drastic step of handing in his resignation. This was where the victim said the men who had assaulted him 'were not boys to be messed with'. The most serious allegation concerned the circumstances in which the victim had withdrawn his statement. It had also included serious delays and a failure to take witness statements.

Byrne/McGinn summed up the deficiencies in a less than forthright manner: 'The original investigation was not carried out in a timely and professional manner and falls below the minimum accepted standard.'

Yet the O'Higgins Commission in 2016 would eventually point out a number of flaws in the original investigation, including:

1. the inappropriate withdrawal of the complaint
2. the inordinate delay
3. the failure to take statements adequately
4. the failure to act on the numerous requests for an investigation file

5. the lack of supervision of the probationary guard by his unit sergeant
6. the failure to act on a direction from the superintendent
7. the loss of the original statement of withdrawal, a most essential exhibit
8. the failure to enter the matter in the PULSE system for many months.

Byrne/McGinn did not explicitly find in the case that McCabe's complaint was upheld.

The Byrne/McGinn report's findings on the dangerous driving incident at Lakeside Manor was another eyebrow-raising affair. This was the case where the patrons ejected from the nightclub drove at people standing near the entrance. The report stated: 'It is clear that no proper management of this investigation took place, as stated by Sergeant McCabe in his complaint. When the matter was highlighted by this investigation to divisional officer Cavan/Monaghan, it then received the necessary attention it required.'

Part of the lack of 'proper management' discovered by Byrne/McGinn included a failing on McCabe's part for not briefing his superintendent on the incident in writing. Once again, the investigation of McCabe's complaints was finding that he himself bore some culpability.

The O'Higgins Commission would find that McCabe 'would certainly have found it bizarre if he thought his complaint would be interpreted as being partly against himself'.

Not only that, but there wasn't agreement between AC Byrne and Chief Superintendent McGinn on whether or not McCabe bore any culpability for the error.

'If the authors of the [Byrne/McGinn] report differ to such a degree on what they intend to convey by stating that there was a lack of proper management, it is unlikely that the reader of the report or those to whom it was addressed could have been assisted,' O'Higgins reported.

Ultimately, Byrne/McGinn didn't find much wrong that required any radical change. As Derek Byrne reported, 'No systemic failures were identified in the management and administration in the Bailieborough district.'

The deficiencies enumerated above were all reported on in the O'Higgins Commission. The commission examined only nine of the forty-six issues that Byrne/McGinn investigated. There has never been an external, thorough review of the remainder of the complaints, but that which has come to light would hardly inspire confidence.

There is no question but that the Byrne/McGinn team, including its principals, worked hard at the investigation. They did uncover some shortcomings, and a review of procedures in Bailieboro was ordered as a result of the team's report. But the quality of the investigation did not withstand outside scrutiny from either the O'Higgins Commission – which commended the principals but criticised various shortcomings – or an earlier inquiry conducted by senior counsel Seán Guerin.

Senior counsel Guerin, who examined Byrne/McGinn in 2014 as part of a broader report into McCabe's complaints of malpractice, found that the only people who were judged to be at fault were the raw recruits or probationers. He got the impression that 'there was, if not an instinctive, at least a routine preference for the evidence of senior officers in respect of whom complaints were made'.

In other words, none of the blame flowed upwards. It was all down to a few young fellas who got things wrong. Guerin found that once senior officers, in particular, provided 'answers' when asked, little was done by way of checking out these 'answers'.

'Ultimately, it appears that conclusions were arrived at as a result of the investigative process without there ever having been a thorough and searching test of the evidence,' he reported.

The senior counsel's overall assessment of the investigation was one that would chime with other internal Garda inquiries, both before and since: 'The overall impression given by the internal garda investigative process was that complaints of matters of concern were put through a process of filtration or distillation so that, by the end of the process, any matters of concern had been removed as a form of impurity, and only what was good was found to remain.'

Or, as the old policing phrase might have it: Nothing to see here, folks. Now move along, please.

The Byrne/McGinn report reached a finale of sorts on 11 October 2010. A meeting was arranged for that day between the two principals of the investigation and Maurice McCabe at the Hillgrove Hotel in Monaghan town. This location had been used a number of times during the investigation. The meeting was scheduled for 7.30pm, although it didn't get underway until closer to 8.30pm.

In his car, McCabe had more evidence of further malpractice. He had, in the boot, two official Garda boxes of over 1,150 PULSE records which he believed showed false inputs, wrongly adjusted information and records that were defective, amounting to corruption. As far as he was concerned, the records could not have been adjusted in error. Instead, it was due to laziness or a desire to cover up the fact that investigations had not been properly undertaken.

Throughout the Byrne/McGinn investigation, during his occasional meetings with McGinn, in particular, McCabe had brought with him, he says, further evidence of malpractice. This was just the latest, although two full boxes of it was by far the largest amount of evidence he had put together.

McCabe was accompanied to the meeting by Sergeant Dominic Flynn, a representative of the AGSI. Byrne and McGinn were the only other two in the room.

McCabe was handed five sheets of paper containing a summary

of the outcomes of the investigation into the complaints. Some had been upheld, others not. There was no indication as to whether there would be further action in relation to the complaints that had been upheld.

Byrne told McCabe that the complaints he had made against superintendents Clancy and Cunningham were unfounded. Both men, the assistant commissioner asserted, were doing a good job.

The two men engaged in a brief question and answer session, dealing with the individual complaints. McCabe was told that he had to accept part of the blame himself for some of the failures. This was the first he had heard that he was to be blamed in some instances. He had never had a chance to defend himself against any such charges.

McCabe was agitated. He felt that he was being blamed for making a mountain out of a molehill. As far as he was concerned, these were very serious issues, yet despite the positive findings in some of the cases, he got the impression that he was being fobbed off, his complaints played down.

He brought up what he saw as AC Byrne's conflict of interest, in which the senior man was, to some extent, investigating himself, since he had been in charge of the division that included Cavan/Monaghan where the alleged malpractice had occurred.

Byrne denied any such conflict of interest. He was adamant that a proper investigation had taken place and the results were rock solid. While all this was transpiring, Dominic Flynn, seated next to McCabe, took notes, and Terry McGinn largely sat back, giving way to Byrne.

Afterwards, McCabe would claim that his concerns and the details of the complaints were brushed over, but AC Byrne maintained that he had responded to all the sergeant's concerns in detail.

Then McCabe said that he was not happy with the outcome and he had further evidence of malpractice and wrong-doing within the force.

He left the room, and returned a few minutes later with the two boxes of PULSE records. He placed the boxes on the table where the other three were seated. He took out a few bundles of files and laid them on the table, pointed to the bundles and said that this was the evidence in question.

There is dispute over what transpired from that point on. McCabe's version has Byrne becoming very agitated, demanding that he hand over the files because they were Garda property.

McCabe says he replied by saying that he wouldn't hand them over since he had lost trust in the investigation, that he would bring them to Mullingar Garda station and Byrne could follow him in his own car. Alternatively, McCabe said, he was willing to drive to Dublin to Garda HQ with the files.

Byrne reiterated that the boxes were Garda property and he was calling a squad car from the local Monaghan station to collect them. According to McCabe, Byrne walked to another part of the room and began making a call.

McCabe decided that he'd had enough. He placed the bundles back into the boxes and made for the door, carrying the boxes in front of him. He would later claim that Byrne intercepted him at the door and said he was going nowhere with the Garda property.

At this stage, Dominic Flynn got to his feet and went to stand between the two men.

'Now, lads,' Flynn said soothingly.

The intervention of Flynn and subsequently of Chief Superintendent McGinn brought down the temperature. Somebody suggested that they all go for a coffee.

'I broke down at that stage and started to cry,' McCabe later revealed. 'We all sat down at a different table to the one we [had] sat at earlier. I told [Assistant] Commissioner Byrne that the information in the boxes would prove me right. I told him that the boxes contained hundreds of innocent members of the public who were on PULSE as suspected offenders for crimes and offences they did not commit. I also told him it contained hundreds of offenders for serious road traffic offences like insurance and dangerous driving which gardaí failed to prosecute,' he said in a statement about the incident.

Within minutes, Byrne put his hand on McCabe's shoulder and said, 'We'll put what happened tonight behind us.' Byrne held out his hand and McCabe shook it. The evening ended relatively amicably.

McCabe was devastated at the outcome, his worst fears realised. He had invested some faith that a high-powered team would uncover the malpractice he had highlighted. But his complaints had been minimised, he was told to bring his search for some culpability to the nearest mirror, and any residual blame was now left resting on the tender shoulders of young and green recruits.

He made a complaint against AC Derek Byrne of assault and false imprisonment arising from the incident at the Hillgrove Hotel. It was investigated, a file sent to the DPP and ultimately a decision was taken not to prosecute. While McCabe harboured a deep sense of hurt at what had transpired, his complaint against Byrne was never going to meet the threshold for further action.

Through his solicitor, McCabe also complained about the investigation and report. The Garda commissioner, Fachtna Murphy, ordered the deputy commissioner, Nacic Rice, to undertake a review of Byrne/McGinn.

McCabe's solicitor wrote to Rice, once more pointing out what the sergeant saw as some of the problems. 'One of the issues he had previously raised was that Assistant Commissioner Derek Byrne was Assistant Commissioner in respect of the area under investigation,' the solicitor wrote.

'His concern was that there was a long delay in the investigation and when he finally received the "Summary of the Findings" that these did not deal with the matters raised. For example, it did not set out the evidence which had been gathered, the identity of and provision of statements obtained, how they were viewed and what reliance was placed on those statements and then ultimately the findings and recommendations.'

Deputy Commissioner Rice did not reinvestigate the complaints. To do so would have involved another huge task. He effectively reviewed Byrne/McGinn over the course of four months, reporting back in March 2011 to Commissioner Martin Callinan, who had taken up the job when his predecessor retired in December 2010.

His report largely gave the nod to the investigation carried out by Byrne and McGinn, but notably placed considerable focus on McCabe, rather than concentrating on his complaints. One passage of the Rice report stated that 'because the investigation was in relation to allegations made by him and to just pointing out that if he was making allegations about other people, he himself should have looked at himself and said hold on, I should have been doing A, B and C.'

This contention should be read in the context of McCabe's record. As pointed out previously, at least four superintendents under whom McCabe had worked in Bailieboro had referenced his performance in glowing terms. Now the second-highest ranking officer in the force was arriving at the conclusion that the sergeant who had complained about malpractice bore some of the blame.

Deputy Commissioner Rice's final verdict was that there was nothing more to see here, everything had been done correctly. On 7 April 2011 Rice wrote to McCabe's solicitor with a brief conclusion to his review: 'The Commissioner has read and agreed with my findings that the investigation carried out by Assistant Commissioner Byrne and Chief Superintendent McGinn was professional, impartial and with propriety.'

Again, three years down the line an outside agent would have a different interpretation of these matters. Seán Guerin reported in

2014 that Nacie Rice's review largely came to the conclusion on Byrne/McGinn that 'all matters were fully enquired into'. Yet Guerin came to his own conclusion. 'I cannot share the view that all matters were enquired into.'

In particular, Guerin referenced the targeting of McCabe with some of the blame. 'Having regard to the apparent failure to give Sergeant McCabe an opportunity to comment on the evidence, and the manner in which "answers" of superior officers were accepted without either testing them too rigorously against other available evidence or giving Sergeant McCabe an opportunity to respond to them, I cannot share the generally approving conclusions of Deputy Commissioner Rice's review.'

And once again Guerin hit on the main theme that none of the blame for anything flowed upwards towards those whose duty it was to supervise probationers or inexperienced guards.

'Neither the Byrne/McGinn report nor Deputy Commissioner Rice's review of it really addressed the extent to which such supervisory sergeants bore responsibility for the issues that arose in the handling of investigations by members under their supervision or the extent to which the District Officer ensured that members in the District were being effectively supervised by their unit sergeants.'

The Maurice McCabe story could and should have ended with the completion of the Byrne/McGinn investigation into his complaints. That may well have been the case if An Garda Síochána operated as it was so designed.

A well-respected sergeant had highlighted issues of malpractice. In another police force, the investigation into his complaints would have resulted in a thorough rooting out of the problems, accountability for everybody concerned, and possibly commendation for the complainant. None of that occurred here.

In another police force, a mid-ranking officer who was highly rated by superiors and trusted by the public would have been taken extremely seriously. He would have been regarded by senior management as an asset who should be used to better the operation of the force. That did not happen here.

In another police force, there would have been consequences for any malpractice found, in order to ensure there would not be similar improper conduct in the future. There would have been a fidelity to the notion that the first objective of the force is to serve the public, not itself. That wasn't the impression conveyed here.

Byrne/McGinn was not a let-down simply because McCabe deemed it to be so. He was not Robocop, nor did he claim to be. He was not pursuing unattainable standards, just reasonable ones. He was not portraying himself as a supreme authority on either public service or policing, but a guard trying to do his best in a difficult job.

McCabe's verdict on Byrne/McGinn couldn't but be contaminated by what he had been subjected to over the preceding two and a half years since he had first made his complaints. An outsider might conclude that after all he had been through, he wouldn't have been happy with the best little report in the world.

Such a conclusion crumbles in the face of the verdicts of senior counsel Seán Guerin in 2014 and Judge Kevin O'Higgins in 2016. Both detected major flaws in Byrne/McGinn that endorsed McCabe's deflated reaction.

There is no tradition of rigorous self-analysis within the Garda Síochána. Any internal reports that have found their way to scrutiny outside the blue wall have inevitably come up short. That's just the way things are done, and Maurice McCabe was not going to change that. Or so it seemed as he went through those dark days.

9

'In An Garda Síochána . . . loyalty is prized over honesty.'
Judge Peter Smithwick

McCabe heard about the death threat from John Wilson. The pair had worked together some years previously. Wilson had his own, relatively minor, issues with the Garda authorities. He had been in a battle to get permission to wear a beard on the job. That marked him out for what passes as a troublemaker in the closed confines of An Garda Síochána.

'I met Maurice McCabe when he was in Clones as sergeant-in-charge,' Wilson said in an interview for this book. 'A couple of months after I started, Maurice called me into his office and told me that he'd been told that I wasn't to be trusted because of the stuff over the beard. He said he'd no problem with me and that I was a good worker who did my job. After that, I had great respect for the man. We were never buddy buddy, but when he ran into his difficulties, I began hearing about what he was up against and I contacted him.'

McCabe was grateful for the support, and in the years to come Wilson and he would find themselves thrust together in another battle with senior management.

All that was ahead of them, but in late January 2011 Wilson rang McCabe and told him about a death threat against him. There had been a meeting a few days previously, a large gathering of rank and file members of the Garda Representative Association (GRA). Somebody brought up the subject of the problems at Bailieboro, and in a follow-on contribution to the meeting a guard said, 'What Maurice McCabe needs is a bullet in the head.'

This was a throwaway comment at a meeting of police officers referencing a colleague. Wilson, who was present, was shocked at what he had heard.

He rang McCabe and relayed the news. McCabe felt a cold chill. Okay, nobody was suggesting that a member of the force was planning on any level to have him shot, but for such an utterance to be made in a roomful of fellow guards was chilling. These were guardians of the law, some of whom actually did have access to firearms. In the heat of emotion where, for instance, one of their number may have been callously murdered, the idea that such a sentiment would be expressed towards a murderer would be understandable, if unacceptable. But the subject of the threat in this case was one of their own, a man who had done nothing more than break ranks to point out where the job was not being done, the public not being served. For that, he was now being subjected to such treatment behind the closed doors of the force, and few appeared to bat an eyelid at the comment. Or else they knew better than to show their real feelings.

McCabe made a complaint about the threat. Two members from Cavan came to his home and took a statement from him. Wilson also supplied a statement about what he had heard and seen.

A few months later, McCabe was informed that the DPP had decided that no prosecution was merited in this instance. McCabe inquired as to whether or not there would be any disciplinary procedure for the man who had made the comment.

This would be standard practise. If a criminal inquiry is completed into a member's conduct, and nothing comes of it, the usual outcome is for the member to then be subjected to a disciplinary inquiry. Just because nothing criminal is detected in an investigation does not mean that there is no disciplinary case to answer.

When he inquired about that, McCabe was told, 'We'll get back to you.' He never heard any more about it. Nobody had ever even suggested that the comment was not made. John Wilson was willing to testify anywhere as to what he'd heard. Yet An Garda Síochána, as a corporate entity, appears to have been happy to let the matter lie once the DPP did not detect a possible criminal offence.

That such a comment would have been made at an official gathering of garda members is a shocking indictment of the culture that exists in the force. One might even be moved to conclude that McCabe was personally disliked by colleagues, that it was something to do with his personality, or record, or interaction with members before he made his complaint. But there is absolutely no evidence that any of this applies. Everything points towards the simple fact that once he had complained, and word got about, he was to be regarded among large swathes of the force as nothing short of a traitor.

The individual, his or her personal traits, character, history – none of those matters. In fact, the attitude towards the guard who breaks from the herd is akin to the famous line from *The Godfather* about the attempted murder of the eponymous godfather, Vito Corleone. 'It's not personal; it's strictly business.'

Most of this stuff goes on behind closed doors, but there is one other recent public example of how this ethic operates. The Smithwick Tribunal was set up in 2005 to inquire into whether there was Garda collusion in the murder of two RUC officers in 1989. In the course of the tribunal, retired superintendent Tom Curran gave evidence of informing a superior officer in the 1980s of intelligence he had received that the Provisional IRA had a mole in the gardaí. Curran was based in Monaghan, and the garda in question was in Dundalk.

Curran related to the tribunal that the assistant commissioner appeared uninterested in this potentially explosive news. When Curran had finished telling him what he knew, the AC had replied, 'How's things in Monaghan, Tom?'

Curran told the tribunal, 'So we discussed activities in Monaghan, but he never mentioned anything in relation to the conversation that I went there to tell him. In a very short time I got the opinion that he didn't want to hear it, so I left.'

Once Curran had delivered that evidence in the tribunal, the attitude towards him from Garda management changed completely. He was no longer inside the family. He had broken the code of *omerta*, which dictates that what is said within the force stays within the force. Counsel for the Garda commissioner treated Tom Curran as a hostile witness.

In his tribunal report in 2013, Judge Peter Smithwick referenced the transformation he had seen before his eyes: 'He [Curran] struck me as an officer of the utmost integrity. I would have thought that he is as deserving of the support of the garda commissioner as any other former officer. However, it seems to me that because he was giving evidence of which An Garda Síochána did not approve, such support was not forthcoming. I regret to say that this suggests to me that there prevails in An Garda Síochána today a prioritisation of the protection of the good name of the force over the protection of those who seek to tell the truth. Loyalty is prized over honesty.'

The judge went on to state that the fact that such a culture still existed today was 'disheartening and depressing'.

While Smithwick and his tribunal were mulling over such a culture, McCabe was living through it.

Around the same time that McCabe heard of the death threat, he got a note from HQ that he was to attend a doctor's appointment. He assumed that it was a regular meeting with a GP, possibly connected to earlier appointments he had with the chief medical officer.

On the day in question he turned up at the doctor's premises and discovered that in fact this man was a psychiatrist. The subtext as far as he was concerned was obvious. On the night in the Hillgrove Hotel in Monaghan he had been emotional during the confrontation with Assistant Commissioner Derek Byrne. Now somebody in HQ had decided that it would be a good idea for him to see a psychiatrist. Maybe it wasn't the force, but him. They were now suggesting that the whistleblower had mental health issues. After largely dismissing his concerns of malpractice, now this. It could easily be interpreted in some quarters that the whole problem had not been malpractice but the mental health of the man who claimed to have witnessed and experienced it. Perhaps he had just imagined the whole thing.

He had a chat with the psychiatrist, who quickly came to the conclusion that McCabe's mental health was fine, even though he was obviously under some stress.

As he was leaving, the psychiatrist jokingly quipped, 'Now don't be assaulting any more assistant commissioners.' McCabe could see the man was only doing his job, and that he knew the score. The referral had been unwarranted, to put it at its most neutral.

The two incidences, the death threat and the referral to the psychiatrist, were now looking like postscripts to the entire matter of McCabe's complaints of malpractice. The outcome of Byrne/McGinn and the review by Deputy Commissioner Nacie Rice had brought Maurice McCabe to the end of the road.

The only outstanding issue was the two boxes of PULSE records he had delivered to Assistant Commissioner Derek Byrne at the Hillgrove Hotel. Those records, McCabe claimed, highlighted further malpractice within the force. There were 1,153 PULSE records in the boxes. By and large these consisted of cases involving road traffic offences, such as driving without insurance and dangerous driving; drug-related offences; and public order offences. In most cases what was involved was a failure by certain gardaí to follow through on an initial detection. It would be difficult to ascribe this to anything other than laziness or incompetence. (These records should not be confused with the 'ticket-fixing' PULSE records in Part II of this book, which was of a different order.)

What the records showed was that cetain aspects of the gardaí's work was not being done properly in corners of the Cavan/ Monaghan division. A member would detect somebody for driving without insurance and record it. There would then often be no follow-up, either to prosecute or to update the record if an insurance certificate was produced.

The same applied to dangerous driving, or the detection of a relatively small amount of drugs, or public order offences. None of these discrepancies were as a result of a garda using discretion, which is perfectly legitimate. Such discretion would be used sparingly and for specific circumstances and would not have generated any PULSE entry.

Bad and all as was the discovery of a cavalier attitude to these types of offences, worse was to emerge from the boxes McCabe delivered.

After the 1,153 records were sent to Garda HQ, a total of 624 were sent back to Cavan/Monaghan once they were identified as having originated there.

The origins of the remainder were not known and McCabe was asked to come to HQ to assist. Initially he said he would but he changed his mind once he heard that over 600 records had been sent back to Cavan/Monaghan. That, as far as he was concerned, was dispatching the corrupt documents back to where they had been corrupted.

As it was to turn out, there was some basis for his concerns. A number of the records returned to Cavan/Monaghan were subsequently updated. The adjustments to the computer system made it look as if there had not been an issue in the first place, effectively covering up for the original errors on the official Garda record.

The O'Higgins Commission confirmed the corruption of the record, but merely noted: 'Serious questions arise as to the integrity of many of the updates themselves.' In reality, the attitude was the same that applied elsewhere – if there's a problem, bury it. If the official record reflects badly on the force, adjust it.

McCabe didn't know that for a fact at the time, but he was certainly prescient in believing that once the records had been returned to the division, there would be no further investigation as to why the cases had not been properly dealt with in the first place.

Those months after the Hillgrove Hotel meeting were among the worst for Maurice McCabe and his family. There had been a belief that something would come out of the inquiry, that he would be vindicated, even if not restored to his former position. While some of his complaints had been upheld, he was left with the impression that the conclusions were reached in a begrudging manner, and nothing would be done about the malpractices. And the suggestion that he himself had been to blame for some of the shortcomings really troubled him.

Then, in the trough of this despair, his worst fears were confirmed. In late June 2011 a notice went up in all garda stations in the Cavan/Monaghan division about the outcome of the Byrne/McGinn investigation. The notice was a communication from Chief Superintendent Colm Rooney.

Re: Allegations made by Sergeant Maurice McCabe
Bailieboro Garda station

On the 24th June 2011 I had a meeting with Assistant
Commissioner Derek Byrne, National Support Services
Garda Headquarters at Monaghan Garda Station. He
informed me that he had completed his investigation into
the complaints made by Sergeant Maurice McCabe. The
findings of the investigation were approved by the garda
commissioner.

The investigation concluded that there were no systemic
failures identified in the management and administration
of Bailieboro Garda District. A number of minor procedural
issues were identified. On further investigation at local
level no evidence was found to substantiate the alleged
breach of procedure. The assistant commissioner further
concluded there was no criminal conduct identified on the
part of any member of the district force.

I would like to congratulate all members who served
in Bailieboro District during the period in question. In
particular I wish to thank Sergeant Gavigan who provided
leadership, enthusiasm and commitment in steering the
station party through the crisis that had occurred. The
findings of the Assistant Commissioner vindicates the
high standards and professionalism of the District force in
Bailieboro. I appreciate the manner in which the members
of the district participated in the investigation, were open
and truthful in their account of events surrounding the
allegations. I hope that the members and their families can
now put this difficult period behind them and continue to

serve the public and their colleagues in an efficient and
professional manner.

Please inform all concerned.

C.M. Rooney, Chief Superintendent

John Wilson spotted the notice in Cavan station and rang McCabe, who couldn't believe what he was hearing. He asked Wilson to fax a copy of it to his father's house, where there was a fax machine. The machine spat out the completed fax, and there it was in black and white. There were no problems in Bailieboro. Every member had acted professionally. There were no breaches of procedure. If one were to take the content of the notice in isolation, one could easily conclude that the investigation had been a waste of time, the allegations a fiction.

Even within the confines of the outcome of the Byrne/McGinn report, the notice couldn't but be read as a distortion. A number of McCabe's complaints had been upheld. The only repercussions for even those upheld complaints would be a few slaps on the wrist for young and inexperienced guards, but they were serious matters.

What of the concerns that Chief Superintendent Terry McGinn had expressed about one incident where a member of the public complained of garda behaviour as being 'symptomatic of a deeper malaise'?

All swept away. There was literally nothing to see here.

The official reaction to McCabe's complaints was probably the blow that finally drained any confidence he had that the problems he had encountered could and should be dealt with. It was all about the whistleblower.

McCabe consulted his solicitor about this latest development. They decided that the only hope of ever accessing the true picture rested with outside intervention. With that in mind, a letter was composed and sent to the Minister for Justice asking that a commission of investigation be set up to examine all McCabe's complaints. It was a long shot, and one that went nowhere. As far as the Department of Justice was concerned, this was an internal Garda matter. It had been examined by a high-powered team of senior gardaí. That investigation had been reviewed by the deputy commissioner. These were the most senior police officers in the country. What more could anybody want?

By then, though, the ground had shifted once more for the troubled sergeant. The force may have concluded its investigation into his complaints, but elements within it were not done with targeting Maurice McCabe.

Maurice and Lorraine were in Enniskillen when he got word of the latest attempt to frame him. The couple had managed to make room for a day's shopping in the North. For Lorraine, the call was nearly predestined. 'Every time we went on holiday, off for the day, even that day we went shopping, something always intruded on us. There was simply no getting away from it.'

This call was from Mullingar station to tell Maurice that a GSOC investigator, Declan Farrell, was looking for him. Maurice let curiosity get the better of him and he rang back. Farrell told him he was investigating a complaint by Mary Lynch, the Kells-based taxi driver who had been viciously assaulted by Jerry McGrath, who went on to commit murder. He added that he was concluding an investigation into garda conduct around the case. One element of Mary Lynch's complaint was that Jerry McGrath had been released from custody within twelve hours of the assault on her. Now the GSOC investigator was saying that he'd been told that McCabe was the garda who had authorised Jerry McGrath's release that day.

The colour began to drain from McCabe's face. He had heard a few titbits about a commotion in the station over the Jerry

McGrath stuff, but he had not been involved. As it was to turn out, he had not even been on duty on the day in question for the good reason that, later on that afternoon, Lorraine had given birth to their youngest son Tom in Cavan General Hospital.

Now, though, he could see immediately what was at work. There was hassle in Bailieboro over this GSOC investigation. In the great tradition of these things, the best approach to dealing with it was to find a scapegoat. And who better than McCabe, the man who had blown the whistle, the rat who prized honesty over loyalty?

He told Farrell he knew absolutely nothing about the matter. Farrell suggested that McCabe think about it over the weekend (this was a Thursday.)

McCabe ended the call. Lorraine knew from the look on his face that the shopping excursion had just been put on hold. He discussed it with Lorraine, this attempt to open up the possibility that he would be disciplined, his record tarnished, a further question mark placed over him.

Then he decided to act. The young garda who had been on duty on the day in question was a man whom McCabe regarded as honest. He phoned the guard, put him on speaker and held Lorraine's phone up to his to record the conversation.

The guard confirmed that McCabe had had nothing to do with McGrath's release and had no involvement in the rest of the case, including the decision to ring Mary Lynch days before McGrath's conviction to tell her that the case wouldn't be going ahead in court that day.

Satisfied that he had once again managed to protect himself, McCabe simply put the matter aside and continued with the day out in Enniskillen.

The following day he got back onto the GSOC man, Farrell, and told him that he had proof of his innocence. Farrell said he believed him. He'd done further digging himself, and found that there was no way McCabe could have been on duty on the day in question.

But that wasn't the end of attempts to drag McCabe into the mishandling of Jerry McGrath. A few weeks later he got a call from Mary Lynch herself. The two had never met. She informed McCabe that she had been told that he was the guard who had instructed another to ring her days before she was due to confront McGrath in court.

This had been in January 2008. Mary Lynch had been told her case was due up the following Monday. Then she got a call telling her that it was off. The outcome was McGrath was convicted and sentenced without her presence in court. She was robbed of her chance to deliver a victim impact statement in which she would most likely also have heavily criticised the guards for how they had handled the case. Her justifiable suspicion was that she was put off going to court in order to save embarrassment for the guards.

Now she was telling McCabe that her information was that *he* was responsible for what she saw as a callous ruse.

Mary Lynch wasn't the only one furnished with the information that McCabe was to blame for her missing her day in court.

GSOC's Mr Farrell had also been told that was the case. The garda who had actually phoned Mary Lynch that day told GSOC that he was acting on McCabe's instructions. He outlined his recollections in a statement: 'Before the court hearing date which was fixed for Virginia District on the 7th of January 2008 I received a phone call from Sgt Maurice McCabe. Sgt McCabe directed me to phone Mary Lynch and to inform her that she would not be required in court because her case was not going ahead and that he Sgt McCabe was going to have this case brought before the Circuit Court in Cavan at a later date. I phoned Mary Lynch as directed and informed her not to attend court.'

This was entirely inaccurate. McCabe would have had no power to get the case into the circuit court. But, apart from that, he had no involvement in the investigation, so would not have been giving instructions related to the case. The guard's recollection may have been flawed, but he did maintain this position years later at the O'Higgins Commission, which ruled that McCabe had no involvement in the Jerry McGrath case.

When Mary Lynch rang McCabe to berate him, she told him straight out what she believed.

But McCabe was on surer ground this time. He had his tape. He allowed Mary Lynch to let off some steam, and then he told her that he could prove that it wasn't him. He kept her on the line while he located the tape recording he'd made of his conversation with the young guard. He held it up to the phone and played the crucial twenty seconds where the investigating guard relates how the whole case had unfolded.

Mary Lynch calmed down. McCabe promised to meet her and go through it in detail with her. A few days later McCabe and John Wilson turned up at Mary Lynch's Kells home.

'They came to me and I said I didn't believe them, that they were guards, and I'd been lied to by guards all the way,' Mary Lynch said. 'But Maurice told me he wasn't there and that he'd had nothing to do with it and he said, "I'm telling you here and now I will not lie to you and anything I say can be proven." Well, the more he talked, I was weakening in my idea that he was lying. The more I spoke to the man, the more I believed him. And he was telling the truth. He didn't lie to me then and as far as I know he never has.'

McCabe convinced Mary Lynch that he'd had nothing to do with her case. Once again, he found himself having to explain to a victim of crime how there had been a serious mistake within the force. Once again he had managed to escape being framed by elements within the force for the error. Once again, his own acumen in realising what he was up against came to his rescue. Without the tape recording, it would have been his word against that of colleagues.

Bad and all as was that effort to shovel blame onto McCabe, it was nothing compared to what would develop in relation to the case of the missing computer seized from a child-abusing priest.

10

The Bishop of Kilmore wanted a computer belonging to the diocese to be returned. He wrote to Cootehill Garda station requesting that a hard drive seized from the parochial house in Kill, County Cavan be returned. The computer had been taken during an investigation into a priest, Michael Molloy, who was suspected of child abuse.

By the time Bishop Leo O'Reilly went looking for the return of the computer, Molloy was already serving five years for defilement of a child and possession of child pornography. Now the computer was required as part of an investigation within the church into an unrelated fraud. Could we have it returned, please? the bishop's letter requested.

The initial response from the gardaí was, computer? what computer? At first, nobody could recall a computer associated with the Molloy case. It certainly had not featured in the charges or brief court appearance where Molloy had pleaded guilty.

Inquiries were made and after some rooting around it emerged that there had in fact been a computer. The only problem was that nobody knew what had happened to it. The computer had vanished. This was a serious matter. A hard drive seized from a known abuser who possessed child pornography had gone missing in garda custody. Somebody had to be held accountable.

Before long, the focus was narrowed down to one man. When it comes to apportioning blame for a terrible oversight with possible sinister implications, what better recipient than the whistleblower?

The Molloy investigation was a bit of a shambles, even if it ultimately had a successful outcome. On 11 September 2007 a man walked into Bailieboro Garda station and complained that his son had been sexually assaulted by Father Michael Molloy. The abuse first came to light when the boy's mother discovered sexually explicit text messages from the priest to her son. Molloy was a 40-year-old native of Clifferna, a townland about ten miles from Bailieboro.

Three days after the complaint was made, the gardaí raided two addresses associated with Molloy and arrested him. Among the items seized were a computer and a mobile phone, along with a shotgun, three rounds of ammunition and a TV/DVD combination player. All the evidence was taken to Bailieboro station.

The computer had some significance. In his statement the boy had referenced one incident of serious abuse having occurred following evening mass in March or April 2007 when he attended the priest's house to install anti-virus software on Molloy's computer. An analysis of the hard drive could uncover the date of installation.

In addition to that, child pornographic images had been located on the priest's mobile phone, giving rise to a strong possibility that more images, more evidence, might be found on the computer.

As such, it could be expected that the computer would be

dispatched to Garda HQ in Dublin for forensic analysis at the earliest opportunity.

Then the computer vanished. The investigation continued, but there was no word further about the computer. It did not feature in compiling the case against Molloy and the computer was never sent to Dublin for forensic examination. Crucially, it was not mentioned in the report on the case compiled for the DPP. When the case came to court, the evidence from the mobile phone was cited, but nothing about the computer. It just disappeared.

The last that was known of the computer was that it was marked as exhibit POS-1 soon after being seized and was handed over with eight other exhibits to the exhibits officer for dispatch to the property room in Bailieboro.

While the computer would not feature in the rest of the investigation, it would later become a major focus in the life of Maurice McCabe, who had had no role in the investigation or in handling any exhibits for the trial.

Molloy was interviewed four times on the day of his arrest. He admitted to having a pornographic DVD and to having exchanged sexually explicit text messages with the victim, but he denied that any abuse had occurred. He called the victim a 'liar and fantasist'. He made no comment when he was shown a recording from his mobile phone in which the victim was engaged in sexual activity with a male.

Once the interviews were completed, Molloy was released without charge.

Some six months later Molloy came to Bailieboro station again, this time accompanied by a solicitor. He made a statement admitting sexual abuse of the boy and possession of the child pornographic images.

This was a major break-through for the investigation. While the guards had the recordings and images seized from the phone, they would ultimately not have been usable as evidence. The warrants that were issued to search the two addresses on 14 September and seize the phone and computer were defective. They had been issued under section 10 of the Sexual Offences Act 1996, which was not applicable in the case. The correct warrants came under section 10 of the Criminal Justice Act 1997. To some this may appear pedantic in the investigation of a serious crime. Yet a Supreme Court ruling in 1990 had determined that evidence obtained by the authorities in breach of a constitutional right could not be used in court. This included search warrants that were defective. (The ruling would ultimately be overturned by the Supreme Court in 2015.) By 2007 this had been long-standing practice and law, which should have ensured that the issuing of warrants – particularly in a serious case – would be carried out with the utmost care.

Such care should have been assured following another high-profile case involving child pornography which had ended in a disaster for the gardaí a few years previously. In April 2004 the trial of Judge Brian Curtin for possession of child pornography at Tralee Circuit Criminal Court had collapsed after it emerged that defective warrants had been used in seizing evidence from Curtin's home. In that case the warrants were simply out of date.

The outcome had led to much breast-beating about how 'technicalities' played such a significant role in prosecutions, but it should also have ensured that any cases involving warrants in relation to suspected child pornography received special attention. Yet such vigilance did not occur in issuing the warrants in the Molloy case.

The priest's confession relegated the significance of the seized evidence and saved the gardaí from major embarrassment.

Within months of the confession, Superintendent Noel Cunningham forwarded the completed garda file to the DPP. Apart from possession of the child pornography images, the charges also included allegations that Molloy had abused the boy on thirty-five separate occasions.

Surprisingly, in light of the seriousness of the charges, the superintendent's report had the following conclusion: 'Summary disposal is recommended in the event of a plea, and the District Court accepting jurisdiction.' This recommendation effectively categorised the offence as minor enough to be dealt with by the district court, which would ensure that any prison sentence could not have exceeded two years, the limit of the district court's jurisdiction. Cases at district court level are also dealt with by a judge alone rather than by a jury.

In his report to the DPP, Superintendent Cunningham gave no reason as to why the case should be heard by the lower court. An inquiry that dealt with this and other cases from Bailieboro years later found the recommendation 'surprising and difficult to comprehend given the gravity of the offences and the strength of the evidence'.

In his defence, Superintendent Cunningham said that he came to his conclusion because of concern for the victim: 'I was conscious that this young man was in a very bad place at this stage,' Cunningham told the O'Higgins Commission of Investigation in 2015. 'I was conscious that he might not be able to sustain, I suppose I'd describe it as the robust cross-examination et cetera that he might be subjected to in the event of a full contested matter'.

The chances of any 'robust' cross-examination were very remote. Molloy had made a confession and in all likelihood was going to plead guilty (as he subsequently did).

Superintendent Cunningham also suggested that the offence might not have attracted a prison sentence longer than that within the district court's jurisdiction. The inquiry did not accept that reasoning either.

In any event, the DPP decided it was too serious for the district court and recommended prosecution by indictment at the circuit court. In December 2008 Molloy was charged with multiple counts of child sexual abuse and possession of child pornography.

Following the charges, Molloy's defence team wanted to examine the exhibits. The exhibits officer at the outset of the investigation had transferred to another station, so arrangements were made for another member to take up that role.

The handover of exhibits to the new exhibits officer took place on 1 July 2009. It was accompanied by a statement from the officer handing it over. No mention was made of the computer that had vanished.

Molloy pleaded guilty to three sample charges on 22 July 2009. In November he was sentenced to five years in prison.

The outcome was a success for the gardaí, although the case had many worrying features. The search warrants had been defective. There was a failure to forensically examine a computer that could have produced vital evidence. The computer was missing.

The other worrying aspect to the case was the recommendation that such serious offences be dealt with by the district court, with no explanation as to why that course should be pursued.

Still, with the case successfully concluded and the priest serving a considerable prison term, that should have been the end of the matter. Until the Bishop of Kilmore came looking for his computer.

The bishop's letter of 21 September 2010 was passed on to Superintendent Gerry O'Brien at Bailieboro, the latest district officer to serve there. He made a few inquiries, tracing the computer from its seizure on the day of the arrest, to being handed over to the exhibits officer. She in turn told O'Brien that she had handed it over to Sergeant McCabe.

The first McCabe knew about the matter was when he received a phone call from the original exhibits officer in early 2011. She told him she had got a letter about the computer, which she had remembered handing over to him. He said he had no recollection of that.

Within days he had got his own letter from the super, asking what he knew about this missing computer. He wrote back and said he knew absolutely nothing about it, had never actually set eyes on the thing.

Some time later he got a text from the original exhibits officer. 'Sorry to land this on ya, but accordin to my notebook the guns, tv and comp were handed over to you. I specifically rem tom murray being here too cos it was in one of the interview rooms and he was lookin at the guns.'

That was news to McCabe. By then, he was out of the loop as to what was going on in Bailieboro, having been long transferred to Mullingar. Still, it now looked as if the garda in question's recollection was in complete conflict with his.

She gave two versions of how she says she handed over the computer to Maurice McCabe. In the text she implied that she had handed it over to him in the interview room in the presence of another officer, Tom Murray.

At the O'Higgins Commission, some seven years after the initial investigation, the exhibits officer said that she had told McCabe that the computer was downstairs in the station's interview room and he responded that he would go and get it and bring it to the property room.

She also produced an exhibits chart for O'Higgins, in which it is stated that she handed over the computer to McCabe. Yet the original exhibits chart had no such entry. A statement she made at the time of the original Molloy investigation contained no reference to the computer. Yet another version of the statement produced during the investigation into the disappearance did include the computer.

Most of those discrepancies were not known to Superintendent O'Brien when he compiled his initial investigation into the missing computer. All he had was the word of the exhibits officer that she had handed the computer to Maurice McCabe, and McCabe's word that she had not.

Based on that, O'Brien wrote a report for the chief superintendent of the Cavan/Monaghan division, James Sheridan.

He set out the original exhibit officer's statement that she had handed over the computer to Sergeant McCabe. The report stated that the computer was of no evidential value, which was entirely inaccurate. It hadn't been forensically examined, so could not be determined whether or not it had been of evidential value.

O'Brien went on to say that he had interviewed Sergeant McCabe but the sergeant could give no explanation for the missing computer, although he did remember the shotgun and ammunition which were exhibits in the case because another officer had commented on them at the time.

Superintendent O'Brien concluded that Sergeant McCabe was in breach of discipline because he had failed to properly record an exhibit he had received. He made no recommendation about the exhibits officer.

In the complicated mechanisms of the force, the affair then moved to the chief super appointing another superintendent from outside the division to examine if there had been a breach of discipline.

Detective Superintendent Tom Maguire was drafted in. He conducted a paper review of the case. He didn't interview anybody, not McCabe, not the exhibits officer, nor even the officer in charge of the Molloy case, Sergeant Kevin Gavigan. Based on his review, Maguire came to the same conclusion as his colleague O'Brien: McCabe, and McCabe only, may be in breach of discipline.

The next step in the process involves a specific investigation into the officer who is suspected of a disciplinary breach. If it is found that the facts stand up, the officer is then disciplined.

Amazingly, Tom Maguire was also appointed to conduct this phase. He had, in his inquiry, concluded that McCabe was in breach, and now he was going to rigorously examine the facts to see if his conclusion was correct. Since he had already expressed an opinion on the alleged guilt of McCabe, he should never have been appointed to this phase of the investigation, which would make him in one sense both prosecutor and judge on McCabe's alleged guilt.

In February 2012 Maguire rang McCabe to tell him that he was now investigating him for a specific breach of discipline. McCabe was at home when Maguire phoned, working in a shed at the rear of his house. He was thrown by the call.

'That's not fair, Tom,' he said. 'It's just not.' Maguire was non-committal, said he was just doing his job. He told McCabe that he would be in touch about a formal interview.

McCabe asked him was anybody else being investigated. 'No' came the reply.

A week before he received that call, McCabe had made a complaint about ticket-fixing and abuse of the penalty points system (which will be dealt with in the next chapter). As far as he was concerned, this was no coincidence. They were out to get him.

A month after the initial contact, Superintendent Maguire met McCabe to hand over the 'disciplinary pack' that would form the basis of the case against the sergeant.

By now McCabe was in a state of constant stress. He had never been disciplined in his career. There was a matter of professional pride, but also a burning sense of injustice. He had had nothing to do with this accursed computer. The whole affair, as far as he was concerned, was being used as a stick to beat him with. He decided he was going to fight it.

He contacted his solicitor Seán Costello to set up a strategy. The first move was to ask for discovery of all the documents associated with the case. An opinion was also sought from a barrister as to the legality of what was afoot. The opinion was stark: 'I think we are all agreed the investigation has most likely been promoted by virtue of the fact that Maurice McCabe availed of the confidential reporting regulations and charter,' the lawyer wrote. 'Indeed the investigation has all the hallmarks of a shambolic exercise.'

The case dragged out for over a year, during which time McCabe's name within the force was reaching new lows. Throughout 2012 he was involved in attempting to highlight the widespread fixing of speeding tickets by senior officers within the force. While his name was not publicly known, practically every senior officer who had been dragged into the ticket-fixing scandal – over 100 superintendents – knew who he was.

The discovery process was drawn out and not all McCabe's requests were met. The formal interview continued to be postponed, mostly by Superintendent Maguire.

In the course of this investigation Maguire came across the conflicting statements that the exhibits officer had provided, the first from 2007 in which she made no mention of the computer, and the second which included it. Maguire wrote to the chief superintendent saying the conflict was 'a matter of concern', but nothing was done about it. Instead, all the focus remained on McCabe.

By late 2012 things were looking grim for the sergeant. The discovery had not thrown up anything that would vindicate him. One Friday afternoon in November he travelled to Dublin to consult with his solicitor. There was little that came out of that meeting to comfort him.

On the way home, he stopped in the Phoenix Park and tried to ring the exhibits officer, just to run the whole thing by her again. There was no answer.

That weekend was black. He could see no way past what, as far as he was concerned, some of his fellow guards were doing to him. The year he had spent trying to fight it had cost him over 5,000 euro between legal fees and his trips to Dublin. And he knew that if they managed to get him on this, they would then go to town on him. His credibility would be shot, but his character would also have been assailed.

On the Sunday evening he told Lorraine he was going out: he had to see somebody about the case.

He was gone for over seven hours. He didn't bring his mobile phone with him for fear it could be tracked. After driving for some time, he pulled into a car park, got out of his vehicle and walked across to sit into another. The driver turned to him and they shook hands. As the wind howled outside and rain lashed down against the windscreen, Maurice McCabe unburdened himself to the other man, another member of the force.

They had known each other over the years. There was mutual respect between them. The other man, who for obvious reasons wants to keep his identity secret, didn't mince his words.

'They're laughing at you,' the man said.

'Who?'

'Some of the lads. They know you'd fuck all to do with that computer thing, but that makes it all the better for them.'

Back at home, Lorraine was beginning to worry as the night rolled on and there was no sign of her husband. Stress levels were high within the house, prompting the darker strains of an imagination to run wild. Would he be coming back at all? The fact that he had left his phone behind began to play on her mind. Where would this all end?

Eventually the headlights from his car appeared through the rain. She went to the door, reaching to assure herself that it was him and not somebody dispatched to deliver bad news.

Maurice walked in, bedraggled and soaked. He threw a folder down on the kitchen table and broke into a smile.

'The Molloy file,' he said.

The file answered a number of questions for him that went to the heart of how he would defend himself. It showed the defective warrant, which offered one possibility as to why the computer might have disappeared. If it wasn't going to be allowed as evidence in court, then somebody may well have decided that the best course was to make it disappear and so save embarrassment.

There was nothing in the file to suggest that the hard drive had been forensically examined.

Crucially, the file showed that after its initial seizure, there had been no further mention of the computer. Why would that be so? How come nobody associated with the case had asked at the time what became of the vital exhibit? Why was there no reference to it in the file sent to the DPP? There was nothing there saying, 'By the way, a computer had been seized, but we appear to have mislaid it.'

All of which gave rise to the question that if this was a case of the sergeant in charge of the station – McCabe – simply mislaying a vital exhibit, why had nobody asked after it during the rest of the investigation?

The formal disciplinary interview finally took place seven months later on 21 June 2013 in the Bloomfield House Hotel in Mullingar. McCabe handed in a robust written submission in which he complained about the disciplinary process, pointed out that he had had absolutely nothing to do with the Molloy investigation, and made a number of complaints about how that investigation had been handled, and particularly how the file had contained no reference to the computer.

A month later he was informed that he was not in breach of discipline. One central reason given for the decision was 'the obvious inconsistency in the evidence of Garda Killian [the exhibits officer], the only evidence against Sergeant McCabe'.

So ended for McCabe and his family a time laden with stress and tension, the outcome of which could have ensured that not only would his record be sullied, but he would be associated with a computer that was suspected of containing child pornography.

As it transpired, Superintendent Tom Maguire had ensured that an injustice would not be perpetrated. It had, once more, been a close-run thing.

The O'Higgins report in 2016 found the computer affair disturbing. 'It is difficult to understand why Sergeant McCabe was the only person subjected to disciplinary proceedings for the loss of the computer as Garda Killian was the exhibits officer in the case,' the report stated. It went on to say:

> It was the first time in his long career that he faced such proceedings. He was, quite rightly, exonerated.
>
> Sergeant McCabe knew that he did not have custody of the computer and that he had not been guilty of any neglect of duty.
>
> Sergeant McCabe formed the view that there may have been a "plot" against him and that other members of An Garda Síochána "went all out to blame him".
>
> While there is no evidence to establish any concerted attempt to blame Sergeant McCabe, it was understandable that he might connect the commencement of disciplinary proceedings with the complaints he had made a short time earlier and that he might feel aggrieved.

The report also stated that the affair was 'very stressful' and was exacerbated by 'delays and difficulties' in the disclosure of relevant documents and information to Sergeant McCabe.

What if McCabe hadn't been on the ball? What if he hadn't had recourse to a colleague who was able to assist him by getting his hands on the original case file?

On the basis of some media coverage at the time, one can reasonably speculate that disciplinary findings would have found their way onto the front pages of some national newspapers or onto the RTÉ *Nine O'Clock News*.

Headlines like 'Whistleblower guilty for loss of child porn computer' would have tripped lightly across some keyboards, which would undoubtedly have dealt a severe blow to McCabe's credibility, as well as his reputation as an upstanding citizen and garda. The spectre of being wrongfully associated with such activity could quite easily destroy a man and his most intimate relationships. It would also have coloured media coverage of his allegations about ticket-fixing, and might well have scared off some politicians who were beginning to champion his cause.

All of which would have gladdened the hearts of those who wanted the troublesome cop to just back off and leave things as they were.

Such a scenario is purely in the realm of speculation, but it is worth mentioning in the context of all that McCabe had been subjected to, and all he would face over the years to come.

PART II

BREAKING OUT

11

'Bees attacking livestock'
Motorist's reason as to why his speeding ticket should be cancelled

By the beginning of 2012 it was all over for Maurice McCabe. He had lost. His efforts to have malpractice highlighted, the force reformed, were dead. There was no more he could do. Byrne/McGinn had ruled that there were a few minor issues, and Chief Superintendent Rooney's letter effectively conveyed to everybody in the division that it was all a figment of McCabe's imagination. The matter was closed.

And yet. 'It was never over,' Lorraine says. 'Even when there was nowhere else to go, it was never over with Maurice. He was like a dog with a bone once they had dragged him that far into it. What was done was wrong and he wasn't going to just lie down and die in the face of it.' In January 2012 two encounters opened up new avenues down which he could attempt to have his concerns vindicated.

The first involved one Oliver J. Connolly. A lawyer of some repute,

Connolly had been appointed to the office of confidential recipient in 2011, when his predecessor, Brian McCarthy, had stepped down.

McCabe had had previous contact with McCarthy, whom he found receptive and professional. It hadn't been his fault that the office as designed was flawed.

Now there was another man in the job. John Wilson, with whom McCabe had been in contact over the previous few years, asked him to meet this Connolly.

'I introduced Maurice McCabe to Oliver Connolly,' Wilson told the author. 'I went to Oliver Connolly in December 2011 about another matter and we got chatting about various things. I told him that Maurice was suffering badly and getting desperate about what he was being put through. Oliver Connolly said he'd like to meet him and I told him I'd arrange a meeting.'

They met in Dublin. McCabe found Connolly to be a receptive man with a professional manner. Within a few weeks McCabe had come across a reason to call Connolly. He had another complaint of malpractice to make.

His old super at Bailieboro, Michael Clancy, with whom McCabe had had major professional issues, was up for promotion. The Byrne/McGinn report had found that Clancy bore no culpability for any of the transgressions in Bailieboro. (The later O'Higgins Commissionre did not find Clancy guilty of malpractice either, although it questioned some of his decisions.) There was no reason why he should not have been in line for promotion.

That wasn't how McCabe saw it. As far as he was concerned, Byrne/McGinn had not properly investigated malpractice. Clancy, he believed, should not be promoted.

Under the Garda charter, an officer on a promotion list should be investigated in certain circumstances. According to the charter, 'If a member on a promotion list is guilty of or is suspected of any conduct that would render the member unsuitable for promotion, it will be the duty of superiors to report the matter at once.'

To McCabe's way of thinking, this might open up the possibility of having his complaints examined again. However, part of this new complaint involved accusing the commissioner, Martin Callinan, of corruption, for putting forward Clancy's name for promotion. McCabe was implying that the commissioner knew that Clancy had engaged in malpractice.

All this was unfair to both men. Clancy had not been deemed guilty of any malpractice. And Callinan, for his part, did not actually select the officers to be promoted. That was the job of government, although the commissioner did have a major influence on the outcome.

McCabe's decision to address his sense of grievance illustrated the straits of desperation he was now negotiating. He believed that what he had complained about to Byrne/McGinn had substance. If they weren't going to deal with it as he saw fit, then he felt forced to try another way.

This new complaint against the commissioner would, according to law, have to be investigated by the Minister for Justice. McCabe's hope was that any agency outside the force considering this would also look in a balanced manner at his original complaints of malpractice.

He was now upping the stakes. This sergeant, from a rural outpost in County Cavan, was accusing the commissioner of An Garda Síochána of corruption. McCabe compiled a list of the twelve worst cases of malpractice that he believed backed up his argument. These included ten that had been examined by Byrne/McGinn, the Mary Lynch case, and the case of the missing computer.

He met Connolly and handed over a written complaint and the dossier of a dozen cases. On 23 January 2012 Oliver Connolly forwarded the complaint to the office of the Minister for Justice,

Alan Shatter. After consulting with his officials, Shatter asked that they seek the opinion of the Garda commissioner. This course of action was perfectly correct under the existing law.

The commissioner replied four days later. He set out how, while the complainant wasn't identified, he could make an educated guess as to who it was. McCabe's fingerprints were all over it. The commissioner pointed out that eleven of the cases had been dealt with. The remaining one concerned the computer. 'It is apparent the investigation was efficiently and speedily carried out and resulted in the priest being sentenced to five years concurrent sentences in Cavan District Court,' Callinan wrote. It is unclear if the commissioner had any knowledge of the shortcomings in that investigation.

He concluded that he was satisfied that 'no evidence was found of any wrong-doing (corruption or malpractice) on the part of Superintendent Clancy'.

Shatter was satisfied with the response. He wrote to the confidential recipient Connolly on 3 February to tell him there was no evidence to support McCabe's allegations.

Six days later McCabe met Connolly in Killiney Castle Hotel in south Dublin. As shown in earlier chapters, McCabe was surreptitiously recording most of his interactions to do with his case. He hadn't recorded meetings with Connolly's predecessor, Brian McCarthy, but this time he decided to record the meeting with Connolly. Some might put it down to paranoia, but by 2012 McCabe knew that, whether or not he was paranoid, there was no doubt that some were out to get him. So he resolved to have a contemporaneous record of every interaction, even those with individuals whom he trusted such as Connolly.

After the men went through the formalities at the Killiney Castle, Connolly read out the letter he had received from the minister.

McCabe was devastated. 'Sure it's a joke really, Oliver. When you see it. Like, the minister should go to someone independent to look at it. Like, what do I do with all the falsification of records and now even the minister is now saying, now saying that everything was okay.'

Connolly replied, 'What he's saying basically is that there is no actual evidence against the commissioner.'

'He is believing the commissioner and not me. So it's a joke, isn't it really, Oliver?'

Connolly was non-committal. He attempted to appease McCabe's anger.

Later in the conversation, Connolly made a statement that would end up being quoted under privilege in the Dáil.

'I'll tell you something, Maurice, and this is just personal advice to you. If Shatter thinks you're screwing him, you're finished.'

Connolly has never confirmed or denied making the comment. His position thereafter was that the meeting was confidential and he felt obliged not to break that confidentiality and felt betrayed that the other party had. (A request to Oliver Connolly for an interview for this book met with no response.)

The comment is no reflection on Alan Shatter. It was an opinion delivered in a context where Connolly appeared to be trying to mollify McCabe and steer him away from, as Connolly saw it, driving up further blind alleys.

The meeting finished with no resolution. McCabe's latest complaint had run into the sand. It had been a desperate attempt by a desperate man. It wasn't his finest hour, but by early 2012 he had been attempting to have this stuff addressed for nearly four years, and was continually running into brick walls.

The men departed amicably. In time, though, Connolly's comment about Shatter would act as a crucial event in the unfolding of McCabe's story.

While that episode was unfolding, McCabe found himself drawn into another area of malpractice. In early 2012 a young garda came to him with a problem. He had issued a speeding ticket to a motorist some weeks previously. He had entered the details in the PULSE system, but a recent glance at the file on the system had revealed that the Fixed Charge Notice (FCN), as the ticket was officially known, had been cancelled. It turned out that a superintendent based in the greater Dublin area had 'hit the button', the expression used for wiping the notice from the system.

This meant that the motorist escaped three penalty points being applied to his driver's licence and a fine of €60. The garda who had issued the ticket was frustrated that a senior officer, outside his district, had seen fit to cancel the ticket without bothering to contact him. What was the point of detecting speeding if this was the outcome?

McCabe was surprised rather than shocked. He had been in the force long enough to know that tickets sometimes had a way of disappearing. There was a time when the quashing of tickets was looked on as a pretty standard element of policing. Many people knew a garda who would offer to have a ticket 'squared'.

That was back in the days when road safety was not considered to be a serious matter, despite a rising death toll. In 1998, the year the government launched its blueprint on road safety, entitled 'The Road to Safety', there were 458 deaths on the roads of the state. At the time there was a growing awareness that the level of fatalities was not acceptable in an alleged civilised society.

To that end, a penalty points system was introduced in 2002. The system provided for the application of points to a driver's licence for a number of offences, the most prominent being speeding.

Two, three or in a few instances up to five points would be attached to a licence depending on the offence. Once a driver reached twelve points, his or her licence was automatically suspended for six months. The range of offences attracting points was expanded the following year to include driving without insurance, failing to wear seatbelts, and careless driving. Today there are in excess of 60 offences that carry a penalty points sanction. Apart from the deterrent effect, the penalty points system also came into play in acquiring insurance, with a hike in premiums likely for those with points on their licence. The system, along with the establishment of the Road Safety Authority in 2006, led to a significant drop in road fatalities. By 2012 the annual number of deaths had been reduced to 161.

Against that background, the old culture of fixing tickets was thought to have faded away. Only a garda of the rank of superintendent, or, in some instances, an inspector, could kill a ticket. And a genuine excuse for doing so would have to be given.

Now McCabe had been approached by a member who felt his work was being entirely undermined. Fixing a ticket without even bothering to contact the detecting officer showed contempt for the whole system.

Once again the sergeant was faced with a fork in the road. He could tell the young garda to keep the head down, try to get on as best he could in his job and ignore the dark side of things. Realistically, though, after all he had been through, was he now going to turn away when something else was brought to his attention?

He did a bit of digging. He checked the name of the offending motorist whom the young garda had detected. The man's surname was unusual, and after further digging it emerged that six different people with the same surname had had tickets squared by the same senior officer. These offences had been detected in Dublin where the senior officer was based, but also in Cork and the Midlands, outside his area. It didn't take a genius to figure out that in all likelihood this officer had some form of a relationship with the family in question.

Curiosity prompted McCabe to dig deeper. He quickly narrowed his focus. In particular, he examined cases where motorists were detected on more than one occasion. He also came across numerous cases where members of the force and their families had routinely had tickets fixed.

There were two serious issues here. The dominant one was safety. The raison d'être for the penalty points system was to enhance road safety. If a slice of the population were able to continue behaving as if the new regime did not apply to them, then it followed that the roads were less safe than most people imagined.

The other issue was revenue. Each fixed charge penalty came with a €60 fine. While this was designed as a deterrent, it was also revenue for the state. If thousands of notices were being cancelled on spurious grounds, then the state was losing out on that money.

Before long, McCabe began to notice a few trends in the tickets that were cancelled. The first of these concerned repeat offenders. A sample of the cases extracted from PULSE show how repeat offenders were dealt with through cancellations.

- A man involved in state security had his notice cancelled in 2011, with the reason 'intruder at his home'. A month later his wife's notice was terminated by the same garda with the comment 'cancelled'.
- One motorist had four notices terminated in three months in 2010.
- A female motorist had four notices terminated in 2011. Twice the comment box was blank, meaning that no reason at all was provided. (The PULSE system requires a comment within the box, outlining the reason for termination. But if the box is clicked into with a mouse, and the space bar tapped a few times, the computer allows the record to proceed. A large number of terminations had nothing in the comment box.)
- A husband and wife in the north-east had four tickets cancelled in two years. Twice, the comment box was blank,

the third recorded the reason merely as 'cancelled', and the fourth was 'called to a medical emergency'.

– A motorist with 'an insulin-dependent son' had an 'emergency call to hospital', but he was detected twice in the same day.

– A motorist in Cork had three notices terminated within a week. The first two had 'cancelled' in the comment box, the third had 'comprehensive letter' explaining why all three had occurred.

– A motorist on Dublin's north side had terminations for five notices over nine months. The first three had a blank comment box, with 'medical emergency' in the other two.

– A motorist in the south-east had three notices cancelled, the first two with no reason attached, and the third recorded as 'speeding due to illness'.

– A driver for a public service transport company had two notices cancelled in 2010, both with the reason 'unfamiliar with route'.

– A woman in South Munster had three notices terminated in the space of a year. The comment box recorded the reason as 'A&E nurse'. There was no indication whether the nurse was speeding to an emergency or merely going to or from hospital, or whether she was even on duty at the time of the detections.

The bizarre explanations sometimes given for cancelling fixed charge notices was another trend that piqued McCabe's curiosity.

There are genuine reasons for cancelling. The most common is 'medical emergency', which would typically involve a motorist speeding to a hospital or for medical attention. While this reason is self-explanatory, it did pop up a lot in McCabe's investigations, often without any supporting evidence for the emergency.

There are other genuine and allowable explanations, such as the offending vehicle having been stolen at the time, or a motorist being ticketed erroneously for breaking a speed limit in a particular location.

A number of cancellations McCabe came across had the reason as 'other', which can cover a multitude. But it was the bizarre reasons that really took his eye. He suspected that these explanations were merely inserted in the comment box as a top-of-the-head excuse to cancel for a favoured motorist.

Among them were:

- 'Delivery of clothes to St Vincent de Paul'
- 'On the way to work' [with no further explanation]
- 'Philanthropic benevolence' [this motorist was detected speeding at 156km/h in Carlow]
- 'Public interest [chairman of local voluntary organisation in County Clare']'
- 'Returning from funeral' [this incident was recorded at 4.30pm and a speed of 150km/h]
- 'Medical certificate for holding mobile phone'
- 'Telephone call to hurry home'
- 'Phone was in handset, confirmed by garda' [in other words, a motorist was detected using his phone by a garda, but when asked about it by the senior garda, the rank and file member stated that he hadn't seen what he had recorded that he'd seen!]
- 'Car broken down, assistance needed'
- 'Family difficulty'
- 'Bees attacking livestock' [the motorist here was a farmer]
- 'Late for swimming lesson'

A number of cases had no reasons at all attached to their file, with the comment box simply left blank.

Another category of cancellation that kept popping up was that of gardaí terminating notices for colleagues. Often the reason for cancelling was inserted as 'on duty', with nothing to support such a contention. In a number of instances of which McCabe was personally aware, he checked and found that the member in question was off-duty at the time of the detection.

Many other cancellations of notices where gardaí were the offending motorist had no explanation attached. Among those uncovered by McCabe were:

- One member was detected four times in three years. The reason for each termination was 'emergency'.
- One notice for termination of an offence in the midlands was authorised by a senior garda in a specialist unit in Dublin who had no professional connection to the motorist garda.
- A garda's case in Portlaoise was dealt with by a senior garda in a Dublin station.
- One member was detected four times. Each case was dealt with by the same senior garda. The first three had no reason in the comment box, the fourth had 'operational'.
- A garda driving a commercial vehicle – which is against the force's rules – had his notice terminated.
- A senior garda in a midlands station terminated the notice for a member in the north-east with the reason 'received call that house being burgled'.
- A garda in Leinster had three notices terminated, two with the reason 'garda on duty', and the third 'incorrect registration showing'.
- The comment box on another member's case had the following: 'Spoke with member concerned, now satisfied that he was not using phone.'

– One garda's reason for termination was 'taking a statement', while another was 'on duty in connection with the Royal visit'. [Garda Commissioner Martin Callinan said he himself had a fixed notice terminated after receiving it for speeding on his way to a meeting.]

A feature that kept cropping up in the records was that senior gardaí were cancelling notices outside their own areas. According to the rules, this was to be done only in exceptional cases, but McCabe saw that it was happening all over the place.

The picture that was emerging was shocking. McCabe knew a certain amount of this had gone on despite the heightened awareness of the importance of the penalty points system, but he had never thought it was as extensive as this. This whole business differed from the kind of malpractice he had been highlighting. This involved what he believed was corruption at senior management level. Those fixing tickets were not the rank and file, who formed the bulk of his complaints of malpractice in criminal investigations. This was all about senior officers enjoying the perks of the gig, with scant regard for the consequences of their collective action.

To bring this issue further would be to take on senior management. After all he had been subjected to, was he prepared for such an endeavour? McCabe's musings on the subject, particularly with Lorraine, kept returning to a simple question: could he live with himself if he did nothing about it? After everything he had experienced and learned since he broke with the herd? The answer was obvious.

Once he resolved to act, the issue was how exactly to go about it. His experience thus far persuaded him that it would be entirely pointless to bring this issue to the attention of his superiors.

With this in mind, he decided that his best port of call was the

Houses of the Oireachtas Public Accounts Committee. If the force was not going to examine the issue, then it was up to some outside body to do so.

McCabe travelled to Dublin and met the secretary of the Public Accounts Committee in Leinster House. He outlined the quality and quantity of information he possessed. The secretary told him that he should go to the Comptroller and Auditor General, whose office was tasked with accounting for public money.

McCabe crossed the Liffey to the office on the north side and was met there by an official. He outlined that he had collated information on the abuse of public money through the ticket-fixing.

'Have you evidence?' she asked him. He sat down and, over the course of two hours, went through the detail of what was contained in his dossier. The official suggested that there certainly appeared to be significant abuse. She took possession of the dossier and said she would be in touch.

Around this time, McCabe found that he had a kindred spirit in attempting to uncover this latest example of corruption. John Wilson, who had stayed in touch with McCabe through his travails, came on board.

McCabe told him what he had discovered about the penalty points and ticket-fixing. Wilson did his own checking and came up with other cases that looked to be well outside the acceptable scope of legitimate cancellations.

'We got talking about the squaring of the tickets,' Wilson remembered. 'I went back to work and did a bit of checking on PULSE and I came up with a load of high-profile names who benefited, most of whom were mentioned in the Dáil a while after that.'

The two men decided that it would be entirely pointless to bring the matter to the attention of Garda management. The only alternative was to approach a politician, something that was provided for under the Garda Síochána Act 2005. To do this would be to take the matter into a new realm. Politicians dealt with their business in the public domain. Were they prepared to go down that route? With little alternative in view, with little hope of the matter being scrutinised internally, there was really no choice.

Once they decided to embark on that course of action, there was only one politician to approach.

12

'Honest gardaí are being undermined. Those gardaí need protection.'
Mick Wallace TD

Clare Daly had already got into her stride as a TD when she first encountered Maurice McCabe.

She had been elected to the Dáil for the first time in the 2011 general election, but her political activism went way back to her student days, when she was elected president of the students' union in Dublin City University.

After college, she took a job in Dublin Airport and became heavily involved in trade union activity. Her natural home was the Joe Higgins-led Socialist Party, for which she was elected in the Fingal local authority area in three successive elections, beginning in 1999.

In 2003 she, along with others, including Higgins, was jailed for a month for refusing to obey a court order in relation to bin-charge protests. She was elected to the Dáil for the Dublin North constituency on her fourth attempt in 2011.

Many saw her as Higgins' natural successor whenever he decided to hang up his parliamentary spurs.

Then in the summer of 2012 Daly's career took a different direction. An issue had arisen over Mick Wallace, an independent TD for Wexford, who had formed a close alliance with Daly and her colleagues since his election.

Wallace's path to national politics couldn't have been more different from Daly's. He was a former developer, a species ordinarily regarded by the Socialist Party as highly suspicious, if not anathema to any notion of social equity. But Wallace was a developer with a difference, one whose commitment to building was matched by a unique political and social interest. With long tangled locks of blond hair and a penchant for pink t-shirts, he was always ready to give his take on the world when a microphone hovered into view.

By 2011 Wallace's business had gone to the wall. Like the majority of his colleagues in building, he had over-borrowed, and when the tide rushed out on the building boom, he was left high and dry. By then he was a regular media presence, particularly on the *Tonight with Vincent Browne* programme on TV3. It was during an appearance on the show on 5 February 2011 that he announced that he was going to run for the Dáil in his native Wexford. He topped the poll in the constituency with 13,329 votes, surfing a wave of disaffection with the body politic as a result of the economic collapse, recession and a burning resentment over shovelling the banking debt onto citizens.

A few months after he was elected, a different picture began to emerge about Wallace's business. He faced financial ruin over bank debts he had run up. Things went from bad to worse for the developer turned politician. In June 2012 it was revealed that his company owed the Revenue Commissioners €2.1 million in tax, interest and penalties, because of under-declared VAT liabilities. Wallace admitted that when his business had run into serious difficulties following the financial crash in 2008, he had made false declarations.

Daly refused to distance herself from Wallace, but by doing so found herself in conflict with her party colleagues. By the end of the summer she had come to the conclusion that her role in the Socialist Party was no longer tenable, and on 1 September the party revealed that Daly had resigned.

The previous year, before all the travails with Wallace, Daly was appearing on *Tonight with Vincent Browne* one night when her contribution grabbed the attention of Maurice and Lorraine McCabe at home in Cavan. The topic under debate concerned shortcomings with the gardaí, and McCabe had noticed in particular that Daly knew what she was talking about when plenty of others either skirted around the issue or were simply waffling. He phoned Clare Daly's office the next day and arranged to meet her. A few weeks later, McCabe went to Leinster House and they met in her office.

'He told me what he'd been through with the Byrne/McGinn investigation and how it hadn't got to the bottom of things at all,' Daly told the author. 'He didn't really want me to do anything at that point; he was just keeping me in the loop. I did write a letter to the deputy commissioner Nacie Rice about it and got a reply from him, but there was nothing else at that stage.'

In July 2012 McCabe and Wilson travelled to Leinster House and met Daly. They had compiled a dossier of the worst cases they had come across in relation to the ticket-fixing and showed it to her. This time, Daly's reaction was one of pure shock. What was before her was actual detail, easily digested and comprehensible.

'We had another meeting after that up in Virginia,' Daly said. 'Mick Wallace and myself went up and we met John [Wilson] and Maurice in the home of this couple who'd been having their own problems with the gardaí. We got a really full picture of the whole thing on that occasion. It was really shocking.'

*

As was his wont, McCabe didn't rest on his laurels. By August 2012 he had not heard back from the C&AG. He decided to try the Department of Transport, to see if anybody there had any interest in road safety. He was met by a senior official, who listened and viewed the dossier. He told McCabe that he would contact the Department of Justice about the matter.

That day was 10 August 2012. McCabe remembered it because he was on the street when he got a call telling him that four men, including three brothers, had been killed in a road traffic accident outside Tullamore. As a member of the traffic corps in Mullingar, he was only too aware of the devastation that was now being visited on yet another family. The news also gave him renewed conviction that the path he was embarked on would contribute in its own way to improving safety on the roads.

He had one more call to make, but this one would not be in person. On the Monday following his day in Dublin, he rang the Taoiseach's office and got particulars for dispatching an email.

From: Maurice McCabe
To: Taoiseach's Office
Sent: Monday, 13 August 2012, 2:40pm
Subject: re- Highly Private and Confidential

Hi -----,
I refer to our phone call just now.
I attach a document entitled 'ticket-fixing' which amounts to about 20 pages.
   This email and attachment must remain highly confidential as if my name gets out I would be finished policing in An Garda Síochána and the backlash would be unbearable.
Regards,
Maurice McCabe

Apart from the standard acknowledgement of receipt of the mail, nothing more came of it.

Summer turned to autumn with little sign of progress. McCabe wasn't aware of it but behind the scenes there was movement. The dossier had been passed to the Department of Justice and from there onto the Garda commissioner's office. The minister asked whether there was something to it.

Meanwhile, McCabe kept trying. In October he contacted Conor Faughnan, the high-profile director of consumer affairs in the Automobile Association. The pair met in the Applegreen motorway services hub on the M4 in County Westmeath. McCabe told him who he was and what he was about. Faughnan asked McCabe if he would meet a friend of his, Noel Brett, chief executive of the Road Safety Authority. No problem, said McCabe; he'd meet anybody who might be in a position to help.

A few days later McCabe got in touch with Brett. The latter was in Naas and lived in Mayo, so the pair agreed to meet in the Longford Arms hotel in Longford town.

'He showed me the dossier,' Brett said. 'He was really clear that he'd gone through the chain of command. I would have pushed him quite hard and satisfied myself that he genuinely believed what he was at and that he had evidence to back it up. I explained to him that he was alleging wrong-doing and possibly criminal behaviour and the loss of money to the exchequer. I told him that I felt obliged to inform GSOC and that I felt obliged to refer the matter to the Comptroller and Auditor General and I did that in both cases the following morning.'

McCabe had of course already been in contact with the C&AG but now the comptroller would be getting the information from the head of a statutory agency. McCabe left Longford that night in a positive mood after a ninety-minute meeting. Brett was a genuine man as far as the sergeant was concerned, someone who would actually attempt to do something.

Brett also phoned the chairman of the RSA, broadcaster Gay Byrne, and asked that they meet urgently. Byrne was a high-profile figure in the battle to alleviate suffering on the road.

The pair met in Buswells Hotel, opposite the gates of Leinster House. After Brett had briefed him and showed him what McCabe had uncovered, Byrne said he was shocked. 'I was agog at the whole thing,' Byrne later said in an interview with the *Irish Examiner*. 'We all knew what went on if you knew a guard or somebody who did, and things got fixed, but what was amazing and astonishing was the extent of it, the number of people and particularly repeat offenders who were getting away with this.'

McCabe was at home on the last day of October 2012 when he heard on the radio that the Garda commissioner had appointed a senior officer to examine allegations about the abuse of the penalty points system.

The officer appointed was Assistant Commissioner John O'Mahony, who had a long and distinguished record of service in the force. O'Mahony's team included five chief superintendents, six superintendents, together with their respective staffs and an incident room staffed by a further seven officers. In terms of application of resources, this was going to be a major job which, it could be expected, would leave no stone unturned.

McCabe was not informed of this development. Having not been kept in the loop about the inquiry that was underway, he fired off another email to the centre of power.

Date: Mon 05 Nov 2012 14:12
From: Maurice McCabe
Subject: re Complaint

To: Taoiseach's Office
Private and Confidential

Hi -----

I feel that I have been fobbed off with emails hoping I would go away. In July 2012 I reported to An Taoiseach's office serious corruption, perverting the course of justice and misappropriation of public money. I was told in emails that the matters were brought to his attention. I mentioned that I brought these matters to Minister Shatter's attention in January 2012 but he was told there was no evidence to my allegations. Minister Shatter may have been misled.

It is almost 4 months since I reported the malpractice to An Taoiseach's office and no one has ever contacted me concerning the allegations. I have recently asked a question four times and An Taoiseach's office refused to answer it. The numerous emails will show my frustration in trying to get the practice stopped. I can now report that the Road Safety Authority put a halt to the corruption last week when contacted by myself.

As previously stated, one million euros has been misappropriated since I told Minister Shatter and over €100,000 has been misappropriated since I told An Taoiseach's office. Both offices failed and refused to order a halt to the illegal and criminal terminations. Any normal person reading my email attachment would be shocked at its contents. Perhaps both offices were kept in the dark by garda authorities.

My complaint is

1. Why did An Taoiseach's office act this way?
2. Why has no one ever contacted me concerning my allegations?
3. Was An Taoiseach aware of the allegations of malpractice?
4. Why did no one take the allegations seriously?
5. Why had it to take the Road Safety Authority to halt the corruption?
6. What is really happening with my complaint?

I hope my complaint remains private and confidential.
Regards,
Maurice McCabe

He received the standard response acknowledging his mail and pointing out that it was a matter for the Department of Justice.

By then, a small band of politicians was formulating a strategy. The dossier presented by McCabe and Wilson had provided Clare Daly with ammunition. She consulted with Mick Wallace, and also shared some of the information with another independent, Luke 'Ming' Flanagan.

Flanagan had been a somewhat colourful addition to the Dáil since his election in 2011. He had first come to public attention as a campaigner for the legalisation of cannabis a decade earlier. He was known as 'Ming the Merciless', a character from the old Flash Gordon television series, because of his style of facial hair. On one occasion when he refused to pay a fine for possession of the drug, his father intercepted to save Luke from a spell in prison. Flanagan senior was thereafter known as Ming the Merciful.

Since those days, Ming had evolved into a serious politician. He was elected in Roscommon-South Leitrim against the odds in 2011. After entering the Dáil, he formed a close alliance with Wallace and Daly.

The other TD to get involved was Joan Collins, another first-timer in the Dáil. She was elected as a member for Dublin South-Central and was aligned with People Before Profit, the group that had grown out of the old Socialist Workers Party.

John Wilson had met Collins and provided her with the names of high-profile people who had benefited from terminations. By now, word had seeped out into the media that the beneficiaries were well known. On one level this gave added impetus to the story. Here was an example of the divisions in society that had been repeatedly referenced since the economic collapse in 2008 and subsequent deep recession. If you were a well-known individual or high-ranking in society, you could get your speeding ticket fixed.

In time, this perception would be shown to have been skewed, but it gave further legs to the story when it was in its infancy.

In the Dáil, Daly and Wallace made a number of efforts to have the ticket-fixing matter addressed but without success. One tactic the pair tried was to put down a question for the minister for transport and tourism, Leo Varadkar – whose brief included road safety – and then veer off that subject and onto the ticket-fixing once an exchange opened up across the Dáil floor.

On 27 November 2012 Wallace attempted this with a question relating to the tourism element of Varadkar's brief. After an initial response, he dropped the tourism and launched into a broadside: 'I submitted a question on the termination by the Garda of more than 100,000 fixed-charge penalties from 2008 to 2011, but it was rejected by the Department. The money lost to the State would have paid for 500 patrol cars. Garda have approached me, as a Member of the Oireachtas, to express their great concern that honest garda are being undermined by this activity. It is corruption and should be investigated.'

Varadkar responded that he was aware of the issue and had referred it to the Department of Justice, but further discussion was ruled out by the Ceann Comhairle (chairperson).

The story finally got a full airing on the floor of the Dáil on 4 December 2012. The afternoon attendance in the chamber was sparse as the House debated the household charge, a contentious form of property tax that was about to be introduced.

The session was being chaired by the Leas Cheann Comhairle (assistant chairperson), Michael Kitt, and was centred on a question from Fianna Fáil's Environment spokesperson, Barry Cowen.

Kitt was opening up the floor to deputies who had requested to speak on the matter. Little did the deputising chair know that he was about to be ambushed.

> **Michael Kitt:** Five deputies are offering and I ask for their co-operation. I call on Deputy Mick Wallace, followed by Deputy Clare Daly.

> **Mick Wallace:** The Reporting of fixed charge penalties on a massive scale has been ignored by the government since last January and we are blocked from discussing that in this chamber. A public inquiry is now needed. Honest gardaí are being undermined. Those gardaí need protection. They went to the garda confidential recipient and did not get any satisfaction or protection. Instead, they got a warning when one of them said to one of the gardaí, 'I'll tell you something. If Shatter thinks you're screwing him, you're finished.' That is a disgrace.

> **Kitt:** Deputy, please, we are on the household charge. I call on Deputy Daly. Is this the same issue?

> **Clare Daly:** This is a matter of national interest. Honest gardaí are being victimised because they have uncovered systemic abuse of motoring charges and terminations of those of some very powerful and influential people in the state, including members of the judiciary.

Kitt: Deputy—

Daly: Judge Devins has been named in the newspapers, as have sports figures and other officials, including garda.

Kitt: I ask the deputy to resume her seat.

Daly: We have been denied the opportunity to raise this issue in other ways ....

Kitt: No, I ask the deputy to resume her seat.

Daly: We are talking about the loss of millions to the state.

Kitt: This is question time and we are on Deputy Barry Cowen's question on the household charge.

Daly: We have tried to raise this issue and garda are being undermined.

Kitt: I ask the deputy to resume her seat. I call on deputies Brian Stanley, Joan Collins and Luke 'Ming' Flanagan.

At this, Brian Stanley, Sinn Féin deputy, got to his feet and asked a question pertaining to the household charge. After his brief contribution, it was Joan Collins' turn to speak.

Joan Collins: I also want to raise the national issue in respect of penalty points.

Kitt: Please, deputy, no.

Collins: It is outrageous. We have been trying to get this issue on the agenda and I submitted it as a topical issue.

Kitt: We are on a question about the household charge.

Collins: There are fixed-term notices and judges are giving down charges ....

Kitt: The deputy can talk to the Ceann Comhairle ....

Collins: ... to people with penalty points and Judge Devins is named in this. It is outrageous.

Kitt: I call Deputy Luke 'Ming' Flanagan on the household charge.

Luke 'Ming' Flanagan: I would also like to talk on the issue of corruption when it comes to removing penalty points from people's licences.

Kitt: Deputy, no ....

Flanagan: This country should protect whistleblowers but it has never done so.

Kitt: This is an orchestrated campaign.

Flanagan: This is one of the reasons we are in the hole we are in.

Kitt: I ask the deputy to resume his seat.

Flanagan: We need to protect whistleblowers, not punish them. We are being denied the right to talk about corruption. What is new? Nothing.

Kitt: This is question time.

Poor Michael Kitt. The Leas Cheann Comhairle had expected a quiet afternoon. Instead, he had sustained a rapid-fire assault from the independent benches.

Wallace had included mention of a comment attributed to Oliver

Connolly, the confidential recipient, and both Daly and Collins had mentioned the name of Judge Mary Devins under parliamentary privilege.

Despite this guerrilla tactic, there was not much take-up on the issue. The press reported the intervention the following day, but the issue of ticket-fixing had been around for a while.

The following Tuesday the matter was raised in the Dáil again, this time by Sinn Féin's Pádraig Mac Lochlainn. In response, the Minister for Justice, Alan Shatter, divulged some of the figures he had received in an interim report from Assistant Commissioner O'Mahony: 'From the interim report I received I have noted that some of the cancellations of fixed charge notices relate to ordinary individuals who are not VIPs or other such individuals.

'At least one person has been unfairly named in this House. The individuals to whom I refer are those in circumstances in which a car identified as speeding is not the actual car owned by an individual who has received a ticket. There have been other instances, including one in which a young child was being taken to hospital in an emergency.'

Later in the day the matter was raised again. Joan Collins once more introduced some high-profile names: 'This is not a question of a few celebrities such as Ronan O'Gara, Paul Williams or Mary Devins, whom I mentioned last week, or other judges or multiple gardaí.'

That was enough to prick Shatter's sense of outrage.

'I must object,' he told the House. 'This is outrageous. The deputy is deliberately trying to force the recording of names, contrary to the rules of this House, into the record, to the detriment of individuals who cannot defend themselves.'

Shatter had a point. Privilege was being used in a manner that could be judged to be unfair. The individuals concerned had no right of reply, and it could be argued that they were being placed in a highly invidious position.

Why should any of them be forced to come out and deny that they had received a termination? What if they had received a termination that was entirely appropriate and within the rules?

On the other hand, Collins was using the privilege of the House to highlight an issue that, in her opinion, was not being investigated in official circles.

Up in Cavan, McCabe had just returned home from a break in Germany. He brought himself up to date with the proceedings in the Dáil and was dismayed that once more it appeared that his concerns were not being properly addressed. During this period he was in constant contact with Wilson, one of the few members in the force in whom he could confide. Neither man knew where this was going to go. Both were fearful at this stage that the O'Mahony inquiry would be a whitewash.

Around this time, Wilson had been discovered printing out records from the PULSE system: 'I had been confronted by an inspector in Cavan [station] and challenged about downloading stuff from PULSE,' Wilson said. 'He asked what I was doing and I told him I was carrying out inquiries about corrupt terminations. He asked who I was giving them to and I wouldn't give him any names.'

Two days later, both men were separately asked to be available for a chat when their respective shifts were completed.

That, as far as each was concerned, most likely meant they were about to be suspended. McCabe was in a tizzy. His career was unblemished. He had done everything by the book in attempting to highlight the wrong-doing. Yet now they were about to put him in cold storage.

Already there had been an attempt, as he saw it, to discredit and discipline him by linking him to the missing computer that had been used by the convicted sex-offending priest. There had been attempts to draw him into the blunders that had led to Jerry McGrath being free on bail when he killed Sylvia Roche Kelly. Now this: another attempt to do for him on a basis that he could not fathom.

Throughout the day, he and Wilson were in constant contact. For whatever reason, Wilson was dealt with first. This meant that he would be in a position to convey to McCabe what was in store for him.

'I got the call saying that there was correspondence from the commissioner there,' Wilson said. 'I thought I was going to be suspended, so I phoned McCabe and filled him in.

'Once I got back to the station, I went in and the order was read out to me warning me about accessing PULSE. I rang McCabe and told him we weren't being suspended.'

McCabe breathed a sigh of relief. He steeled himself for the meeting and half an hour later popped his phone into his breast pocket, pressed record and entered the superintendent's office. He was met there by Chief Superintendent Mark Curran and Sergeant Paddy Guinan, the divisional clerk.

The chief super was brandishing a sheet of paper, from which he began reading how the Garda commissioner had taken legal advice and had information that McCabe had been printing out records from the PULSE computer system.

Then he formally gave McCabe the commissioner's direction.

> **Chief Superintendent Mark Curran:** The direction is as follows: The commissioner is now directing you to desist from the practice of accessing PULSE and/or disclosing to third parties sensitive personal data regarding the cancellation of fixed charge notices by members of An Garda Síochána. If you have any further concerns and without prejudice of your rights under the Confidential Reporting Mechanism, such matters can be brought to the attention of Assistant Commissioner

John O'Mahony, Crime and Security, who will fully investigate those matters.

[Further conversation]

McCabe: But I didn't do any of that.

Curran: Well, I'm only telling you that that is the directions from the commissioner.

McCabe: And what happens under the Garda Síochána Act, where you are allowed hand over stuff, under section 62 and the whistleblower charter. What about that?

Curran: I think you need to raise that with Assistant Commissioner Mahoney. Honestly that might be the way you pursue it.

McCabe: That's a serious accusation.

Curran: The directions on it, and just to make sure we are both clear, I'll read it out to you again.

McCabe: No, I am very clear. He is accusing me of handing stuff over.

[Curran then reads out the first paragraph in the report again to explain what McCabe is being accused of by the commissioner. And then reads out the direction again.]

McCabe: So he is saying I did that.

Curran: The commissioner has facts on which he is basing these comments on. So I'll read it out one more time so you understand. [He reads it all out again.]

McCabe: He is basically saying that I gave the information to somebody else, so the whistleblower charter is gone, finished, cause he is saying there. If the Data Protection Commissioner asks me for stuff, what do I do? Do I say no to him? He has asked for stuff.

Curran: No, no, don't. If you want authority to do anything or if you have an issue there in relation to those matters, you can talk to Assistant Commissioner John O'Mahony. Or you can send your concerns here in relation to that.

McCabe: So I can't go near the whistleblower charter anymore? Obviously!

Curran: You cannot.

McCabe: I can. [Curran reads out the report again.] He's after accusing me of stuff there that I didn't do, and that is shocking. The only person I forwarded stuff to was An Taoiseach, so I'll have to take it up with him. Cause he must be the third party. Shocking stuff.

Curran: I know, but that's his legal advice.

McCabe: But even the Data Protection Commissioner, he asked me for stuff, so what do I say to him – no?

Curran: Well, that's the instruction and you'll be in breach of discipline and any other possible acts if you ignore it.

McCabe: So am I allowed email Enda Kenny about that?

Curran: I can give you an answer, my own personal answer, but I think you should address it with John O'Mahony. The direction is down here that he will deal with your concerns.

McCabe: Shocking stuff. So basically, I can do nothing.

Curran: What you need to do is do what you're meant to do, your day-to-day duty.

McCabe: Oh, and not report anything which is wrong which—

Curran: This is a direction from the commissioner. You are searching PULSE for a particular reason.

McCabe: I got a complaint in relation to that from a garda. I carried out my duty.

Curran: Did you report that?

McCabe: I carried out my duty.

Curran: Did you report it here?

McCabe: I carried out my duty. I carried out my duties in relation to that.

Curran: Did you report it thr…ough the channels?

McCabe: I carried out all my duties in relation to it.

Curran: OK.

McCabe: I used the whistleblowing charter. Let's not argue. As regards the last paragraph, you'll have no issue with me here anymore.

Curran: That's all I want to know.

McCabe: You won't, chief, you won't, no. But it's just amazing. I did not think it was that, I thought it was something ….

Curran: No, you should follow that; it is a direction.

McCabe: Yes, it is, and I will follow that. I won't disobey any direction and you can make note of that, Paddy. I won't disobey any directions in relation to that. You have my full compliance. But I'm just amazed, but sure ....

[Small talk]

McCabe: Do I get a copy of that?

Curran: No.

McCabe: OK, well it won't happen anyway. I give you my word on that. It's not your problem anyway. You were sent to read it out to me.

McCabe left the room and went to his car in the station car park. He felt shaky, as if another Rubicon had been crossed.

In his mind it was as if they were determined to come after him. If they couldn't get him one way, they would try another. He was a persona non grata, who had to be either destroyed or driven from the force. At least he hadn't been suspended. At least he had been spared another torturous, long drawn out process to clear his name.

As he left Mullingar and headed for the drumlins of Cavan, his mood lightened. After all he'd been through, shipping blows like that had become just part of another day.

Back in Dublin, independent TDs Daly, Wallace, Collins and Flanagan had put out word that a media briefing would be held to disseminate more high-profile names who had benefited from the wiping of penalty points.

The meeting was held on 20 December, and attracted a large

media presence. But, much to the disappointment of the assembled hacks, new no names were introduced.

The purpose of the gathering was to dispute the information put out by the Minister for Justice which suggested that only 300 suspicious cases had been uncovered, of which 197 required further explanation. Mick Wallace said they were now calling for a public inquiry to examine the issue in a forum that would enjoy at least some modicum of confidence among the public.

As everybody went on leave for Christmas, there was a sense that perhaps this penalty points thing wasn't going anywhere. There had been a long tradition in the country of controversies blowing up, being fixated on for a brief period, and then quietly disappearing. Perhaps this was going to be another one.

13

'Can you advise me as to where I can turn to next?'
Maurice McCabe to Taoiseach Enda Kenny, 24 April 2013

McCabe worked through Christmas 2012, from 20 December to St Stephen's Day. He did ten-hour shifts across the seven days. The reward at the end was a stretch of free days to catch up with his family.

There was to be no respite for McCabe, however. Over the first three days off work, he received a number of calls from senior officers. He didn't answer any of them. As far as McCabe was concerned, he was on downtime, catching up with his family over the fag end of the festive season. He felt entitled to do so and refused to respond to work calls.

On 30 December two officers showed up at his home: Superintendent Pat McMenamin, district officer for Mullingar, and Inspector Jarlath Folan, an inspector at the station.

Lorraine went out to meet them. She told them Maurice was

asleep. In reality, he simply was not going to give them the satisfaction of meeting with them while he was off-duty. In his experience it was unheard of for officers to visit a member's private home unless it was connected with a criminal matter. He hadn't committed any crime. What could be so important that couldn't wait until he was back in Mullingar garda station in the next few days?

The two officers were perfectly courteous, even trailing a whiff of apologia. Lorraine could see they were taking no pleasure in the tidings they had been dispatched to deliver. They told her they were instructed to inform Sergeant McCabe that another order had issued from HQ in relation to his access to PULSE. The restriction was now to be extended. He would not be allowed any access to the computer system unless it was under the supervision of another ranking officer.

Being denied access to PULSE meant that McCabe simply could not do his job. Practically every officer in the force needs to access PULSE on an almost daily basis. For a sergeant in a traffic unit, the requirement is even greater.

For example, each morning McCabe would be obliged to brief and update those coming on duty about incidents from the day before. Without access to PULSE, that basic duty could not be performed.

Equally, when guards would phone their sergeant to check a registration number or the background of a particular driver, he would be unable to do so. In more serious cases – and one was to occur for McCabe within weeks of being taken off PULSE – a guard would ring in and ask the sergeant to access the details of an individual driver who had been killed, in order to locate and inform the next of kin. Without access to PULSE, that could not be done.

McCabe would now have to go to work wearing a metaphorical blindfold, with one hand tied behind his back.

Meanwhile, among those who were championing his cause, there was another surprise just around the next right turn.

The squad car came to a halt behind Clare Daly and indicated that she should pull in. This was at a quarter past midnight on the morning of 29 January 2013. She had just taken an illegal right turn.

Daly was driving home from a friend's house on the South Circular Road in Dublin. She was not familiar with the locale and may well have been unaware that she was restricted in turning at that junction.

The garda officer breathalysed Daly. She had a cold at the time, and had earlier accepted the offer of a hot whiskey in the house she was visiting.

The breathalyser result was inconclusive, so the gardaí told her they were taking her to the local station, Kilmainham. Daly was arrested and handcuffed. She objected to being handcuffed but was told it was standard procedure.

In fact, gardaí rarely handcuff women when arresting them for an offence such as suspected drink-driving. Garda code regulations specify that a number of suspect types are exempted from being handcuffed when arrested.

The categories of suspects exempted include women, children, older people, and soldiers in uniform. Unless any who fall under these categories are behaving violently or believed to present a risk to public safety, they tend not to be handcuffed. There was never a suggestion that Daly comported herself at the scene other than in a respectful and responsible manner.

It is not known if or when exactly members of the force recognised Daly as the deputy who was making noises in the Dáil about the cancellation of penalty points.

She was driven to Kilmainham station and placed in a cell. A doctor took a urine sample. Daly was told she could contact her solicitor, but there was no reply from the number. She then gave the number of her fellow TD Mick Wallace but was unable to get a response from him either.

At around 1.30am Clare Daly was released. It had been a relatively short interlude in her life, but a shocking one. She was confident that she had not been over the drink-driving limit, but had been arrested and handcuffed. As a public representative, that did not look good.

Within half an hour of Daly leaving Kilmainham, the details of her arrest were entered in the PULSE system as per procedure. What was highly unusual was that in the following hours there were 36 different views of the file on the system. Officers from stations in Dublin city centre, Coolock, on the north side of the city, and Newbridge, Co. Kildare all took a peek. What prompted their curiosity is unknown.

Much later, when the Garda Síochána Ombudsman Commission (GSOC) investigated the incident, the officer in Newbridge claimed he had 'a particular interest in traffic-related incidents'.

The media was first alerted with a phone call to the *Irish Daily Star* newspaper from a phone located in an unlocked office in Kilmainham station. That was at 11am on 29 January.

A few hours later the details of the arrest were emailed to a senior officer at the station. It was procedure – and still is – to inform a senior officer of any incidents involving a politician. (As will be seen later, such a policy would be dragged into the public glare a few months later concerning Mick Wallace.)

That email was forwarded to 57 people within the force. The subsequent GSOC investigation would identify 145 people who were in possession of the information by that afternoon, but in all likelihood it was many more. The Garda Press Office began fielding calls from reporters at 2pm.

A few hours later, Daly got a call from an RTÉ journalist and decided to go on the *Six One News*. She told of the hot whiskey she had and that she would take responsibility for the matter if she was over the limit. As it would turn out, she was well below the legal limit.

The fallout from the matter did not end there. At 7.30pm Wallace got a text from a reporter: 'Sympathy for Clare?' A few hours later, Daly received a text from the same reporter: 'Understand you rang Mick Wallace TD on your allowed phone call by gardaí. Why was that?'

There was more. A tweet was sent to Daly from a Twitter account belonging to a detective who knew the reporter who had contacted the two TDs. 'How big was that hot whiskey? Boiling a bottle of Jameson and swallowing it doesn't count as 1.'

A further tweet from that account said Daly was 'a media-hungry attention-seeking savage complaining about information being given to the media hilarious'.

Another said, 'Probably a bit too late night or in the night to expect certain TD's to be sober at this late hour.'

When the matter was investigated by GSOC, the detective in question suggested that his Twitter account could have been hacked. When he was asked for his phone, he replied that he no longer had it.

The source of the media leaks was never identified, but what had been afoot was obvious. Elements within the force had combined with elements in the media to target Daly in a grievous manner, rushing to get the news out into the public domain before she could address it herself. In the nature of these things it is the first headline, the first angle of a story, that tends to have the most lasting impact.

Not just that, but the whole incident was mined for gossip in connection with Clare Daly's decision to phone her Dáil colleague. There was also the basic but fundamental issue of the privacy to which any citizen is entitled.

It may well be a coincidence that Daly was by then involved in the attempt to highlight the ticket-fixing. If you believe in coincidences of this nature.

The episode was troubling for Daly, but it also put her in the spotlight for people who had their own grievances with the force.

'After the arrest, loads of people began contacting us because they saw it as me being targeted, so they came to us with their problems about the Guards,' she told the author.

'There was big and small stuff, some of it shocking and some a bit crazy. But we had to act, so we organised a meeting in the Red Cow [a hotel on the old Naas Road]. The place was packed out the door. Some of the stories were heartbreaking. And there was a lot of it there. We had five meetings in all and the shortest length of any of them was five hours. All of that started tying into the ticket-fixing stuff for us as well then.'

Less than six weeks after Daly's arrest, another of the band of independent TDs was to find himself with his own headline. A Sunday newspaper reported in mid-March that Luke 'Ming' Flanagan had benefited from having had tickets cancelled not once but twice in recent years.

Flanagan's first reaction was to deny the report on Twitter, but then he caved in. He suggested that a local garda and council official had been involved in having the tickets cancelled – which was denied by both – but then conceded that in the first case, dating from 2011, he had written to the local superintendent requesting leniency for the offence, which was for holding a mobile phone while driving. Flanagan was perfectly entitled to write, and the superintendent was entitled to cancel the ticket. In most of the cases causing controversy, no such written petition was made to the district officer as per procedure. Flanagan did as any other citizen would do in seeking to have his ticket cancelled. Still, it didn't look good.

The affair was deeply embarrassing not just for him but for the colleagues with whom he had highlighted the ticket-fixing.

After the furore over it – including a slot on the *Tonight with*

Vincent Browne programme in which Browne roasted him, Flanagan did step back from the campaign.

The first leak of the O'Mahony report found its way onto the front page of *The Irish Times* on Wednesday, 10 April, under the headline 'Inquiry Finds No Evidence Of Corruption On Penalty Points'.

The piece, written by crime correspondent Conor Lally, bore a strapline under the heading proclaiming, 'Some gardaí were liberal in complying with pleas but didn't benefit'.

The copy began: 'A garda investigation and report for the Government into the quashing of penalty points from drivers' licences has found no evidence of Garda corruption.

'It concludes there is no criminal case to answer by any gardaí or those whose points were terminated and that no gardaí received any reward, monetary or otherwise, for clearing points from licences.'

The article went on to detail that there would be tightening of the rules and greater auditing of the system. Apart from that and the fact that the Minister for Justice intended publishing the report, it was a case of nothing to see here; move along now.

The main message was writ loud and clear. There was no corruption. No money changed hands in return for fixing tickets and quashing penalty points. The main problem had been that some gardaí were too 'liberal' in interpreting their right and duty to cancel tickets in particular instances.

This was a theme that would be writ large once the report was published the following month, but the first leak set the tone: those behind the leak got out their message loud and clear. There was no corruption, no money changed hands.

The straw man was the word 'corruption'. For most people, that word, when referenced in public life, suggests the exchange of money for favours. Neither McCabe nor Wilson ever suggested that such transactions had taken place. It was simply a case of senior officers abusing their position to do a favour for family and friends as a matter of course.

The impression that what was at issue was 'money for quashing points' was reinforced with the strapline stating that gardaí 'didn't benefit'. Again, there never was a suggestion that benefits were received. All that was involved, as far as the leaked version of the O'Mahony report suggested, was 'a liberal interpretation' of the rules in response to 'pleas'. And we all know that people don't 'plea' for something unless they're desperate, or placed in an invidious position, like having to rush to hospital with a sick child or perhaps a frail elderly relative.

McCabe was at work in Mullingar on the morning the piece was published in *The Irish Times*. He read it twice. He couldn't believe it. The investigation had been completed, yet he had never been contacted. He had been waiting for the call to ask him to sit down with the investigators and explain exactly how he had come to his conclusions.

McCabe had done his homework. He had gone back over the material that had formed the basis for his allegations and assured himself that everything was as he had presented it. There was no possibility that he was getting only half the picture. There was no question but that the cancellations he had highlighted were extremely dubious at the very least.

Now it was emerging that he was not to be interviewed. The complainant, the person who had initiated the whole process, was not going to be asked for his point of view.

One word kept flashing through his mind: whitewash.

He and Lorraine mulled over the predicament for more than a week. He was also back and forth with Wilson, who had come to the same conclusion as McCabe had. The following Wednesday, during his lunchbreak, McCabe picked up the phone and rang Garda HQ in the Phoenix Park and asked to be put through to John O'Mahony.

The assistant commissioner wasn't available but he returned the call later that afternoon. 'John,' McCabe asked him, 'what's the story? The newspaper says your report is finished but nobody came and asked me what I knew.'

Later, at the Public Accounts Committee, O'Mahony would say that his reason for not contacting McCabe and Wilson is that both had made their complaints anonymously, and he was precluded from presuming whom exactly the 'anonymous authors' were. That reasoning is flawed. Officially, the complainants were anonymous, but management in the force, all the way up to the commissioner, were aware of their identity. Proof of this was evident from the orders the previous December and January to McCabe and Wilson restricting their access to PULSE. Everybody knew who they were, and if the assistant commissioner had been so minded he could have at least approached them.

There is an alternative explanation for the failure to contact either man. If McCabe in particular, but also Wilson, had been approached and told the investigators what they knew, the information would be officially in the hands of the investigation team. They would then be obliged to act on it.

For instance, in the unlikely event that the high-powered team did not know how to trawl through PULSE, following particular names of repeat offenders, and spotting patterns, McCabe could have informed them. With that detail of information at their fingertips, the investigation team would have been in a position to carry out a more comprehensive investigation than was actually done. All that, though, would emerge only later.

On the phone O'Mahony said that if McCabe wished to speak to some of the investigation team, he would send two of them down to Mullingar to meet him.

'But the report is done,' McCabe replied. 'What's the point of that if it's all done.'

McCabe was hopping. Experience over the previous six years had told him that an internal report into the workings of the force was unlikely to uncover the extent of wrong-doing as he saw it. But in this case, with the publicity and the intervention of politicians, he had believed there was some hope of the full story being dragged out into the open.

Now this. McCabe drove home after work and discussed developments with Lorraine. She was just as agitated. Once more he sought solace in contacting the force's political masters.

From: Maurice McCabe
To: Taoiseach's Office
Sent: Wednesday, 24 April 2013
Subject: Penalty Points Investigation

Dear Taoiseach,
Today, 23/4/13 I contacted the office of Assistant Commissioner John O'Mahony at 1pm. Assistant Commissioner O'Mahony returned my call at 5pm.

I requested to know why I was not interviewed concerning the Penalty Points Investigation and asked if in fact I would be interviewed soon, seeing as I was the principle [sic] person who had reported the malpractice. Assistant O'Mahony stated that he had completed his investigation and the report was with the Minister. The Assistant Commissioner stated that he was of the opinion that the Commissioner Callinan had informed me in December that if I had any concerns regarding the investigation I was to contact Assistant commissioner O'Mahony.

I informed him that this was not correct, that a Chief Superintendent had given me as gagging order for reporting the matter to your office and had stated I was not allowed to avail of the Confidential Recipient or section 62 Garda Síochána Act 2005 without contacting Assistant Commissioner O'Mahony first.

I again regard that I was concerned, and seriously concerned, that I was never contacted or interviewed and I informed the Assistant Commissioner that I had seen tens of thousands of corrupt terminations on PULSE and I hoped his report would reflect this. Alarmingly, he then asked me if I wanted to speak to someone on his investigation team. I ended our call having expressed concern about him not interviewing me.

Taoiseach, I had concerns when I previously brought the matter to the confidential recipient, I had concerns when I previously brought this matter to Minister Shatter, I had concerns when I brought it to your attention, I had concerns when I brought the matter to the Comptroller and Auditor General, I had concerns when I brought this matter to the Transport Minister, I had concerns when I brought this matter to the Data Protection Commissioner and I had concerns when I brought the matter to the Road Safety Authority. Why then would I suddenly stop my concerns when I persisted with reporting this corruption for almost a year?

It is my belief that the Assistant Commissioner O'Mahony should have interviewed me concerning my allegations and in keeping with fair procedure and natural justice. I reiterated to him that I stood by my allegations.

Can you advise me as to where I can turn to next?

Regards,

Maurice McCabe

There was no way the Taoiseach's office was going to involve itself with an internal Garda investigation, but McCabe felt he had to put it on the record. If nothing else, at this stage of the whole affair, mailing the political leaders of the country provided a vent for his frustration.

The sense of injustice wouldn't leave him alone. The following week he emailed the Minister for Justice.

From: Maurice McCabe
Subject: Fwd: re- Penalty Points Investigation
To: Minister for Justice's Office
Sent: Mon 29 April, 2013

Dear Minister,
I refer to my previous email and wondering if you had received it.
   It is so annoying and so wrong that I have been totally excluded from the penalty points investigation. I was central to the whole investigation and the only conclusion I can come to is that I was purposely excluded for fear what I would come out [sic] and reveal the truth.
   I ask one question, Minister! Why were the CA&G, Data Commissioner, RSA and Public Accounts Committee shocked at the level of corruption? Because they saw the evidence?
Regards
Maurice McCabe

The standard reply acknowledging receipt of the mail was forthcoming once more. After that for McCabe, there was nothing for it but to wait for publication of the report, depressed in the knowledge that it was not going to provide a full picture of what exactly was going on.

14

'Whistleblowers also have responsibilities. Their concerns must be real
and genuine, and based on evidence rather than conjecture.'
Alan Shatter

The O'Mahony report was published on 15 May 2013. A covering
letter with the report from Commissioner Martin Callinan laid out
what was at stake. The most grievous allegations had been levelled
at a number of senior gardaí, 'inclusive of grave assertions citing
criminality, corruption, deception and falsification committed
by named and unnamed officers by virtue of their discretionary
terminations of Fixed Charge Notices'.

Could it be more serious? Short of being associated with violence
of one sort or another, this was about as serious an accusation as
could be levelled at any upstanding citizen, not to mind a law
enforcement officer.

Yet the commissioner's letter went on, 'No evidence has been
adduced to suggest any act of criminality, corruption, deception or
falsification as alleged by the anonymous author.'

That statement summed up the tenor of all that was to follow. What kind of individuals, let alone fellow officers, would make such allegations based on what appeared to be falsehoods?

The investigation had uncovered a very minor issue, one of 'certain departures from administrative procedures'. In 'a small number of instances (3) possible breaches of discipline have been identified', in which files were forwarded to the assistant commissioner of internal affairs.

Hints of incredulity at the allegations were detectable in the statement issued that day by the Minister for Justice. Alan Shatter said he accepted the findings of the O'Mahony report, which he intended to forward to the Garda Inspectorate.

Then he turned to the whistleblowers. 'I believe that there should be a supportive environment in the Garda Síochána and every workplace for whistleblowers who have genuine concerns over apparent wrong-doing ... but whistleblowers also have responsibilities. Their concerns must be real and genuine, and based on evidence rather than conjecture, especially when the allegations made are of widespread criminality in the authority responsible for enforcing the law and are therefore such as to be likely to undermine trust in and respect for that authority. They should also be mindful of the rights of others.'

The theme of an absence of evidence of any 'corruption' was taken up by the media. On RTÉ's *Six One News*, political correspondent David Davin-Power said that the report suggested the whole affair was 'a bottle of smoke'.

Such a conclusion was entirely reasonable if one took at face value the report and the interpretation of it by those responsible for policing in the country.

The report covered a period from 1 January 2009 to 30 June 2012. In that time a total of 1,460,726 fixed charge notices were issued.

Of these, 95.45% were processed through the system without being terminated, or 'cancelled', as described in some instances. The remaining 66,407 were terminated, but, taking into account matters like system failures and the subsequent production of tax and/or insurance, the number of terminations at issue was actually 37,384 in the three-and-a-half-year period.

McCabe and Wilson had made complaints about 2,198 terminations. Of these, 661 were terminated by the three officers who had been identified as having breached administrative guidelines. The remaining 1,537 were then examined and of these, 89% were found to have been strictly within guidelines. That left 198. The terminations there were attributable to officers acting outside their districts, and a failure to create and retain audit material, showing the reasons why the termination or cancellation occurred.

Looked at in the light of the figures, the ball of smoke analogy fitted perfectly. What was the big deal? For example, garda family members receiving terminations accounted for just seven, over three and a half years, from a force of 13,000 members.

Just to be sure to be sure, the investigators also conducted a random audit of 1% of all terminations, accounting for 672 cases. Again, very little of significance was unearthed.

Viewed within the parameters of the investigation, one could well conclude that there was nothing to see here. However, such a picture is one of broad brushstrokes, avoiding the detail that might show things in a different light.

The rigour, or lack of it, applied by the investigators was neither obvious nor accessible to anybody reading the report. For instance, 89% of the relevant cancellations brought to light by McCabe and Wilson were deemed to have been within regulations. So when a member of the force was caught speeding and he gave the excuse that he was on duty, was this accepted at face value? Was any effort made to check if he had been on duty at that time? McCabe in his initial investigation found it easy to determine whether or not that was the case, but O'Mahony did not.

Then there were repeat offenders. Once a termination under dubious circumstances was detected, was any attempt made to check whether this individual was a repeat offender?

What about the 'medical emergencies'? How many of them were examined to determine whether or not they were genuine? Furthermore, how often was supporting documentation provided with an application to cancel?

All these matters could have been pursued with little effort. A computer whizz was not required to follow the online trail within PULSE. If McCabe had been consulted during the investigation, he could have set out in easy steps how this might be done, lest there be any doubt at all.

Instead, it appears that the investigators merely followed up on the specific cases that were complained about and took a random sample of other terminations without really looking into the detail of what exactly was going on.

None of this was explored when O'Mahony's report was published, but much of it would come to light in a series of reports by outside bodies over the following years. For some reason, the business of detection appears to have come easier to those who were not members of An Garda Síochána, a reality that doesn't reflect well on either the rigour of internal investigations or the capabilities of trained police men and women.

The media's reaction to the O'Mahony report chimed with that from official sources. The *Irish Independent*'s headline typified the general tone: 'Garda Penalty Points Investigation Finds No Evidence of Corruption'. The story began, 'Allegations made by garda whistleblowers that led to an inquiry into the quashing of penalty points have been found to be "seriously inaccurate and without any foundation".'

So it went throughout the day. There was nothing to see here, apart from a few disgruntled cops – one of whom was no longer even a cop because Wilson had by then retired – who appeared to have acted with malice and scant regard for the rights of their fellow officers, not to mind the good name of An Garda Síochána.

Up in Cavan, McCabe was devastated. Was this the end of the matter? He knew that the report was not presenting the full picture. He knew that the truth was still humming away in the bowels of the PULSE system. He knew that a lot of senior officers were sagging with relief.

Perversely, he felt sympathy for the three senior officers, a superintendent and two inspectors, who had been targeted in the report. Sure, what they did was wrong and they should be made accountable, but they were not alone. They were the scapegoats, as far as McCabe was concerned, to ensure that the majority would walk away scot-free and the system would continue to function as before.

On another level it was déjà vu. This was Byrne/McGinn all over again. The wagons had been circled.

The day wasn't done yet though. Politically this story had a long way to run, and the distance was about to be extended by none other than the Minister for Justice.

Alan Shatter had been appointed minister for justice in the Fine Gael/Labour coalition government following the 2011 general election. He was well suited to the portfolio. Over thirty years he had combined a very successful career as a TD with partnership in his own legal firm, Gallagher Shatter. Once in the cabinet, he set about developing a reputation as a reforming minister. He moved to revamp the immigration system and received plaudits from many non-governmental organisations working in the field.

He also went where none of his predecessors had dared to go in tackling the legal system, his own bailiwick, with particular emphasis on the huge costs of accessing the courts. In this, he made a lot of enemies in the legal business, but he appeared determined to drive through necessary reforms.

So it was that he had all the hallmarks of a highly accomplished minister for justice when the Garda controversy began appearing like a dark cloud on the horizon. In time, it would prove to be his biggest challenge, but in May 2013, on publication of the O'Mahony report, it looked like just another issue on his busy schedule.

On the morning of the publication, Mick Wallace had been interviewed on Pat Kenny's programme on RTÉ Radio 1. On the basis of all he had heard about the imminent report, Wallace called it a 'whitewash'.

The following evening the matter featured on RTÉ television's *Prime Time* programme. After a report on the O'Mahony inquiry, Kenny – who was doubling up on his radio work – interviewed Shatter and Wallace.

'Do you accept you went off half-cocked on this?' Kenny asked the Wexford TD.

Wallace took it in his stride. 'No. The whole element of discretion … there's no legislation in place to justify the use of discretion. There's lots of protocols, advice on how things can be done.'

Wallace went on in that vein, explaining how the use of discretion had been abused once the fixed charge notice, or ticket, was in the system. Then Kenny turned to the minister.

'What occurred here was that Deputy Wallace and others made wild and exaggerated claims,' Shatter said. 'I took those allegations with great seriousness, as did the Garda commissioner. We have had a full, comprehensive investigation under an assistant commissioner, five chief superintendents and a team of gardaí over five months. What has been established is that the wild claims were untrue and what has also been established is that some gardaí didn't follow procedure, that some acted outside their district, and that in some cases records weren't adequately held.'

After further exchanges, it was Shatter's turn again to put forward his case. 'Deputy Wallace seems to have a problem with gardaí exercising discretion. There were circumstances here in which a child was sick, an individual was sick and they were speeding. There's a two-stage process. A ticket issues and you have 28 days to raise it. I would accept there are some individual decisions made that should not have been made. As Deputy Wallace knows, without issuing tickets garda exercise discretion. Deputy Wallace was on a mobile phone last May and he was advised by gardaí who stopped him that the fixed ticket charge could issue and he would be given penalty points, but the garda, I'm advised, used his discretion and warned him not to do it again.'

Wallace didn't miss a beat in his reply, most likely because he didn't know to what exactly the minister was referring.

'That's news to me. With regard to discretion, once it goes on the system, they should go to court to deal with it,' he said.

Kenny knew immediately something big had just happened. 'Are you not concerned that the minister should know about your private business dealings with the gardaí?' he asked Wallace.

'I'm not remotely concerned,' Wallace replied.

But Kenny wouldn't be deflected. 'The minister has thrown in a grenade about you benefiting from the gardaí ....'

Wallace shrugged. 'That's news to me, Pat.'

What had started out as a post-mortem on the penalty points controversy had suddenly seen the matter come alive again.

Shatter's revelation about Wallace's minor indiscretion threw up a number of questions, most notably: how did the information get into the hands of the minister for justice?

As seen earlier in the case of Clare Daly's arrest, a policy was in place within the gardaí that any incident involving a politician should be reported to the district officer and on to HQ. Daly's case was a potentially serious one of suspected drink-driving. Now it looked like even an innocuous incident involving a politician, which gardaí at the scene believed didn't merit any action, was also passed up through the ranks.

What did that say about the running of the force, the force's interaction with its political masters, the retention of intelligence on politicians?

Did the Garda commissioner or one of his subordinates regularly or under particular circumstances convey intelligence to the minister about political opponents, or even political colleagues?

Then there was the matter of Alan Shatter's judgement. A highly intelligent, long-standing politician with a professional grasp of the law thought it acceptable to broadcast information that he had acquired in his ministerial capacity.

The O'Mahony report had shown Wallace's allegations to be empty, and now he, Shatter, would expose the force's biggest critic as a hypocrite.

Even within his own party, some would see Shatter's actions as a highly questionable tactic in order to score a political point.

Up until this juncture, the minister could claim to have done everything by the book. He could claim, with some justification, that he had handled matters no differently from how any of his predecessors would have done.

Now he had overstepped the mark.

Wallace's initial reaction after the programme was one of disbelief. 'I hadn't a clue what it was about,' he said. 'For about the first twenty-four hours after *Prime Time* I thought that Shatter had made it up. But then it came back to me.

'The year before I'd been in the right-turn lane at the Five Lamps [on Dublin's north side] with the window rolled down. I was on the phone and the squad car pulled up beside me, so I threw it down on the seat. The lads looked across, and one of them says, "How's it going, Mick? How's the politics treating you?" We had a few words and the lights changed. That was it.

'At that point I wasn't involved in the ticket-fixing stuff and I'd always had a good relationship with the Guards, through the building work, dealing with permits and road closures and that. A lot of them knew me, so on one level I wasn't surprised they said nothing about the phone. It wasn't a big thing.'

But after the *Prime Time* programme, it quickly became a big thing. The political fallout was swift. Fianna Fáil's Justice spokesman, Niall Collins, applied the boot liberally. He said that the minister was 'apparently relying on private information provided to him by the gardaí'.

'Fianna Fáil holds no brief for Mick Wallace, but the issues raised by Mr Shatter's intervention are more important than party politics or the hypocrisy of the Dáil technical group. They include the security of citizens' private information, the right to due process and the use of private details for political purposes.'

Wallace said he intended lodging a complaint with the Standards in Public Office Commission and the Data Protection Commissioner. (In time, the former body would reject his complaint, while the latter would uphold it.)

The controversy dragged on for a few days. When it hadn't been extinguished by the following week, the minister felt compelled to address it in the Dáil chamber: 'I regret that comments made by me may have inadvertently resulted in concerns being expressed that I am prepared to use confidential Garda information to damage a political opponent,' he said. 'Nothing could be further from the truth, but I am happy to offer reassurances to Deputies on this point. I give a solemn assurance to the House that I am not in the business of receiving, seeking or maintaining confidential, sensitive information from An Garda Síochána on Members of this House, the Seanad or anyone in political life, nor are gardaí in the business of providing it.'

Shatter went on to point out that section 41 of the Garda Síochána Act provided for the minister to receive information from the gardaí on particular matters: 'However, all Members of this House and I can agree that it would be absolutely abhorrent if An Garda Síochána were to collect information on anyone, regardless of whether he or she is involved in public life, for political purposes. There is no question of that happening. There are simply no circumstances in which I would countenance the abuse of Garda powers.'

Then he dealt with how and why exactly the information had been conveyed:

During the course of one of our conversations in which a number of matters relating to the reports on the fixed notice charge issue were discussed, including circumstances in which gardaí exercised their discretion on traffic offences, the incident involving Deputy Wallace was mentioned by the Garda Commissioner.

I most certainly did not request any information on Deputies and no big issue was made of the incident involving the Deputy. I have no doubt that the Garda Commissioner was mindful that Deputy Wallace might make public reference to the incident as part of the public controversy which was ongoing about fixed charge notices and, in these circumstances, he had a duty to mention it to me.

It is important to see this matter in perspective and context. Deputy Wallace and his colleagues put in the public domain a whole range of allegations about the operation of the fixed charge notice system and they had no way of knowing if they were true or not, many of which have since been disproved. They wanted to put in the public domain information on third parties, implying wrong-doing on their part, with no basis for any assertion of wrong-doing …

The minister then went on to address Wallace personally.

'If Deputy Wallace believes I did him a personal wrong by mentioning it, I have no problem in saying I am sorry.'

This admission received an immediate riposte from independent Kerry South deputy Michael Healy-Rae. 'That's a first,' he said.

There was a brief kick to the controversy when it emerged that Shatter had a few years previously been stopped at a random checkpoint in Dublin city centre and that he had reportedly reacted with indignation to a request that he be breathalysed. There was little to the whole incident, though, and it would not have merited a mention had he not been in the spotlight over his *Prime Time* revelations.

Overall, it looked as if that was the end of the matter. Like much in Irish public life, things began to move on despite an unsatisfactory resolution to the whole affair.

Two weeks after the publication of the O'Mahony report, the *Irish Examiner* ran a piece based on sample cases and touching on the shortcomings of the internal Garda report as laid out above. It referenced an examination of over 100 terminations that should have been available to the internal inquiry.

Included were a series of incidents involving repeat offenders, bizarre excuses and cancellations for members of the force. Few of these had appeared in the O'Mahony report and the article raised a question about the thoroughness of the report. But the media and political caravans were already back on the road, moving on to the next issue.

15

'... no one has been victimised ... And there is no basis for alleging that anybody has been victimised.'
Alan Shatter

The controversy around the ticket-fixing scandal was beginning to have an impact in the Mullingar garda station, where McCabe worked. Up until that point, he had managed alright in Mullingar. Since mid-2008 he had been working as a sergeant in the traffic division in the busy Westmeath town. The resentment and anger generated by his complaints in Bailieboro had not followed him across the midlands.

Now that was changing. The sergeant-in-charge in Mullingar at the time was Kieran Williams. Soon after he arrived in Mullingar, McCabe told Williams of his own history, and Williams did not have a problem with it.

'There was no ill feeling towards Maurice when he arrived first,' Williams said in an interview for this book. 'In a busy station, fellas have less time to be looking at other fellas. I can say that he blended in really well and was accepted. I used to organise to get the skippers [sergeants] to go out together every so often, and Maurice came with us and he was well received. I suppose in one way he was lucky that I was sergeant-in-charge because when he told me what had happened in Bailieboro, I wasn't that surprised.'

Things changed in 2013, however, when the ticket-fixing issue seeped into the public domain. A few of the guards in Mullingar had been the recipients of suspicious cancellations. Word began to spread that Sergeant McCabe was the one making all the noises. At that stage McCabe's name was not publicly associated with the issue, and wouldn't be until his appearance before the Public Accounts Committee the following January.

But his identity was known among large swathes of the force. And it didn't take long for word to get to Mullingar that the man causing all the trouble was one of theirs.

'For some of them, Maurice became an enemy within,' Williams said. 'Anybody who associated with him also became an enemy of sorts too. If you were seen as friendly towards him, you were blanked but there was an element of fear there too because nobody wanted management to think that they were friendly towards him. If somebody was having a cup of tea with him and one of the management saw it, that fella might think, "Jesus, they think I'm friendly with him. That's no good."

'It didn't apply to everybody in the station but there was enough of them. As for me, I hadn't done anything wrong in relation to tickets. I couldn't see what he [McCabe] had done wrong except highlighting practices that were wrong. I saw no reason to treat him any different to every other member.'

There were others in the force who knew McCabe and retained friendship and ties with him. Williams, however, was a rare example of a member who wasn't afraid to be publicly associated with the sergeant.

The atmosphere that McCabe was enduring in Mullingar was difficult, but at least he could deal with it. On another level within the force, he was the subject of an even greater foe – the malicious rumour.

Word was about that Maurice McCabe had serious questions to answer in relation to child sexual abuse. The genesis of this rumour may have been the allegation made against him in 2006. Ironically, at the time anybody within the force who had known about that allegation had sympathy for McCabe. Few believed it had substance. A thorough and expedited investigation had dealt with it and the DPP had ruled not just that there was no proof of the allegation, but even if there had been, it would not have constituted a criminal office.

Such details were known in Cavan/Monaghan, but details are the first casualty of malicious rumour. McCabe was discommoding a lot of people. He was exposing powerful officers as having had at best a cavalier attitude to road safety because they were cancelling tickets. Wouldn't it be handy if the fella had some serious questions to answer himself? Besides, who would believe a 'paedophile' about the comparatively harmless business of fixing tickets?

The rumour spread far and wide. It was known within media and political circles. Not everybody believed it, but enough did to put a question mark beside McCabe's name.

The most cursory analysis of the rumours throws up the one question that few appeared to be asking – if McCabe really had questions to answer, why would he, an apparently intelligent man, go on a kamikaze mission, taking on Garda management across the country?

Equally, the question might have been asked about the evidence. Surely, of all agencies, the police should be able to uncover at least a shred of evidence that could be exposed publicly to blacken McCabe, if that was the purpose? But the malicious rumour does not dwell on relevant questions.

In McCabe's case, the rumour served to put him beyond the pale as far as some were concerned, a figure to avoid for others. In attempting to discredit his character, the rumour was working away through conspiratorial whispers and throwaway asides.

The temperature in the ticket-fixing story dropped during the quiet summer months of 2013, and by late August it had retained as much heat as a damp Irish summer.

McCabe got on with his job, attempting to do the best he could, given his restricted access to PULSE. As the school holidays ended, he contacted the Comptroller and Auditor General's office once more to see how it was dealing with the complaint he had delivered over a year previously.

He phoned more in hope than expectation. He had received a patient and sympathetic reception on his initial visit to the office, but the O'Mahony report and the fallout from it had left him with low expectations of anything more happening. This time he poured out his frustration to the same official he had briefed on that first day. He pointed to instances in the O'Mahony report which he believed were in complete contrast to the dossier in the C&AG's office. The response was a plea for patience. 'Hang in there,' the official said. 'Our report will be out within the next few months. Trust me.'

Up at Garda headquarters the publication of O'Mahony and the minister's decision to refer it to the Garda Inspectorate had prompted a modicum of action. Management in the force decided to issue fresh guidelines on how and why tickets could be cancelled.

The new guidelines represented little more than cosmetic changes to the system, however. McCabe must have smiled wryly when he saw the gentle revamp. How were things going to be tightened up when there wasn't even acknowledgement of the extent of the problem in the first place?

Just over a month later, on 1 October, the C&AG report into ticket-fixing was published.

It found that only one in five of the tickets issued had resulted in a fine and the attachment of penalty points. Some of this was attributable to lazy follow-ups, more was the result of a dilapidated system of summonsing. But there was also considerable blame placed on the termination of tickets by senior officers. In this analysis, it differed considerably from the O'Mahony report.

While the overall number of terminations was confirmed at around 5%, the manner in which they occurred painted a different picture.

In keeping with the C&AG's role as the accounting watchdog for public money, the tone of the report was dry and confined strictly to how notices were terminated. No blame was attached to any individual or management figure:

'The operation of the FCPS (Fixed Charge Penalty System) does not accord with the termination policy as articulated in the manual in some key aspects,' the report stated. 'There is evidence that the policy on termination of cases is not being applied consistently. In the same cases reviewed for this examination, a significant proportion of cases appear to have been terminated in circumstances that do not satisfy the stated policy.'

A 'significant proportion' was a long way from O'Mahony's 'certain departures from administrative procedures'.

The report outlined some of the reasons applied for terminating notices. These included:

- Driver speeding on way to hospital or GP appointment or visiting others in hospital (26)
- Driver acknowledged that tax not paid when stopped but was subsequently paid covering period when stopped (13)
- Nine cases where speeding was acknowledged but gave reason

as the road was wide or quiet, rushing to pick up a relative from a bus stations, being late for a religious ceremony, being late for a swimming lesson, being on 'urgent domestic business and the speedometer not working'.

— Four cases where the driver acknowledged that an offence was committed and stated that the driver did not see the red light, the driver accidentally exceeding the speed limit, there was a lack of concentration by the driver, who had other things on her mind.

Few of these examples – which were only a sample – had appeared in O'Mahony. By the time the C&AG report was published, the controversy had been public for nearly a year. In that time, sources familiar with the PULSE system confirmed that the level of medical emergencies as excuses for speeding had plummeted. Either the publicity had made the country a lot healthier, or there was a clampdown on using that excuse as a bogus reason for cancelling tickets.

The C&AG report concluded: 'The rate of terminations in many districts is too high to be reflective of "exceptional circumstances". Absent and inadequate records and the recorded facts of many cases give rise to concerns that many cases have been terminated without cause.

'Furthermore, there are grounds for concern that certain "outside-district" cases were terminated without appropriate authority.'

The C&AG report was a resounding vindication for McCabe and Wilson. In their opinion, this was a lot closer to the real picture of a culture where those on the inside track had had their tickets cancelled.

The following afternoon the report reached the floor of the Dáil through Sinn Féin Justice spokesperson Pádraig Mac Lochlainn, who was addressing Alan Shatter. He described the findings as 'absolutely shocking'. He went on: 'And Minister, you know that two garda whistleblowers brought this wider issue into the public domain last year. You and the garda commissioner, I believe, sought to undermine their credibility, talked down the numbers that were involved and now we see very clearly that they have been vindicated.

'And Minister, will you now apologise to the two garda whistleblowers for the attempts by yourself and the garda commissioner at that time to discredit them, to undermine the scope of what they were bringing into the public domain and acknowledge that they were right?'

That day in the Dáil was a significant one in the trajectory of Alan Shatter's ministerial career. He was now faced with some evidence that the internal garda report did not present a full picture of the malpractices. He could have taken stock and reassessed any conclusions he had drawn four months earlier when O'Mahony was published. A man of Shatter's considerable intellectual gifts could have weighed up the situation and tapped into the political acumen that thirty years in the business confers on practitioners.

He could have moderated his stance. He could have tasted a little humble pie.

Instead, he whipped out his metaphorical six-shooters.

Shatter rose to his feet and defended the O'Mahony report, claiming that the C&AG report confirmed the findings of O'Mahony. Such an interpretation was based on the fact that both reports concluded that only 5% of fixed charge notices had been quashed within the system. That observation was correct, but it missed the point that where O'Mahony had unearthed a few unripe apples, the C&AG saw the whole orchard as being in danger of contamination.

Shatter went on to train his guns on the whistleblowers.

'Perhaps most significantly, the member of An Garda Síochána making the allegations rejects all of the findings of the O'Mahony report and continues to claim that there has been widespread corruption and criminality on the part of senior members of the Garda Síochána. These are exceptionally serious allegations for which the O'Mahony report found no basis in fact. My department has written to the member concerned, urging him to come forward with any evidence that he may have to justify these allegations. And indeed, it's open to the member concerned to make an appropriate presentation if he chooses to do so before the Joint Oireachtas Justice Committee but in fact that has not yet occurred.'

The Socialist Party's Joe Higgins got up and addressed the same themes as had Mac Lochlainn, putting particular emphasis on the plight of the whistleblowers: 'Now Minister, you said that the conclusions of the Comptroller are in line with the findings of the report by the Assistant Commissioner O'Mahony. Clearly that is not the case, Minister, and that is easily documented. So I invite you to get your department to go through it with a fine-tooth comb to revise your view on that.

'You do say it is only fair to acknowledge that these reports and the findings and recommendations are in response to allegations by whistleblowers. My word. Minister, I want you to go the extra mile. Be generous here. Okay, maybe they didn't get everything absolutely right but the vast substance of what they said has proved to be absolutely honest and true and they have been victimised.

'And you have to stand up and champion the right of people in vulnerable positions to come out for the public good. So I'm asking you to do that today and to apologise for wrong comments you made yourself castigating these people.'

Shatter was having none of it.

'Can I firstly say to Deputy Higgins, no one has been victimised; no one has been victimised, Deputy. And there is no basis for alleging that anybody has been victimised. The allegations that were made were taken very seriously.'

He continued on through a response that was typically long for these kinds of debates, before winding towards a conclusion: 'So let me just say, that in conclusion, in so far as individuals who raised issues are alleging that the Garda reports published are untrue, let them bring forward the chapter and verse and proof of that. I'm open to being convinced, but they haven't done so. Indeed, having engaged with members of this House, and published material, they didn't cooperate with the Garda investigation that took place.'

The debate fizzled out after that, with few present realising on the spot the significance of what Shatter had just said. He had effectively accused McCabe and Wilson of breaking Garda rules by failing to co-operate with an internal Garda investigation.

Not just that, but the suggestion that they did not co-operate also casts a dull light on their motivation for coming forward. Who but somebody with nefarious motives would make a song and dance about these issues and then, when the matter was finally being investigated, turn on their heels and walk away from it?

In the chamber, Shatter's utterance was insulated by parliamentary privilege. If he had issued the same allegation outside its confines, there is little doubt but that he would have attracted legal action for slander from both McCabe and Wilson.

The significance of what had been said wasn't lost on McCabe once he'd read the transcript. He contacted Wilson and they chewed it over. He contacted his legal team, where his worst fears were confirmed.

His interpretation of Shatter's statement was correct and it was insulated from legal retribution. McCabe felt the slur keenly. He had, over the course of a long, harrowing journey since first raising concerns, conducted himself entirely within the law. He had not been subject to any disciplinary action within the force, despite being the focus of widespread animus.

He had ensured that he didn't give an excuse to management in the

Garda Síochána to attack him in any manner. He had followed the letter of the law in bringing his concerns to Clare Daly TD. Section 62 of the Garda Síochána Act 2005 states that a Garda member may disclose confidential information to 'a member of either of the Houses of the Oireachtas where relevant to the proper discharge of a member's functions'. Who could argue that highlighting a misuse of power within An Garda Síochána amounted to a proper discharge of a member's function?

Yet now the Minister for Justice, the nominal head of criminal justice and policing in the state, had not only just called Maurice McCabe's motives into question once more, but he had asserted that he had failed to co-operate with the internal Garda inquiry. The sense of futility tightened. He couldn't rid himself of the feeling that he was inside a large silo, banging his head off steel walls, screaming at the top of his voice, but nobody beyond was within hearing.

During his Dáil contribution, Alan Shatter had made reference to McCabe's right to address the Joint Oireachtas Committee. The idea appealed to him. If the whole thing could finally get an airing in public, it might awaken wider society to what had been going on within the force.

But reflecting on the prospect, McCabe began to consider another committee. So far the only entity to come close to identifying the problem had been the Comptroller and Auditor General. That report would now be referred to the Oireachtas Public Accounts Committee (PAC) for examination. Why not approach that branch of the House of the Oireachtas and explain that he could bring them through the detail of the report, and fill in the blanks left by the accountants?

The PAC had been one of his first ports of call the previous year when McCabe was trying to awaken the state to what was afoot. He picked up the phone and got in contact with the secretary once more. Now that things had advanced, and the C&AG's report would be before the committee, could he meet with the chair to discuss the matter?

A few weeks later he met by appointment John McGuinness, the Fianna Fáil deputy and chair of the Public Accounts Committee. McGuinness had an interesting record. Under the previous Fianna Fáil leader and Taoiseach Bertie Ahern, he had been an outspoken critic of how his party was running the country. He had a particular issue with the level of public spending which he predicted, correctly, would be unsustainable. As such, he had been a member of an awkward squad within the party, which at the time would have had no difficulty being accommodated in a Ford Fiesta.

In 2011, when Fianna Fáil suffered catastrophe at the polls, its seat numbers plummeting from 77 to 20, McGuinness had managed to hang on to his seat.

The position of chair of the Public Accounts Committee is in the gift of the leader of the opposition, and Micheál Martin handed the job to McGuinness. Some speculated that Martin wanted the Kilkenny man as far away from the front bench as possible, yet engaged in some worthwhile business which would ensure that he wouldn't be making waves in the parliamentary party.

McCabe and McGuinness met in Buswells Hotel, across the road from the gates of Leinster House. They sat in the busy hotel lobby. All around them, the officer corps of the political and media world moved about their business. Some might have wondered who was the man John McGuinness appeared to be deep in conversation with, but most would have dismissed him as a constituent or possibly a civil servant.

McCabe brought a dossier of some of the more outrageous examples of the ticket-fixing malpractice. He went through it with McGuinness, and then sat back.

McGuinness paused, then looked McCabe in the eye. 'I've

listened to you for forty minutes and you're not mad and you're not bad,' he said.

McCabe nodded. He didn't have to ask the politician to elaborate. He was well aware that his reputation was being trashed by elements within the force. You don't point an accusing finger at a large cohort of senior officers and expect no retaliation. That a politician would have been in receipt of rumours that the two whistleblowers were either mad, as in running off with half-cocked accusations, or bad, through pursuing some nefarious agenda, was no surprise.

McCabe handed the dossier to McGuinness, suggesting that he should go through it in detail. The pair left on good terms. McGuinness expressed the opinion that he would like to see McCabe giving evidence before the committee if the sergeant was positively disposed to doing so.

The meeting between the pair was reported in the *Irish Examiner* a few weeks later, on 9 November 2013. That newspaper report was read in Garda HQ in the Phoenix Park with a sense of growing trepidation. There had been rumours that McCabe was persisting with his complaints, but an appalling vista was now opening up. Could this internal matter be aired in public before an Oireachtas committee?

Commissioner Callinan was due to appear before the committee on 23 January to discuss the C&AG report. That was a straightforward matter, nothing that the commissioner couldn't handle.

But now this. McCabe was wresting control on the issue away from the commissioner. It was bad enough that he had gone to the Comptroller and Auditor General, but bringing his complaints directly to politicians who operated in the full glare of public view was simply not on.

On 15 November Martin Callinan wrote to the Data Protection Commissioner, Billy Hawkes, to complain about a sergeant in his force handing over documentation to McGuinness. Information that was the property of An Garda Síochána had been passed to a third party. This action contravened data protection law, Callinan suggested.

Hawkes examined the complaint and agreed. Both men then contacted John McGuinness separately. 'I am of the view that these files, containing personal data, are files which I am responsible for and accordingly should be returned forthwith to me,' Callinan wrote. 'Unfortunately, I am not in a position at this juncture to identify whether the person who has furnished this information to you is an employee of mine or not.' (This was a highly unusual statement. He knew that the files had been handed over only through the pages of the *Irish Examiner*, which also reported that it was McCabe who had handed them over. Yet Callinan was suggesting that while he accepted the newspaper report on the handover, he was not sure who had done it. All he had to do was call in McCabe and ask him whether or not it was he.)

The letter went on, 'I can confirm that my prior authority was not obtained before this data was furnished to you.'

The letter from Hawkes to McGuinness was of a similar character.

The ball was now in McGuinness's court.

He sought his own legal advice on whether he and the committee could view the material and allow it to form the basis of a hearing with the whistleblower who had presented it. In doing so, the Fianna Fáil TD made plain that he would back away from this issue only under protest.

On 27 November he received the legal advice from a parliamentary adviser that the committee was within its right to examine the dossier McCabe had supplied.

A sample of the material was examined and the committee agreed to edit it in a form that would redact any names of motorists benefiting from cancellations.

Meanwhile, despite the prospect of possibly getting a public airing, McCabe was still put out at what the Minister for Justice had alleged about him in the Dáil.

On 3 December 2013 he dispatched another e-mail to the Department of Justice, pointing out that the minister must have been misinformed when he had alleged that McCabe had not co-operated with the Garda investigation: 'I'm very concerned that somebody has told Minister Shatter information about me of a very serious nature and I am being refused the right to know the identity of the person or persons who advised him. I want to know now who advised Minister Shatter of this and when. If you refuse to give me this information, I would like to know the reason why you are refusing me? I have the right to know who passed this information to Minister Shatter and when.'

Christmas came, offering respite from the whole affair for all those concerned. Twelve months previously the festive season had been one of high stress for McCabe, sandwiched as it was between the two directions restricting his access to PULSE. The length of a year had not lost the ticket-fixing as a political story. Things had moved on from what McCabe regarded as the whitewash of the O'Mahony report. The truth was moving closer to the surface, bursting for air.

16

'Frankly, on a personal level, I think it's quite disgusting.'
Martin Callinan

Labour TD Kevin Humphries takes credit for first using the phrase 'ambulance chasing' in describing the Public Accounts Committee under John McGuinness.

By early 2014 it could well be argued that the PAC was in search of trouble for business. McGuinness and his committee had conducted public hearings with a number of high-profile individuals covering relatively new territory for the committee.

Problems had arisen in the charity sector about overpayments to senior executives. A number of executives were hauled in. There were problems with top-ups for people working in the health sector. Then there was Irish Water, the newly established vehicle set up to manage and develop the country's water structure. Irish Water was fast becoming one of the most unpopular brands in the country, as a result of revelations about excesses within the body, allied to a growing public opposition to water charges. Some argued that certain members of the PAC were using their position to grandstand in public hearings.

The new approach could be attributable, to some extent, to the chairmanship of John McGuinness. He had long been a critic of spending in the public sector. Now he was in a position to scrutinise such spending and he wasn't holding back.

Apart from McGuinness, the committee included a number of very able politicians, including a few who were regarded as masters of finding themselves in the limelight. On the government side there were Fine Gael deputies Áine Collins, Paul Connaughton, John Deasy, Simon Harris, Eoghan Murphy and Kieran O'Donnell. The Labour Party's complement consisted of Derek Nolan and Gerald Nash. Fianna Fáil was represented by McGuinness and Seán Fleming, while Sinn Féin had its deputy leader, Mary Lou McDonald. The only independent deputy on board was Shane Ross, who had been elected in 2011 after a long career as a senator. He was also a high-profile journalist who had broken a number of stories about the misuse of public funds, most prominently in the state training agency formerly known as FÁS. This committee had its share of able deputies and strong characters.

Ross and McDonald had been to the fore in their performances over the previous few months. Both were able and on top of their respective briefs and managed to extract information for the cameras.

The media also played its role in bigging up the committee. After all, the PAC was operating in a Dáil where there was a huge government majority, and in which the opposition was scattered and fragmented. As such, the PAC offered a rare glimpse into how the state was being run.

In the week running up to the Garda commissioner's scheduled appearance on Thursday, 23 January 2014, the PAC received further documentation from McCabe. The committee began its discussions on whether or not to hear evidence from the sergeant. No firm conclusion was reached by the close of business on the Wednesday evening, but McGuinness was of the opinion that they would be hearing from McCabe.

The following morning, Commissioner Callinan arrived at Leinster House for his appearance. He was accompanied by his deputy, Nóirín O'Sullivan, his press officer, Superintendent David Taylor, and a platoon of assistant commissioners and senior officers, including John O'Mahony.

Four windowless rooms in the basement of the new wing of Leinster House, known as Leinster House 2000, are reserved for committees. The seating is designed in an oval arrangement, under a low ceiling, with a small media/public gallery to the rear of one end. Among the mainly journalists in the gallery was John Wilson, now a civilian, who was coming to hear at first hand what the Garda commissioner had to say about his involvement in blowing the whistle. Also present in the gallery were TDs Mick Wallace and Clare Daly.

At some point before the meeting got underway, the Fine Gael TD John Deasy bumped into a senior garda. Three years later he revealed what exactly transpired: 'Before the meeting I was approached by a very senior guard and he proceeded to make some very derogatory comments about Maurice McCabe. The nature of which were, Maurice McCabe couldn't be believed and couldn't be trusted on anything. They were very, very derogatory. It was a serious attack and very strongly worded.'

Deasy also said, on that later occasion in an RTÉ interview, that he and other members of the PAC formed the view that there was a campaign in the Garda Síochána to undermine McCabe's character.

At the outset of the hearing, chairman John McGuinness noted that the committee had made a decision on whether to hear from the whistleblower. They had, he said, the previous night 'agreed to engage again with one of the whistleblowers because he had asked to come before us. We agreed that we would hear his evidence on Thursday next. I think the commissioner should be aware of that.'

He also noted that the committee had received 'further information from Mr Wilson and a Mr McCabe'. This was the first time that Maurice McCabe had been identified publicly. The release of the name sent a frisson through the press benches. While everybody in media, politics and policing were by then aware of Maurice McCabe's identity, the naming in an Oireachtas committee was a nod to making it known to the wider public.

The commissioner opened with a statement that set out the findings of the O'Mahony and C&AG reports, showing where they correlated but ignoring the glaring difference between the two. He concluded, 'I think we have shown with our swift action in relation to the findings of the O'Mahony and the Comptroller and Auditor General reports, we are committed to ensuring that the fixed charge notice system is operated in an effective and efficient manner – fairly and consistently – so as to ensure it has the confidence of the public and, most importantly, that it continues to play an important role in improving road safety by reducing poor driver behaviour.'

Labour's Derek Nolan was first up with the questions. He had a particular issue over the commissioner's interpretation of the word 'corruption'. Since the publication of O'Mahony – and even preceding it – all the emphasis on the investigation was that no corruption had been discovered.

Nolan wanted to know whether corruption was confined to receiving a benefit. There was some discussion over that before things moved on to the detail of the report.

The questioning went on in that vein, including queries about how rigorously the O'Mahony investigation had been, whether, for instance, it had uncovered many cancellations for families of garda members. (Seven cases had been uncovered, and AC John O'Mahony pointed out that it was difficult to identify whether a beneficiary of a cancellation was related to a serving member.)

Callinan made plain his backing to anybody who brought forward instances of wrong-doing, pointing out that during his career he had been involved in the jailing of colleagues for wrong-doing, which was, he said, a painful exercise.

That point was well made but it ignored what was at the heart of McCabe's complaints. McCabe wasn't suggesting that elements in the force were consorting with criminals. The corruption he was talking about was malpractice, covering up shoddy work, abusing the penalty points system. There was an obvious distinction.

Callinan also maintained that the whistleblowers were not operating with the full gamut of information when they had identified what they thought were erroneous cancellations: 'It is very clear that in a substantial portion of the allegations the people who complained about corruption, malpractice, cancellations of all types had very limited access to the decision-making process,' he said. 'They simply did not have access, to put it in a nutshell. They opened a screen in the PULSE system and looked at a snapshot of the actual event but they did not see the complete picture.'

This was an unusual defence. The complete picture should be available to anybody examining the file on the PULSE system. This would include, for example, whether written petitions had been made for a cancellation.

Now the commissioner was implying that the whistleblowers had grabbed pieces of information and run off half-cocked to politicians shouting about corruption.

After further discussion on the matter, Chairman McGuinness intervened and pointed out that one of the whistleblowers (McCabe) had provided much more than just a screenshot from PULSE: 'I was struck by a number of examples that were contained in one of the whistleblower's reports whereby a senior person [in the force] had his or her penalty points struck out because he or she was on his or her way to court. The whistleblower went to the bother of finding out that there was no court sitting on the day in question. He also went to the bother of looking into a situation where a garda who was stopped did not receive penalty points because, it was stated, he was on duty. Apparently several penalty points were at issue here. The whistleblower states that he investigated the case and found that the garda was not on duty when the incident took place and it did not take place in an area where he would normally be working. In fact, he was on sick leave.'

Repeatedly, Callinan said that unfortunately he did not have access to the information that was in the hands of the committee. This was an amazing admission. McCabe's information came from within An Garda Síochána. The commissioner had access to all information within the force. And his assistant commissioner had conducted a high-powered investigation into the ticket-fixing. How could a lowly sergeant easily access such information, yet it had not been excavated by the commissioner's high-powered investigation?

John McGuinness framed the obvious in another question to the commissioner: 'Would it not have been possible to bring in the two serving gardaí before one of them retired and have a man-to-man discussion with them in regard to their duty, as they saw it, to report what they considered wrong-doing and, in some cases, what was described as corruption under the definition we gave earlier? As proper members of the force, willing to give this information, they have put their jobs on the line. That is what happens to whistleblowers – they sometimes become the victim. Was it not possible within the force to create a situation where they were brought forward in order to give that information?'

Callinan referred to the confidential recipient system and also said that his door was and always had been open.

The longer the proceedings went on, the bigger appeared to be the chasm between the scenario presented by the commissioner and what Maurice McCabe was alleging.

One painted a picture of an open door through which rank and file members would be ushered with a warm welcome to reveal shortcomings within the force which should be redressed. The latter picture was one where the bad stuff was swept under the nearest carpet and any further inquiries treated as a personal attack on the force.

As the morning turned to afternoon, the questions moved on to one of the two most vocal members of the committee, Shane Ross.

> **Ross:** We are talking about whistleblowers. If they feel there is something wrong in the system and they are in search of wrong-doing, does Mr Callinan think they should not do it?
>
> **Callinan:** No, I am not saying that. What I am saying is that if they have specific knowledge that there is a particular person or persons involved in wrong-doing, they should report the matter to the appropriate authority in order to have the matter investigated. The appropriate authority is up through the system.
>
> **Ross:** If they do not have confidence in the procedure, what course of action should they take then?
>
> **Callinan:** They should then move through the confidential recipient process.
>
> **Ross:** What would they be expected to do if they do not have any confidence in the procedure?
>
> **Callinan:** These are the systems we have in place.
>
> **Ross:** I know, but if they do not have confidence in those procedures, surely the only option open to them is to pursue it in the way they did.

Callinan: No, I do not agree with Deputy Ross.

Ross kept going. He put it to the commissioner that the men were perfectly entitled to come to the Public Accounts Committee with their complaints.

In doing so, he opened up a door through which the commissioner of An Garda Síochána strode, unaware that he was in danger of walking himself out of a job.

Callinan: Of course Deputy Ross is entitled to his view and I respect it but is it not extraordinary that it is just two individuals that are making these huge allegations of system failure, as Deputy Ross has referred to them, and that it is not dozens or hundreds of other members of An Garda Síochána who are making similar allegations?

My position is very clear. Anyone who makes any report of wrong-doing to me, I will deal with it very seriously. I am sure I speak for my officers beside me and elsewhere when I say that is the case. We will not be isolating anyone who makes a complaint of wrong-doing against another member of the force.

We have many examples within the disciplinary process where we deal with people who transgressed every year. We are certainly not perfect, nor would I ever profess to come before this committee and say so. We have difficult problems. As one can imagine, in a force of over 13,000, dealing with such complex issues, of course we will have difficulties.

However, the Deputy should be very clear that, from my perspective, as Commissioner of An Garda Síochána, I will not allow anyone reporting wrong-doing to be bullied, harassed, intimidated or whatever adverb or adjective the Deputy chooses to use. That will not happen on my watch.

Clearly, here, however, we have two people, out of a force of over 13,000, who are making extraordinary and serious allegations. There is not a whisper anywhere else or from any other member of the Garda Síochána, however, about this corruption, malpractice and other charges levelled against their fellow officers. Frankly, on a personal level, I think it is quite disgusting.

The remark had eyebrows shooting for the low ceiling. The Garda commissioner was characterising the actions of McCabe and Wilson in the lowest terms possible. After four hours of relative restraint in his characterisation of the two men, this was a revelation that left no room for doubt. It was a remark that would come back to haunt Martin Callinan.

The other revelation in his answer was the assertion that he would not allow any so-called whistleblower to be 'bullied, harassed, intimidated' on his watch. McCabe, observing proceedings on the television at home, couldn't believe what he was hearing. The commissioner's stated determination to protect whistleblowers from reprisal was completely at odds with McCabe's experience over the previous six or so years. If Martin Callinan was determined to ensure that whistleblowers were properly regarded and respected, then he was falling down on the job.

The assembled media had their line with the 'disgusting' remark, but there was one other matter to be addressed, and it fell to Mary Lou McDonald to do so.

She wanted to know whether or not the internal O'Mahony investigation into the affair had contacted the man who had made the complaint, on which she questioned O'Mahony.

McDonald: Am I right to state that at no stage in the course of Assistant Commissioner O'Mahony's investigation did he speak to or interview the whistleblowers?

O'Mahony: That is correct.

McDonald: Why was this the case?

O'Mahony: First and foremost the documentation provided to the Commissioner and subsequently to me was unsigned and unattributed. I proceeded with my examination on the basis I was dealing with anonymous allegations.

McDonald: I thank Mr O'Mahony.

O'Mahony: I became aware during the course of the investigation there had been an incident, as the Commissioner described.

There had been an incident, as the Commissioner described, and I was also aware that both of those persons had been issued with a direction that if they wanted to make their complaints, I was available to receive them. I waited for their contact but it did not come.

During the course of the investigation, around February 2013, one of those whistleblowers had extensive contact with a chief superintendent who was investigating the complaints about confidential fraud reporting. I was aware of that process and of the complaints he had made in that regard, and that the complaints mirrored strongly some of the issues I was investigating.

McDonald: Mr O'Mahony still did not speak to him.

O'Mahony: No, I did not speak to him.

Two salient points were extracted from McDonald's questioning. In the first instance the investigation team did not contact McCabe because officially they did not know that he was the source of the allegations.

This is a quite extraordinary claim. In December 2012 and January 2013 McCabe and Wilson had been subjected to orders restricting their access to PULSE on an allegation that they had been downloading material and disseminating it. This material was the evidence of widespread ticket-fixing. Yet the assistant commissioner who was investigating the matter at the time claimed that he didn't make the connection that those two individuals were the anonymous authors of the allegations. Perhaps he should have contacted his boss, who quite obviously was aware that only two members in a force of 13,000 were engaged in highlighting these matters.

O'Mahony also revealed that he expected the complainants to come to him rather than he, as the investigating authority, approach them to see what it was all about. Don't go out and question people who might know something about the subject of an investigation. Wait for them to call you.

The assistant commissioner did note that McCabe had contacted him in February 2013 when the latter read in the media that the investigation was completed. Interestingly, O'Mahony didn't express any shock when this anonymous author revealed himself in the phone call.

It may well be that the assistant commissioner made a genuine oversight in failing to contact McCabe and Wilson. It may well be that he felt constrained because officially the two men were anonymous, even if every last one of the force's 13,000 members was aware of their identity.

However, the alternative explanation, canvassed earlier in this book, is difficult to dismiss. If the men had been contacted, they would have produced information that would then be officially in the hands of the investigation team. This information was easily accessible in the PULSE system if one was minded to apply some basic rigour in seeking it out. But if it were officially one of these handed to the team, they would be obliged to act on it. Such a course might have produced a radically different report, highlighting much wider abuse.

The meeting came to a close at 2.50pm, the commissioner having been under sustained questioning since 10 o'clock that morning.

As the politicians, media and police spilled out of the committee room and mounted the stairs from the basement, there appeared to be a consensus about the hearing. It was not a good day for the commissioner. It was not a good day for An Garda Síochána.

Afterwards, outside the committee room, McGuinness spotted the commissioner and, as was customary after such hearings, he went over to thank him. The commissioner was with Nóirín O'Sullivan and David Taylor, who both listened as McGuinness and Callinan had a few words.

Maurice McCabe and his wife had watched the whole thing at home. Afterwards, he was pleased with what he had seen. As far as he was concerned, Martin Callinan had done little to damage him or his claims in any substantive manner. He found the 'disgusting' remark offensive, and the talk about disciplinary action interesting. If there had been any chance that disciplinary action could have been initiated against him over this matter, it would have occurred long ago. He was secure in the knowledge that the law was on his side here and that there was precious little Garda management could do to prevent him from bringing it into the open.

He wasn't there yet but if things went according to plan, he would be getting his chance before the committee in a week's time.

17

'... it was a question of did I believe the Garda commissioner or did I believe Maurice McCabe?'
John McGuinness

There was wall-to-wall coverage in the media the day after Martin Callinan's appearance at the PAC. As is often the cases in the aftermath of major political theatre, the occasion was probably best captured by Miriam Lord of *The Irish Times*. Under a headline, 'Move along, there's nothing to see here, says garda commissioner', she wrote:

> Before the most powerful committee of the national parliament, the Garda Commissioner stood his ground and all but told the representatives of the people to keep their noses out of police business.
>
> 'My force. My officers,' he said, at one point.
>
> Martin Callinan was correct, in as much as he is the commander of the force. But it is not his force. They are not his officers. It is our force. They are our officers.

Which is why his evidence to the Dáil Public Accounts Committee yesterday was so troubling. He finds the actions of 'so-called whistleblowers' who chose to take their grievances outside the blue brotherhood nothing short of 'disgusting'.

There is nothing, it seems, that cannot be sorted within the confidential confines of the organisation. There is a system in place. Whistleblowers should use it. To do otherwise, to step outside 'the system', is a step too far.

Lord reflected the general sense that the commissioner had emerged with his reputation damaged.

The other issue that received prominence was the commissioner's strong view that Maurice McCabe should not appear before the committee. This, Mr Callinan had asserted, would be an unprecedented challenge to his authority within a disciplined force.

That matter was broached with Shane Ross on RTÉ's *Morning Ireland* in the wake of the commissioner's appearance.

'We want to hear the views of the whistleblowers,' Ross asserted. 'My personal preference is that it should be held in public.' (At this point, the possibility of John Wilson appearing before the committee was still being considered.) Ross went on to give his view on the demeanour of the commissioner at the previous day's hearing. 'He was almost disdainful of the Public Accounts Committee,' the TD said. 'And went on to say they [the whistleblowers] should be dealt with by me, myself. It's a great pity he used such language and went on to say he was being usurped by subordinates as if they were second-class citizens.

'They tried the confidential method which was unsatisfactory, so what other option was open to them? We want to challenge them the same way we challenged the Garda commissioner yesterday.'

On the programme it was mentioned a number of times that this matter was now destined for the courts. There was certainly a real possibility of such an outcome at the time. The commissioner had consulted with the attorney general as to whether he could or should challenge the appearance of one of his officers before the committee.

Heading for the Four Courts could prove risky to the commissioner. What if, as would be likely, McCabe was called to give evidence in court? There was much that a disgruntled garda could reveal in court about what exactly went on behind the blue wall.

The commissioner might well have had that prospect at the front of his mind when he phoned John McGuinness the morning after his appearance, requesting a meeting. While the legal route held dangers, he could try to convince McGuinness that it wasn't in the committee's best interests to hear from McCabe.

Callinan hadn't received any reply from McGuinness by the time he left to go to Dundalk for a press conference to mark the first anniversary of the death of Detective Garda Adrian Donohoe, who had been murdered in the course of a robbery in County Louth. Nobody had as yet been charged with the murder.

While in Dundalk, he received word from McGuinness that he could meet him, but he was under some time pressure. They agreed to come together in Bewley's Hotel, at Newlands Cross, on the Naas Road outside Dublin.

Callinan had a dilemma. He really wanted to talk to McGuinness, but that would necessitate delaying the press conference, tearing back down to Dublin and back up again. He concluded that it would be worth it and made the arrangements.

That afternoon, McGuinness arrived in the car park ahead of the commissioner. He saw Callinan's car pull in, the commissioner in the passenger seat beside his driver. Callinan spotted the politician and got out of his vehicle and came over. He sat in beside McGuinness, who quickly realised that the meeting he had scheduled for the hotel was going to take place in his car.

The pair spoke for twenty minutes. Callinan was anxious that the committee not allow his sergeant to appear before it. He gave the impression that the committee members didn't know who they were dealing with in the person of McCabe. He conveyed to McGuinness that McCabe was not to be trusted.

Three years later, McGuinness gave a statement to a tribunal of his version of what transpired:

> Mr Callinan asked if I was aware of issues surrounding Mr McCabe's personal life. I stated that I had heard vague rumours and gossip that Mr McCabe had abused someone and that he was a paedophile but that I had been assured by Mr McCabe that these rumours were lies, that he had heard them before and that they were malicious falsehoods. Mr Callinan stated to me that the rumours were true, that Mr McCabe had sexually abused someone and that he was not a credible person.
>
> Mr Callinan stated that an investigation into Mr McCabe's activities was underway. Mr Callinan then asked me was I aware that Mr McCabe had sexually abused family members. I was shocked and extremely troubled by what Mr Callinan was telling me because the allegations being made were extreme and the person relaying them to me, as well as the fact that an investigation had commenced, was the Commissioner of An Garda Síochána.

Callinan has vehemently denied making these comments to McGuinness. One way or the other, the allegations outlined by McGuinness were the subject of rumours circulating at the time, and malicious falsehoods of the most grievous manner. It is difficult to imagine anything more vicious to be propagated about an innocent person.

Once the meeting was finished, the commissioner got on the road back to Dundalk. Later, in the County Louth town, he remembered Garda Donohoe: 'His murder had a profound impact not only on his colleagues in Dundalk, but also on the wider An Garda Síochána family. It had an impact not only on the lives of those he positively affected in County Louth through his work, or through his involvement with the GAA community, but also countrywide.'

The commissioner was reported to have delivered his speech in a genuine, heartfelt manner. His plaudits for a member who had died in the line of duty were in sharp contrast to his alleged attitude to another officer who felt he was doing his duty by highlighting malpractice within the force.

Callinan's attempts to dissuade McGuinness from hearing from McCabe was just one of a number of strands of pressure being brought to bear on the committee. In the days after Callinan's appearance before the Public Accounts Committee, and before McCabe's scheduled appearance, the pressure was seriously ramped up. High-powered elements within both the gardaí and the government were determined that it wouldn't happen.

There were fears over what McCabe might say. Would he attempt to throw out high-profile names of those who'd had their tickets cancelled in dubious circumstances? Would he use the public forum to launch a personal attack on the commissioner? Could he be trusted?

Since their initial meeting in Buswells, McGuinness had been in regular contact with McCabe. He trusted him. He could understand why others, who knew McCabe as this faceless whistleblower, the subject of dark rumours, might not have the same insight.

'After my meeting with Martin Callinan, I had to make a decision,' McGuinness said in an interview for this book. 'I could either trust Maurice McCabe or believe what I was hearing about him, particularly that he was not to be trusted. I had heard the rumours. I knew who was lined up against him. It wasn't just the senior management in the Guards, but a lot of people in Leinster House as well.

'But I'd met him, I was getting to know him. Everything he had presented me with stacked up. The evidence of what he was talking about was there in black and white. So by then for me, it was a question of did I believe the Garda commissioner or did I believe Maurice McCabe? I believed McCabe. After that, my job was to convince those on the committee who were wavering that it was in our best interests to hear what he had to say.'

By the following Monday, the heat was further intensified. Alan Shatter announced that he was inviting the Garda ombudsman GSOC to investigate concerns around the ticket-fixing issue.

Many saw this as another attempt to thwart the PAC from hearing from McCabe. As such, it showed the government rowing in behind the Garda commissioner.

Later that day, McCabe was in contact with John McGuinness. The politician told the sergeant that it didn't look too good for his scheduled appearance. As things stood, McGuinness reckoned the vote would go against any appearance.

The parliamentarians from the government parties were coming under pressure to vote against it. In this, the Fine Gael members were more resolute than their Labour Party colleagues.

The legal adviser for the Houses of the Oireachtas was advising that there could be unforeseen legal issues with the Garda sergeant's appearance.

On Tuesday Alan Shatter was interviewed on *Morning Ireland*. He was asked why it had taken him until now to bring in the ombudsman, and whether it had anything to do with the proposal for the PAC to question McCabe.

He replied that he couldn't have referred to the ombudsman

before this point. 'That would have been an abuse of the legislation,' he said. 'We now have the Garda engaged in a political controversy which is completely undesirable. The vast majority of members of the Public Accounts Committee go about their business in an appropriate way but a minority are making public comments outside the realm of the committee. I concluded it is desirable in the public interest that these matters be taken to the Garda ombudsman. It couldn't previously have been done.'

For many observers, the gesture smacked of an attempt to head off the PAC at the pass.

In Mullingar station, at around the same time Shatter was being interviewed, McCabe was called in to a meeting with the divisional head, Chief Superintendent Mark Curran. The senior officer read out for McCabe a communication from Garda HQ. It relayed that McCabe was a valued member of staff and he could, if he so wished, nominate any officer to act as a go-between with senior management to convey his concerns over the ticket-fixing.

McCabe asked for a copy of the communication, but the chief superintendent said his instructions were to provide it only verbally.

McCabe left feeling deflated. Now that it looked as if his efforts to bring the ticket-fixing issue to an Oireachtas committee were dying, the commissioner was offering an olive branch of sorts. Form told McCabe that it was little more than an empty gesture. He had been down this road before. Once the political storm passed, it would all be back to 'as you were, lads'.

That evening McGuinness was hard at work with his committee. He had presented a version of McCabe's dossier on the ticket-fixing to the members. The information made it plain that there was a case to answer, and that McCabe had a number of those answers.

After further discussion, the mood began to shift. A failure to have the matter thrashed out would look bad. There was a serious issue of the abuse of public money involved. In the end, a compromise was suggested. The committee would hear from McCabe, but it would be in private session and confined to systems, practices and procedures, with a warning that no names be mentioned in evidence.

The majority of the Public Accounts Committee were now on board. The Labour Party members in particular were always wavering between supporting the government line, as expressed through the Minister for Justice, and rallying to the standard of accountability. Their votes and a few from the Fine Gael contingent changed the perspective.

It was a victory for McGuinness. He rang McCabe and told him that he would see him on Thursday. McCabe was over the moon. The conditions suited him perfectly. He didn't want a public palaver, and he certainly had no interest in mentioning specific names as beneficiaries of the system.

The news that the Public Accounts Committee was going to hear from the Garda sergeant made the *Nine O'Clock News* that night.

The following morning, McCabe was back at work in Mullingar, and was told once again that Chief Superintendent Curran wanted to see him. Another communication from HQ. This time, though, the tenor was the polar opposite to that which had been dispatched twenty-four hours earlier.

The chief super read out the communication, which informed Sergeant McCabe that he should consider his position. His actions were going against the explicit wishes of the commissioner. There could be consequences for such an action in a disciplined force. He should get some legal advice on the matter. Once more, McCabe's request for the written version was denied but he was allowed to take detailed notes of the statement's content.

McCabe asked Chief Super Curran if that meant he would be disciplined. Curran, who was merely conveying instructions from HQ, said he couldn't give guarantees one way or the other.

McCabe left the room even more deflated than he had been the previous morning. The thought of being disciplined went to the core of what it meant, for him, to be a guard. He had never been disciplined in his career. He had never broken the rules. He had been a good cop, and now they were saying that if he continued down the road he was embarking on, he may well have a stain on his record.

He rang Lorraine and discussed it. 'I was in favour of it, no matter what they were threatening to do to him,' she said. 'He had come this far and he couldn't let them stop him now. This was his chance to tell somebody outside the Guards what was really going on. He had to do it.'

McCabe consulted with a few other family members. The balance of opinion was with Lorraine. But what if they disciplined him? Well, that would be a reflection on the force, rather than on his actions.

Still, the guard inside him wouldn't leave his conscience alone. His record meant a lot to him. He wanted to tell the PAC what exactly was going on, but not at the expense of a black mark on his record.

In the afternoon he went back to the office of Chief Super Curran to get clarity on the prospect of being disciplined. This time Curran said he had received his own clarity. No, McCabe would not be disciplined if he went before the committee.

This time McCabe left the office with a giddy sense of achievement. It was going to happen. Finally, he was going to be heard.

On one level, the forthcoming appearance was daunting. His name had been in the public domain since the previous Thursday, but he would have to be prepared to be caught on camera in Leinster House.

He would do what he could to avoid it, but he sure as hell wasn't going to run away from a camera, as if he had something to hide. The thought of the spotlight being trained on him was discomforting, but in the context of what he and his family had been through, it was relatively small potatoes.

He and Lorraine discussed what he should wear. He was appearing in a professional capacity, an acting member of the national police doing the duty he had sworn to do. To appear in full uniform might come across as provocative to the commissioner. That wasn't his style. But neither was he going to walk into this committee as a lay person. He was a guard. He was acting as a guard, in the best interests of the force.

He decided to wear his garda shirt, tie and trousers and a plain blue jacket. That way he wouldn't be making a statement for the cameras. But once he got into the committee room he would take off his jacket and give evidence in the uniform of the garda that he was.

The veteran socialist TD Joe Higgins rang McCabe at home in the morning. Higgins had been in touch with him over the preceding weeks, offering support. Now he suggested to McCabe that if he was interested, he, Higgins, could pick him up somewhere in Dublin and drive him right into the Leinster House car park. This would avoid any media scrum at the gates.

McCabe was grateful for the offer, but, after brief consideration, he turned it down. He had seen plenty of television images of a person of interest being driven past the cameras. The subject was usually either somebody in power at the centre of a controversy or a criminal being brought to book. He was neither.

He would walk into Leinster House to do his duty.

He left Lough Sheelin around noon and drove to his twin sister Patricia's house in Harold's Cross.

From there Patricia drove him, in her car, as far as St Stephen's Green. He told her he would text her when he was done. Patricia drove off and McCabe made his way down Kildare Street, a rucksack slung over his shoulder, butterflies flapping like clappers in his stomach. This was it.

It took the cameramen a few minutes to realise that their prey had arrived. A team from TV3 caught him within yards of the gate's entrance. He kept walking, head up, through the flashes, through the sound of film being reeled off, as if he was an exotic creature who had just landed from Hollywood or outer space.

Maurice McCabe had never been in Leinster House before, so he missed the pedestrian entrance and had to turn back. Now he saw a guard there, and asked was this where he entered. His colleague nodded, and in he went.

He walked across the Leinster House frontage, yards from the plinth where politicians had in recent days been feeding the media their views of the Garda whistleblower. And then he was gone from sight, through the doors of Leinster House 2000 and down into the bowels of the building, in the recent footsteps of his boss, the commissioner of An Garda Síochána, but with a very different tale to tell.

There was one sharp contrast between the choreography of McCabe's appearance and that of the commissioner seven days before. When Callinan sat before the committee, he was joined by a phalanx of colleagues and assistants: half-a-dozen uniformed assistant commissioners or senior officers sat on both sides of him or behind him. This is relatively standard when witnesses appear before the committee. They have colleagues or assistants to help out when the going gets tough. It also projects the image of authority.

Maurice McCabe came in alone. He didn't even have a legal adviser at his side. There was just him and his folder, in which he had notes and records of the malpractice he had been attempting to highlight.

'He sat down on his own, took off his jacket and appeared before us in his uniform,' John McGuinness said. 'Every one of the committee members were present for the meeting, lined up there opposite him. These were politicians like myself who are accustomed to this kind of environment. We have experience in questioning people, holding them to account in a forum like that. It can be a very daunting experience for anybody to come and face that, even people at the head of organisations who have done it previously. Maurice McCabe was on his own. He'd never done anything like this before and yet he was completely assured and coherent.'

Maybe it was a sense of euphoria that calmed McCabe, or maybe it was just that he was certain that he knew exactly what he was talking about and had nothing to hide. Maybe it was the knowledge that truth was on his side. Or perhaps it was the realisation that after six years he had finally arrived at a place where he believed he would get a fair hearing, that what he had to say would be regarded not as a threat but an opportunity to put something right in the business of policing that had been his life.

He gave evidence for nearly three hours. No names were mentioned. There was nothing about the well-known individuals or celebrities who had benefited from cancelled tickets. There was nothing about particular superintendents who had a reputation for cancelling at the drop of a hat. McCabe just went through the issue methodically, using the material that he had supplied to John McGuinness. He showed where there was a trend with certain repeat offenders. He pointed out the anomalies in the cases where gardaí had benefited from cancellations. More than anything, he was able to demonstrate how most of the cancellations simply did not have the supporting evidence required to ensure that they fell within the policy guidelines for cancelling.

Repeatedly, he told members that he loved being a guard, that this was his vocation, and it gave him no pleasure that he had uncovered this level of malpractice.

'I got the impression that on one level he felt he was speaking for the ordinary guards in the country, the type of individuals we know and respect who want to do their best at the job,' McGuinness said. 'He saw what was going on as a stain on the badge and he wanted something done about it. He emphasised his frustration that he hadn't been listened to within the organisation.'

The committee members whose opinions were canvassed by the media after the hearing all said that Maurice McCabe was 'credible'.

In the round, the hearing was a success, for McGuinness as chairman in bringing it about, for the committee in delving into a matter of state accountability, and for McCabe himself.

When he emerged just before 6pm, darkness had fallen. He came out through the pedestrian entrance, the scrum of media on his tail, his confederate John Wilson emerging from the scrum to offer him some physical solidarity. Patricia pulled up in the car, Wilson got him in and slammed the door shut, and then he was off. Job done.

Maurice McCabe's appearance at the Public Accounts Committee on 30 January 2014 represented an ending of sorts for him. Six years after he had begun to highlight malpractice, he got to lay out the particulars to an official body of the state. He did so in an unprecedented manner, going outside the force against the express wishes of the Garda commissioner.

His efforts to have matters examined internally had, in his view, been a disaster. The confidential recipient route had seen him embark on a Kafkaesque journey in which his complaints against malpractice in Cavan/Monaghan had boomeranged.

Then, the ticket-fixing scandal looked as if it was heading down the same blind alley. This time, with the assistance of John Wilson, he had brought the matter as far as he could.

Wilson played a considerable part in the whole affair, according to Clare Daly: 'It wouldn't have worked without John,' she said. 'He's articulate and because he had left the Guards by then he was able to come out and put a public face on it. When we were dealing with Maurice at the time the first issue was any implications for his job. If he had had to break his anonymity at the early stages, there could have been massive implications for him. So it worked well with John from that point of view.'

McCabe's modus operandi was the same as it had been for the complaints that he'd made – and that others had referred through him – in Cavan/Monaghan. He had come into possession of information that pointed to malpractice. The road ahead of him was forked. He could, as he may have done occasionally before 2007, shrugged and moved on, kept the head down, concentrated on his own little patch and internalised any notions of morality or standards.

Now at last he had had his say. He was not, as John McGuinness reassured him when they first met, mad or bad. His years thumping on the blue wall, crying out to be heard, were not the rantings of a malcontent or a crazy guard. At last, somebody in power had listened. At last, the matter could not be buried in a blizzard of spin. He had done his duty.

'Before that meeting, a lot of people didn't believe him,' John McGuinness said. 'Afterwards that changed. The committee members had seen what he was like, that he was a man to be taken seriously. And the fact that he was no longer the anonymous whistleblower made it more difficult for those who wanted to ensure he was ignored.'

Six weeks after his appearance at the PAC, there was further confirmation of the claims he had made. The Garda Inspectorate published its investigation into the operation of the fixed charge notice system. That investigation had been ordered by Alan Shatter on publication of the internal Garda investigation headed up by Assistant Commissioner John O'Mahony the previous year. Now, ten months later, it was seeing the light of day in a transformed landscape. No longer were McCabe and Wilson being characterised as chancers; no longer was the word of the force's official investigation into the matter being accepted as gospel.

The Garda Inspectorate found that 'there were consistent and widespread breaches of policy by those charged with administering' the system.

'With few exceptions, the Inspectorate found no meaningful evidence of consistent quality management supervision of the cancellation process either at Garda headquarters, Regional, Divisional, District or any level that would have detected and rectified these problems.'

Just over half (51%) of the cancelled tickets reviewed had no supporting evidence. In other words, tickets were cancelled in these cases largely on the word of the offending motorist.

Out of nine districts examined by the Inspectorate, only one had a functioning system to properly monitor cancellations.

In terms of cancellations for gardaí, the general excuse was that the member was on duty at the time, yet 'the Inspectorate found little evidence by management to confirm that the member was actually "on duty"'.

The other, and probably most serious, category of cancellations were those for repeat offenders. The Inspectorate examined a number of cases where motorists had received multiple cancellations, usually for speeding. 'In cancelling these FCNs [Fixed Charge Notices] no regard was taken of previous cancellations, the reckless speed detected or to the safety of other road users. The Inspectorate considers that the reckless speeds detected are not commensurate with a real need to put other road users in danger and therefore the FCNs should not have been cancelled.'

In the round, the Inspectorate went much further than the Comptroller and Auditor General's report in blowing the internal Garda investigation out of the water.

By then, the tide had turned on McCabe's endeavours. His appearance at the PAC had been an ending of sorts as far as the ticket-fixing was concerned. It had also, however, pulled a thread attached to the long-dormant concerns of malpractice in Cavan/Monaghan.

That malpractice in criminal investigations was arguably far more important than the ticket-fixing, but had been dealt with internally and swept under the carpet as far as McCabe was concerned.

The controversy around his appearance at the PAC – greatly inflated by the voracious opposition it generated – along with his emergence from anonymity, changed the landscape markedly. Far from reaching a conclusion, the whistleblowing saga was about to take off in a different direction which would have devastating consequences for some powerful figures, in both the government and An Garda Síochána.

18

'They are shocking revelations of incompetence which ultimately led to people being murdered as a result of a failure to act.'
Micheál Martin

On the Wednesday following McCabe's appearance at the PAC, Mick Wallace was addressing the Dáil during a debate on a new protected disclosures bill, designed to protect whistleblowing in any sector.

By then, Wallace and Clare Daly had effectively taken on reform of the Garda Síochána as a political crusade. Through their work, a group called Justice For All had been established, which included over two hundred citizens who had come forward with complaints of what they believed to be Garda malpractice.

'We were talking to Maurice all the time and dealing with all the other cases,' Daly said. 'We were trying to raise these issues in the Dáil but it was only sporadically that we got on to leaders'questions. We had also drafted two policing authority bills.'

On the day in question, Wallace brought up the transcript of the conversation between McCabe and the confidential recipient Oliver Connolly from January 2012: 'Whistleblowers are rare for many reasons, and will become rarer, given how this State treats them. A while back we were given a transcript of a conversation two years ago between Maurice McCabe and the confidential recipient. It is frightening.

'It includes the following: "I'll tell you something, Maurice, and this is just personal advice to you: if Shatter thinks you're screwing him, you're finished." Here is another line: "If Shatter thinks, here's this guy again trying another route trying to put pressure, he'll go after you." Our Minister for Justice and Equality will "go after you". What is going on?'

The chamber was nearly empty during Wallace's address. Yet the TD from Wexford had just pulled a thread that was going to reach into the heart of government and policing.

There was little media take-up of the speech, but the following Saturday the *Irish Examiner* reported on Wallace's comments, putting them into the context of the recent penalty points controversy and earlier reporting on McCabe. The piece was read by Fianna Fáil leader Micheál Martin, who resolved to follow up on it.

The tape was incendiary because it portrayed Shatter as a ruthless politician, which was fodder for his opponents. The nuances involved were ignored. This was not a declaration from the minister that he would 'go after' anybody, but an opinion expressed to that effect from a man who knew the minister, but not particularly well. The portrayal of Shatter in this light was unfair. There is absolutely no reason to believe that Alan Shatter would go after anybody. But in the maelstrom that had been kicked up over the ticket-fixing, it added fuel to a fire that had not yet gone out.

Then, within twenty-four hours of the *Irish Examiner* story, another bomb landed in the public domain. *The Sunday Times* reported that an investigation had taken place the previous autumn to determine whether the offices of GSOC had been bugged.

'The Garda Síochána Ombudsman Commission was targeted as part of a sophisticated surveillance operation, which used "government-level technology" to hack into its emails, wi-fi and phone systems,' the story, written by crime correspondent John Mooney, began.

The revelation drew the Garda Síochána and the Minister for Justice into another police controversy. The minister's first reaction was not to consider whether GSOC, a vital organisation for overseeing the gardaí, had been bugged. Instead, he expressed himself displeased that he had not been informed that GSOC had carried out the investigation.

For the following two weeks, this matter was thrashed out in public. At a time when Alan Shatter and the government were still dealing with the whistleblowers, this extra pressure, and more negative headlines, was exactly what they did not need.

Three days after *The Sunday Times* article appeared, Micheál Martin brought up the Connolly/McCabe tape at Leaders' Questions in the Dáil, the same tape that had received such scant attention the previous week when Mick Wallace had mentioned it.

'I have read a transcript of a conversation between the Garda confidential recipient and the Garda whistleblower, Sergeant Maurice McCabe,' Martin said. 'It makes for serious and grave reading. The import of the transcript is such that the Garda whistleblower is frustrated and there is a sense of disbelief that his complaints are going nowhere. Clearly, the transcript reveals efforts, if not subtle threats, that if the material that the whistleblower had ever got to the media, the Minister, Deputy Shatter, would come after the whistleblower. This is a grave situation in a democracy, particularly given the office involved.'

Martin went on, 'Has the Taoiseach spoken to the Minister, Deputy Shatter, since this was first revealed last week? Has the

Minister spoken to the confidential recipient about this exchange? Is the Taoiseach concerned?'

Enda Kenny replied that he was 'concerned about it. I believe that there is a matter of public interest here of the utmost importance that has to be dealt with.'

The following day Kenny announced that he had asked the Department of Justice to furnish him with a report into the alleged comments on the tape. The same day Shatter addressed the matter.

'There's a reference to some transcript,' he said. 'I'm not privy to the transcript. I don't know anything about the meeting that took place. I don't know how the transcript was created.'

Later that day, the chairman of GSOC, Simon O'Brien, told the Oireachtas Justice Committee that he suspected GSOC was bugged and that it could have been the gardaí. That contribution added further fuel to the bugging controversy.

The entire week was dominated by headlines about Shatter, GSOC, the commissioner, offices allegedly being bugged, the Minister for Justice being described as somebody who would 'go after' you if he thought you were screwing him.

The swirling controversies were giving the impression of a strange kind of chaos at the interface of government and the police force.

Away from the spotlight of the Dáil that week, Micheál Martin had a quiet word with his party colleague John McGuinness.

The Oliver Connolly/McCabe recording had raised Martin's interest in McCabe. What was this fella like? Martin asked McGuinness, who assured him McCabe was a genuine character. Martin wondered would it be possible to set up a meeting with him.

McGuinness made the call and McCabe's reply was that he would meet anybody. An arrangement was made to sit down in Portlaoise on Friday evening, when Martin would be on the road home to Cork for the weekend.

That Friday morning McCabe got some terrible news: one of his best friends had died. He was a highly popular sergeant who had worked in both Cavan and Monaghan. A few years older than Maurice, they had shared an interest in cars, heading over to motor shows in Germany once every few years. The friend had been ill with cancer, but a few days before his death Maurice had been in touch and he seemed to be in good spirits. Now this news, sudden yet not unexpected.

The two men had remained friends since McCabe had first made his complaints. While others blanked him, this friend had stood by him. Frequently, through the years of isolation and stress, they had met up for a few pints or a meal, sometimes in the company of their wives. Now he was gone, taken in his mid-fifties.

Later that day McCabe left home and drove across the midlands to Portlaoise. It was raining hard when he arrived at the hotel in the town centre. He waited in the hotel lobby and spotted Martin immediately when he came through the door. Martin recognised the other man from the television shots of him outside Leinster House on the day of the PAC hearing.

They repaired to a large conference room, which Martin had organised. Martin said he wanted to check whether the transcript that had been aired in the Dáil was a true reflection of the conversation between McCabe and Connolly.

The tape was played, the two men listening, Martin's eyes on a copy of the transcript, the recording playing at a low volume in the big, cavernous room. When it finished, Martin expressed himself satisfied with the result.

'Is there anything more serious than the penalty points?' Martin asked. McCabe said there was plenty, but it had all been dealt with internally, buried as far as he was concerned.

Martin pushed him on what he was referencing. McCabe produced three folders, which he had dusted down and brought along with him. These were divided into those cases that he considered contained serious malpractice, the less serious, and the ones involving the harassment that he had suffered on the job.

Martin began reading and quickly expressed himself concerned. There was a large volume to get through, so he asked McCabe if he could assemble a sample of about ten of the worst cases that were involved. McCabe said that would be no problem. He also aired his grievance about Shatter's comments the previous October in the Dáil in which he'd said that McCabe and Wilson had not co-operated with the Garda inquiry into the ticket-fixing.

That was a slur, McCabe said, about which he was extremely angry. His record in the force was perfectly clean, and he did not deserve to be cast as somebody who would act in a duplicitous or negligent manner.

The pair shook hands and went their separate ways. McCabe drove home through the rain in good spirits.

Over the weekend he assembled the document that Martin had requested, but his mind wasn't on it. The death of his friend and its aftermath was occupying him.

The funeral was going to be a major Garda affair, yet McCabe was excluded from the garda-organised arrangements. He was devastated and angry to be denied playing a part in this tribute to his dead friend.

Such was his anger that he stayed away from the removal. Word got back to him that other colleagues were amazed that he wasn't there, but he was adamant. His friend would not have wanted it like this.

The following day, the funeral was to be held. He was still of a mind not to go, but his father and brother Declan persuaded him to attend.

They arrived in the church early and met with the bereaved family, but then melted back into the general congregation. Afterwards, McCabe decided he wasn't going to the cemetery. He was in his car on the way home when he got a text from one of the organisers, belatedly telling him that he could form part of the guard of honour if he so wished.

Somebody had realised the wrong that was being done by excluding him, but it was too late as far as McCabe was concerned. He kept going, cursing once more the warped notion of loyalty, the circling of the wagons, that refused even to make allowances in times of bereavement.

A few weeks after the funeral, his brother Declan met with one of the guards who had been involved and he didn't hold back in telling him what he thought about what had occurred. The only response he got was, 'Sure, I couldn't have been seen with Maurice.' The fear of being associated with the whistleblower was now even more pronounced.

McCabe travelled to Dublin the following day, Monday, 17 February, to meet with Micheál Martin. He handed over the dossier of the ten worst cases of malpractice and Martin told him that he would be raising the matter at Leaders' Questions in two days' time.

Before then there was another development. Alan Shatter sacked the confidential recipient Oliver Connolly. Shatter set out his reason in a statement confirming the sacking. 'I informed him that in the context of his failure to unequivocally repudiate the content of the alleged conversation or take the necessary action to restore public confidence in the office of Confidential Recipient, I believed his position was untenable and I had no alternative but to relieve him of the position.'

Connolly went quietly. McCabe had some sympathy for Connolly, but he had no regrets about taping their conversation. It was nothing personal. But when you were up against the might of An Garda Síochána, and its influence on the levers of power, every possible caution was required. Connolly has never spoken publicly about the incident.

Following his Dublin meeting with McCabe on 17 February, Micheál Martin wrote a letter for Enda Kenny about the seriousness of the situation. Before doing so, he brought up the issue at Leaders' Questions on the Wednesday.

He told the Taoiseach that he had been given a dossier of ten cases, which included incidents of murder and kidnapping.

'They are shocking revelations of incompetence which ultimately led to people being murdered as a result of a failure to act. It is very serious stuff which the Department of Justice and Equality has had for quite a long time but not acted on.' Martin added that any investigation should be taken out of the hands of the department. He also stuck the knife into Shatter, saying his position was no longer tenable.

Later that day, Martin dispatched the dossier to the Taoiseach with an accompanying letter.

19 February 2014

Dear Taoiseach

I refer you to our discussions this morning during leaders Questions in the Dáil. I met with Garda Maurice McCabe recently and I listened to the audio tape of the transcript involving him and the Confidential Garda Recipient. It is quite startling to say the least and very unacceptable. As you are aware, the transcript is now freely available.

I believe that Garda McCabe is due an apology because Minister Shatter misled the Dáil by saying he did not co-operate with the Assistant Commissioner O'Mahony's recent inquiry. This is untrue and the record should be corrected.

I have also been sent information by email that contains information about eight cases that range from allegations of sexual assault, abduction, hi-jacking, imprisonment and endangerment as well as murder.

*I am attaching them for your urgent attention. The contents of
these cases, the volume of information and the allegations therein
are extremely serious. I believe they deserve an independent
inquiry under the Commission of Inquiries Act. This is the only
way the public can have confidence in the country's justice system.*

*I am available to discuss these serious issues with you if you so
wish.*

Sincerely

Micheál Martin

McCabe followed the events in the Dáil with a sense of disbelief.
First he had been taken seriously by the Public Accounts Committee.
Now this. Had the worm finally turned? Not yet, as events were to
demonstrate.

The McCabe affair was now firmly in the political arena. Therein
every opportunity would be sought to hunt down some political
capital. In particular, Alan Shatter was in the sights of Fianna
Fáil. Micheál Martin's assertion that Shatter should apologise for
misleading the Dáil in effectively slandering McCabe and Wilson
was going to become the focus of attack.

Over the weekend of 22–23 February, word began to seep out
that Shatter would come under enormous pressure on the issue.
Fianna Fáil was going to go all out to force the supremely confident
minister to declare 'mea culpa'. Knives were being sharpened for the
following Wednesday's Dáil proceedings.

Then, on the Tuesday afternoon a story appeared on the RTÉ
website. It reported that commissioner Martin Callinan had written
to Sergeant Maurice McCabe 14 months ago and told him to co-
operate with the [Assistant Commissioner John O'Mahony] inquiry'.

The story had no direct quotes from the commissioner, and was
not an official press release. If it could be verified, it would give

Shatter complete cover for his Dáil utterances that McCabe and Wilson hadn't co-operated.

Strangely, calls to the Garda press office from various media outlets – including the *Irish Examiner* – during the day confirmed that the office had not released any official statement on the matter.

The story, and its assertions, asked more questions of itself than answered anything else. Where did it originate? If this was a direct statement from the commissioner, why were no quotations used? Why was it being published now, just as the Minister for Justice was under political attack?

The occasion of this alleged 'direction' from the commissioner was when McCabe had been called in to a meeting with Chief Superintendent Mark Curran in Mullingar station on 14 December 2012 (as outlined in Chapter 12). The purpose of that meeting was to inform the sergeant that his access to PULSE was being restricted. Now it was being alleged that, on that occasion, McCabe had also been informed that he was being directed by the commissioner to co-operate with the O'Mahony inquiry.

The story was highly damaging for McCabe. It implied that the sergeant had failed to follow a direction from the head of the police force. The implication was that McCabe had in fact kicked up a controversy and then run for cover when it was being examined. It also suggested that his grievance at Shatter's Dáil comments about him was entirely misplaced.

From Shatter's perspective, the story provided political cover. Look, there's nothing to apologise for.

On that evening's *Six-One News*, the story was taken up by the station's political correspondent. 'We're told this evening that Maurice McCabe was indeed directed by the commissioner to co-operate with the inquiry,' he said, referring to the story that had appeared on the RTÉ website. 'Now he [McCabe] didn't in the end give evidence to the inquiry – we don't quite know the circumstances of that – but if, as we're told, there was a direction given to Sergeant McCabe, that obviously provides Alan Shatter with a defence because of course he's in the dock for suggesting that Maurice McCabe didn't co-operate with the inquiry. If he was given a direction and he didn't ultimately give evidence to the inquiry, there's obviously a grey area there, but there is a potential defence for the minister.'

Up in Lough Sheelin, the stress levels had been ratcheted higher. McCabe made some frantic calls to his legal advisers. He knew the story was false. He had not been issued with any direction.

Not for the first time, and certainly not for the last, McCabe gave thanks to his foresight. He had recorded the meeting in December 2012. He had the evidence that the RTÉ story was based on a lie, but what could he do now?

McCabe was faced with an unenviable decision. Does he take on the commissioner of a disciplined force, of which he is a member? He made and took a series of calls from his legal advisers, and, as ever, he and Lorraine delved deeply into the maw of what faced them.

Just before 9pm, Maurice McCabe issued his own statement, an unprecedented move for a garda. It was also explosive, since it consisted of an attack on the truthfulness of a story allegedly originating with the force's commissioner. Included with the statement was a transcript of a recording he had made at the meeting in December 2012 where the commissioner was apparently now saying he had issued a direction to McCabe. The transcript showed that no such direction was conveyed. The statement itself was startling:

> My attention has been drawn by members of the media today to a statement or press release that appears to have been released to the media earlier today in relation to me.
>
> The un-headed statement or press release is, I regret to say, both gravely misleading and false.

It suggests that the Garda commissioner wrote to me 14 months ago 'and told [me] to co-operate with the investigation into the allegation that penalty points had been cancelled'.

It claims that the commissioner 'issued a direction' to me 'to co-operate with the investigation being carried out by the assistant commissioner' and 'directing' me to bring any information or concerns I had 'to the inquiry team'.

It goes on to say that 'the Garda Síochána is a disciplined force and that members are required to comply with directions issued by the commissioner', implying that I wrongfully failed to comply with the commissioner's direction to co-operate.

The statement further suggests that I did not comply with the commissioner's direction during a period when I was on sick leave and that I 'did not contact' the assistant commissioner until 'April 2013, by which time the investigation had been completed'.

I was never directed by the commissioner to co-operate with the O'Mahony investigation as alleged. On 14th December 2012, I was asked to remain back after duty in Mullingar Garda Station to meet with Chief Superintendent Mark Curran. I did so.

When he arrived he read me out a document. I have, fortunately, a full record of what transpired and it is attached to this statement. As appears from the record, the chief superintendent refused my request to furnish me a copy of that document. I presume that this was in accordance with his superiors' instructions.

The fact that I was denied a copy of the direction may have encouraged the author of the statement issued today about me to grossly misrepresent the terms of the commissioner's direction as read out to me and as recorded by me.

I was never contacted by anyone conducting the O'Mahony investigation which completed its report without making any attempt to speak with me or to seek my input or co-operation into its inquiries. I never withheld any information or co-operation from the O'Mahony investigation as is now suggested.

When I learned that its report had been completed without making any attempt at all to contact me, I protested at what had happened, as the record shows. At that point I was offered a totally meaningless opportunity to speak with Assistant Commissioner O'Mahony.

As a member of the Garda Síochána, I have tried to uphold its integrity by complying with my duty and being truthful in my dealings with my superiors and with the public office-holders with whom I have been dealing in relation to these matters.

I must leave it to others to judge whether those standards are shared or have been adhered to by those who issued the false and misleading statement concerning me today.

The statement and excerpts of the accompanying transcript featured on RTÉ television's *Prime Time* that night, with a fuller report in the *Irish Examiner* the following morning. All things considered, the whole affair was an embarrassment for Martin Callinan, but it also raised questions as to the connections between the national broadcaster and An Garda Síochána.

How had the story come about? Where did it originate? And why, once it was publicly called into question by McCabe, did it disappear from RTÉ's website?

McCabe's reaction to the story brought him onto a new level. Now that he was out in the open, he had been forced to engage in a public relations battle directly with his boss, the commissioner. A failure to do so would have seen him portrayed in a highly negative light, based on a complete untruth.

Some of the credit for McCabe's unprecedented reaction to the situation he found himself in must go to his legal counsel, Michael McDowell.

McDowell is a former TD, attorney general and Minister for Justice as well as a senior counsel. He had been advising McCabe since he was first retained some years previously. Now, though, his contribution went beyond that of a standard senior counsel. The story had moved from behind the blue wall out into the open, where it was the subject of both media and political debate and manoeuvring. Here, McDowell's long-standing experience as a politician came to the fore.

No doubt he also relished the prospect of pitching his wits against some in his old stomping ground of politics, and none more so than the incumbent Minister for Justice, Alan Shatter. Irony also attached to the fact that McCabe's complaints were highlighting shortcomings in the An Garda Síochána Act 2005, which had been the first serious piece of legislation to attempt to reform the gardaí, including the introduction of the confidential recipient system of whistleblowing. The minister who had brought in that law was none other than Michael McDowell.

The following day, Enda Kenny announced that senior counsel Seán Guerin would be retained to conduct a 'scoping' inquiry into the McCabe dossier that had been furnished to Micheál Martin.

Also in the Dáil, Alan Shatter made it clear that he was not for turning. He rejected any notion that he had misled the Dáil in declaring that McCabe and Wilson had not co-operated with the ticket-fixing inquiry. And he certainly wasn't going to offer any apology: 'In what I said to the House I relied on material which I received detailing the content of a direction given to Sergeant McCabe on a related matter which included inviting him to participate in the O'Mahony investigation … there is no basis for the suggestion that the Garda Commissioner in any way misled me in relation to this matter. Nor is there any basis for an allegation that I in any way misled the House.'

The Minister for Justice was, along with the Garda commissioner, adamant that the course on which they had embarked was the correct one. If the Garda whistleblower had had any issues, they had been dealt with appropriately. There was no question of anybody being victimised.

So it went in late February 2014, but it wouldn't be going that way for long. The ground was already shifting, and some in previously unshakable positions were about to feel the tremors.

19

'There have been many words used to describe their actions. But if I
was to use one word, the word I would use is "distinguished".'
Leo Varadkar

There wasn't much respite for Alan Shatter on the political front over
the weeks that followed the setting up of the Guerin Inquiry.

On 13 March the Garda Inspectorate's report into the penalty
points system was published. As outlined in Chapter 17, the results
largely vindicated the concerns that McCabe and Wilson had raised.

Commissioner Callinan released a statement in which he said
that he accepted the Inspectorate's report. He also, belatedly,
addressed the concern over his use of the term 'disgusting' during
his appearance at the Public Accounts Committee: 'I want to clarify
that my use of that term was not in reference to the character of
either Sergeant McCabe or former garda Wilson, but the manner in
which personal and sensitive data was inappropriately appearing in
the public domain without regard to due process and fair procedure,'
he said.

The statement raised a few questions. The commissioner had found it 'disgusting' that 'personal and sensitive data' had wrongly found its way into the public domain. Yet he didn't have any problem with 'personal and sensitive' data about Mick Wallace finding its way into the public domain on live television the previous May, data that he had supplied to Alan Shatter, who did the disseminating. Neither did he express any 'disgust' that sensitive and personal data about Clare Daly had found its way into the public domain, almost certainly from one of his officers, after her arrest in January 2013. The commissioner's disgust was highly selective. His statement was also notable for its omission of any apology to Maurice McCabe and John Wilson.

Interviewed on RTÉ News about the Inspectorate's report, Alan Shatter conceded that the two men had got some things right but again he failed to respond to an invitation to apologise to them. 'I'm not getting into that in any detail. My job as Minister for Justice is to ensure we get it right now.'

The publication of the report created a bit of a stir, but the consensus was that things had moved on. Any talk of an absence of accountability was still emanating only from the Dáil seats occupied by Daly and Wallace.

So it went until a significant intervention from, of all people, a government minister.

Leo Varadkar, the Minister for Transport, Tourism and Sport, has a reputation for being frank. Since his portfolio included road safety, he had taken an interest in the ticket-fixing scandal, but until this point had avoided stepping on the toes of his colleague Alan Shatter.

Then, just as it seemed that the whole political caravan was moving on to the next controversy, up pops Leo.

On Thursday, 20 March, a week after the publication of the Inspectorate's report, Varadkar was attending a road safety conference. On the way in he was asked by a reporter whether the commissioner should withdraw his 'disgusting' remark made at January's Public Accounts Committee meeting.

'I think it is very important to bear in mind that the Garda whistleblowers only released information about people after they tried to use the correct procedures and those procedures failed them and when they did release the information, they did it through Oireachtas members, which is provided for under the Garda Act of 2005,' he said. 'So yes, I do think that remark should be withdrawn.'

Varadkar was the first minister to break ranks. Inside the conference he elaborated on his attitude towards the two whistleblowers: 'Speaking on my own behalf and on behalf of the thousands of families who have had to endure the pain and loss that flows from the death of a loved one on the road, I want to thank Sergeant McCabe and Mr Wilson. They may not have got everything right but they did shine a light into a dark place and forced those who would rather turn a blind eye to face up to the truth. There have been many words used to describe their actions. But if I was to use one word, the word I would use is "distinguished".'

With that word, and those that preceded it on his way into the conference, a controversy that was fleeing for the hills suddenly turned on its heels. Reaction was sought far and wide to the breaking of ranks. Almost immediately there was a stampede from Labour Party ministers to line up beside the voluble young Blueshirt.

There had been mumblings at grassroots level within the Labour Party about the silence over how Callinan was dealing with the whistleblowers. Word had come back to sit tight. But now a Fine Gaeler was stealing a march on the road to righteousness.

Eamon Gilmore and Ruairi Quinn were out of the traps like sleepy greyhounds bursting into life. Both said they agreed that Callinan should apologise. Further calls came from their Labour ministerial colleagues Joan Burton and Pat Rabbitte.

Enda Kenny, over in Brussels, was asked for his reaction. He concentrated not on what the commissioner should do, but on what his ministers should not do. He said he'd prefer that 'if any minister who has an issue to raise that they raise it at the cabinet or raise it where we could have discussions and deal with them, rather than have them aired in public'.

In setting this out, the leader of the government was effectively consigning the matter to that quiet and reserved corner of cabinet confidentiality. Yet the issue was not one of policy. Varadkar was simply expressing an opinion based on what he must have observed as a general disquiet among the public – and particularly among those interested in road safety – about how the whistleblowers had been treated.

Alan Shatter stayed schtum. The issue was now driving a wedge across the cabinet table. He had supported the commissioner all the way, and he could hardly do an about-turn at this stage. If he were to echo the growing calls within the cabinet, then an obvious question would arise about his own obligation to apologise for accusing McCabe and Wilson of not co-operating with the internal Garda inquiry.

Up in the Phoenix Park, the Garda commissioner knew that the game had changed. Throughout Friday he was in contact with officials in the Department of Justice as to whether or not he should respond. There would be conflicting accounts as to what conclusion he reached. Later, it would be claimed that Callinan wanted to apologise, but was advised by the department to sit tight. As more ministers took off in Varadkar's wake, an issue might now arise as to whether Callinan's tenure would survive the next cabinet meeting if he weren't to act.

An apology by the commissioner to a subordinate and a retired member would be a humiliating climb-down. From the outset, Callinan had painted the two whistleblowers as malcontents. He had restricted McCabe's ability to do his job. He had attempted to block McCabe's appearance at the PAC. He had briefed against Mick Wallace, who was one of the few parliamentarians who were listening to McCabe until recent months. And now he was faced with the spectre of apologising for what he regarded as a slip of the tongue.

Callinan had the weekend to think it over. The next cabinet meeting was scheduled for Tuesday, which would give him time enough time to craft any statement he might wish to issue.

Little did he know that events elsewhere were about to relegate his considerations over the apology. A new controversy was blowing in across Enda Kenny's desk.

The Ian Bailey case was coming to a head. Ian Bailey had been on the gardaí's radar since soon after the murder of Frenchwoman Sophie Toscan du Plantier in her west Cork holiday home on 23 December 1996.

Bailey, a then 39-year-old Englishman, was living in the area, working as a journalist, among other things. He became a focus of Garda inquiries within days of the discovery of Toscan du Plantier's badly beaten body.

Twice Bailey was arrested in connection with the murder and brought to Bandon Garda station. On the first of these occasions the media was out in force, obviously having been tipped off. On each occasion Bailey was released without charge. The gardaí sent a file to the DPP, which recommended that there was not sufficient evidence to prosecute. Over the years the DPP, on foot of various developments, examined the file at least another five times. On each occasion the result was the same: no charge.

Those are the bare bones of Bailey's experience with the gardaí and organs of state. From his perspective, he and his artist partner, Jules Thomas, had been subjected to a witch-hunt by the gardaí, arrested under false pretences and harassed for nearly two decades. They also claimed that the gardaí had tried to extract false information from a witness, and attempted to coax another individual to give evidence against Bailey by furnishing him with drugs.

Bailey launched a legal action against the state for wrongful arrest and breach of his constitutional rights. By late 2013 his day in court was beckoning. The case was deep into the discovery process, in which each side has to produce material that the other side deems to be relevant to the case.

Bailey's legal team had requested access to any tape recordings at Bandon station dating from his arrests, some sixteen years earlier. In rooting out those tapes, the gardaí made a discovery that was to have major national repercussions. A practice that had persisted since the 1980s of taping all calls into dozens of stations around the country, including Bandon, had largely gone uncommented on within the force. Down through the years, tapes were used and replaced but very little was examined on the recordings, or so it appeared.

Now the discovery process had brought to light the full possible repercussion of this practice. Confidential calls between members and informants may well be recorded and would be liable for discovery in any possible court action. Even more worryingly, the system could have recorded confidential calls between solicitors and clients who were being detained.

The full import of a practice to which nobody had theretofore given much thought was passed up the ranks to the commissioner in November 2013. Callinan immediately ordered that non-999 calls in stations should no longer be recorded. He also informed the attorney general of his decision; her office was co-ordinating the defence against Bailey's action.

Over the following months the gardaí set up a working group to discover and evaluate the full extent of the practice. On 10 March 2014

Callinan wrote to the secretary general of the Department of Justice informing him of the discovery. There followed further meetings between senior gardaí, people from the Attorney General's office and justice officials. Alan Shatter was not informed of the problem because he had left to attend St Patrick's Day events in Mexico.

All this activity came to a head on the weekend beginning March 21, the day after Varadkar's comments had reopened another simmering controversy. Over that weekend, Attorney General Marie Whelan assessed the situation. She considered it grave, with possible far-reaching implications. One appalling vista was that convicted criminals could exploit the situation to claim that their rights had been breached while under arrest, rendering conviction unsustainable.

In the darkest version of this vista, hundreds of criminals could be set free on what the general public would regard as a technicality. It was time the Taoiseach was informed. Later, a commission of inquiry would rule that Whelan had been 'alarmist' in how she had reacted to the news. That reaction, though, would have far-reaching consequences.

Enda Kenny was being driven to Dublin from his home in Castlebar on Sunday morning when he fielded a call from Marie Whelan. She had something to discuss, but didn't want to do so over the phone. They agreed to meet that afternoon.

They met in Dublin. Whelan told him of the unfolding situation. Surprisingly, the Minister for Justice, the line minister for the gardaí, was not brought into the loop at that point.

Later, when asked why Shatter had not been informed, Marie Whelan said that he 'had become part of the narrative'. Her explanation suggests that, as far as the Taoiseach was concerned, his Minister for Justice was no longer a source from which he would seek counsel on matters concerning the gardaí.

On the Monday evening, Kenny met with Whelan, the secretary general of the Department of the Taoiseach, Martin Fraser, and the secretary general of the Department of Justice, Brian Purcell. At that point Shatter was sent for and informed of what was unfolding. He was surprised at the whole turn of events and the lateness of his inclusion in the process.

A decision was taken to send Purcell out to the home of the Garda commissioner and inform him of the 'concerns' about the unfolding controversy. He was to relay that the Taoiseach was unsure if the commissioner would receive a vote of confidence if the matter of his tenure arose at the following day's cabinet meeting.

Purcell did as he was told. In his position, he was in regular contact with Callinan, but this was the first time he had been to the commissioner's home.

He conveyed to Callinan the 'concern'. For anybody with the slightest interest in politics and how it operates, the highly unusual events of that evening signalled that the Taoiseach was effectively providing room for the Garda commissioner to go.

The following morning Callinan announced his retirement: 'I feel that recent developments were proving to be a distraction from the important work that is carried out by An Garda Síochána on a daily basis for the citizens of the state in an independent and impartial manner,' he said in a statement.

Later that day Kenny announced that he was setting up a commission of inquiry into the tape recording of calls to garda stations, to be chaired by Judge Niall Fennelly. Usually, when an issue arises that may demand an inquiry, a scoping exercise is first conducted to check whether it is necessary to set up a full commission. Notably, that was bypassed in this instance.

The following day Alan Shatter finally apologised to McCabe and Wilson in the Dáil. He told the House that he wished to correct his remark on the Dáil record that the two men 'did not co-operate with the Garda investigations that took place'. He went on, 'It was never my intention to mislead the House and I believe it is appropriate that I apologise to both and withdraw the statements made. It was never my intention to cause any upset and, if any upset was caused, I hope that my correcting the record of the Dáil today will put this matter to rest.'

In delaying the apology over a period of months during which it had become increasingly obvious that McCabe and Wilson's concerns had genuine substance, Shatter had done himself serious political damage. Speculation had it that Enda Kenny had either prompted or strongly encouraged him to make the apology in the wake of the Garda commissioner's departure.

Martin Callinan left office on 25 March 2014 with a number of questions in his wake, particularly about how he had dealt with Maurice McCabe. Any answers to those questions to be found in Callinan's personal possession were lost on the day of the commissioner's departure. Later that afternoon Callinan went to a filing unit in the conference room in Garda HQ where he kept his personal papers. He asked a superintendent to get him some black refuse bags.

After being left alone for a time, he handed the superintendent between eight and ten bags filled to the top and knotted, which he asked to be shredded. The contents, he told the super, were personal papers he had gathered over the years.

The contents of Callinan's phone also disappeared. The Fennelly Commission would be told that the departing commissioner handed in his SIM card on leaving, but held onto the phone because it was his own. The card was subsequently destroyed at HQ. Callinan told Fennelly that he didn't know what became of the phone he had kept; he couldn't locate it to help the commission.

In the years that followed, as more detail emerged about the treatment of Maurice McCabe, some curiosity would attach to the commissioner's decision to destroy his papers, and the fact that his SIM card and phone were beyond retrieval. Were there any secrets in there that might have helped piece together the thoughts, words and actions of senior management of the police force at a time when this Cavan-based sergeant was giving them grief?

The other burning issue about Martin Callinan's departure is whether or not he was sacked. The Taoiseach does not have the power to sack the Garda commissioner. That is a function reserved solely for the cabinet. If Enda Kenny had acted outside his powers in removing the head of the country's police force, he would have had no option but to resign.

The matter as to why and how the Garda commissioner left office was shovelled into the Commission of Inquiry, chaired by retired judge Niall Fennelly, which had been set up to examine the tape recording of calls to stations.

In September 2015 Fennelly published an interim report dealing with Callinan's departure. He ruled that he accepted Kenny's assurances that 'he did not, by sending Mr Purcell to visit the commissioner, intend to put pressure on the commissioner to retire'.

In the next paragraph, though, the retired judge had this to say: 'Seen objectively, however, Mr Purcell's message that the matter of the telephone recording was grave and that the Taoiseach might not, at cabinet the next day, be able to express confidence in the commissioner, delivered without previous notice, in person by the secretary general of the Department of Justice, on behalf of the Taoiseach, at the commissioner's home, late at night, was likely to be interpreted as doing just that.'

So the judge accepts that Kenny's intention wasn't to sack the Garda commissioner, but the commissioner was justified in believing that was exactly what was occurring. Mr Fennelly's carefully worded conclusions were at odds with the general belief that Callinan was sacked because the series of evolving controversies demanded a head to take the heat from the government.

The irony was that Callinan had acted perfectly correctly in how he had dealt with the tape recording issue once it was brought to his attention. (In 2017, Fennelly would deliver a final report on the matter exonerating Callinan.)

Martin Callinan's problem was that he had been the focus of controversy for the preceding two months at least, principally over how he had handled the whistleblower affair. Varadkar's intervention had been the official acknowledgement that the public stock of McCabe and Wilson had risen while that of Callinan had gone south.

Once a fresh controversy broke, most observers believe that Kenny saw an opportunity to get rid of a commissioner who had become an embarrassment.

Delivering a head, from Kenny's point of view, might put a lid on all the Garda controversies. Setting up the commission of inquiry in jig time took the latest controversy out of the public domain and behind the commission's closed doors. And then Shatter's apology should reduce any further demands on that front. That, the wisdom of observers concluded, was most likely Kenny's cobbled-together strategy over those few days.

If it was, it didn't turn out to be very successful. The Garda controversy involving Sergeant Maurice McCabe, his complaints and the treatment to which he was subjected, had a long way to run.

20

'The system grinds down any individual who complains, and pretends there is nothing wrong and does so by rubbishing the complainant, his character and his motives.'
Maurice McCabe

The McCabes shed no tears for the end of Martin Callinan's career. From their perspective, the commissioner had utterly failed to live up to his duty to protect an officer who had come forward with complaints of malpractice. Far from protecting McCabe, the commissioner had sought to play down his complaints and branded his actions as 'disgusting'.

It may have been a coincidence, but following Callinan's appearance at the Public Accounts Committee in January, McCabe's sense of isolation on the job grew. He noticed that fewer colleagues were now willing to be seen even in conversation with him. Some, like the sergeant-in-charge Kieran Williams, stuck by him, but those few were more the exception than the rule. McCabe himself felt it was as if the commissioner's 'disgusting' remark at the Public

Accounts Committee was interpreted by the rank and file members as an instruction to have no truck with this maverick.

The attitude to McCabe among some in the station was writ large in the duty detail for the traffic corps one day in early April. A colleague who was quietly sympathetic to McCabe brought it to his attention.

The duty detail set out how many guards were scheduled for work on each shift, including the number of sergeants and rank and file members.

On the detail in question were listed '5 sergeants 9 guards' and beside it, added in felt pen '+ 1 whistleblower'. The insult demonstrated that those who were ill-disposed towards McCabe were now willing to, within the station, intimidate him on such a forum open to all members who worked there.

McCabe complained, but little was done until the story appeared in the *Irish Examiner*. Thereafter, the investigation was stepped up, but the culprit was never discovered.

A parallel investigation to determine how the incident had reached the media was also launched. As is often the way in these things, far more elbow grease was applied in pursuing the leaker rather than the culprit who had done the deed.

Away from work, McCabe felt he was coming under further pressure. After the establishment of the Seán Guerin Inquiry, he had been contacted by the senior counsel. The terms of reference for the inquiry included a stipulation that Guerin should interview McCabe and anybody else he thought might be relevant.

Before the first interview, McCabe supplied the senior counsel with all the evidence he had in his possession. He also included details of the allegation that had been made against him by his colleague's daughter in 2006.

McCabe was aware that that incident had been used in some quarters in an attempt to discredit what he was highlighting. He was perfectly happy for Guerin to go into it in any detail required. He had nothing to hide, and plenty to highlight.

An arrangement was made to conduct the first interview in the Dunboyne Castle Hotel in County Meath. The pair met and shook hands. Early on, McCabe told the senior counsel that he was an open book.

'Be as hard on me as you like,' McCabe said. 'You can test all my evidence.'

'I intended to anyway,' Guerin replied.

They began going through the various cases that McCabe had highlighted. These included the criminal cases he had handed over to Micheál Martin, and the falsification of PULSE records he had repeatedly come across. The subject that was the focus of much of Guerin's questioning was the Byrne/McGinn internal Garda report, which had initially investigated most of the cases that Guerin was now examining. The interview lasted around four hours.

The second day they met at the same venue. McCabe noticed that the tenor of the questioning had changed. The relatively gentle inquiries of the previous day had been replaced by more direct questioning. In courtroom terms, this was more cross-examination than direct evidence. In particular, Guerin explored the issue of McCabe's motivation in bringing his complaints. The counsel was interested in whether McCabe may have harboured a grudge after resigning as sergeant-in-charge of Bailieboro in March 2008.

When he had reverted to being an ordinary sergeant, he was obliged to return to shift work, rather than the office hours of the sergeant-in-charge.

Now the senior counsel, obviously acting on information, was exploring whether this change in McCabe's working life had awoken a grudge against the force. (Ironically, vacating the sergeant-in-charge office meant he had far less working time because he had habitually worked way beyond the office hours, and, as was seen earlier, was often on hand to attend incident scenes at all hours.)

McCabe was taken aback at the directness of the questioning. Yet Guerin was only doing his job. An experienced criminal lawyer, he had been tasked with examining very serious allegations against elements of An Garda Síochána. To have been less than rigorous in parsing every minute detail of the allegations would have been a dereliction of duty.

At the end of the evening, McCabe felt agitated, as if he had been subjected to something of an inquisitorial pummelling. The pair didn't shake hands as they left the hotel.

That meeting was on a Friday and their next engagement was scheduled for the following Monday. Over the weekend, McCabe reflected on what he had been put through. Clearly somebody had been feeding Guerin a line about McCabe's character. To his mind, it was just the latest attempt to blacken him.

On the Sunday, McCabe decided to write a letter to the senior counsel. He wanted to address the questions that had been raised over his motive, but did not feel confident of including all his thoughts unless he put them on paper.

When they met again on the Monday, McCabe handed over the letter.

Dear Seán,

Looking back on our meetings last week, as a general comment I would like to point out that everything I have done has been to try to adhere to the minimum standards of An Garda Síochána. I am not a perfectionist but I am not a crank. You asked me a question probing whether or not I was motivated by a desire to avoid night duty. This related to when you were questioning me about when I left my sergeant-in-charge position and the implications being that my complaints arose by my reluctance to work on Unit D. I am very surprised by this suggestion. I am unsure as to the source of this suggestion. I would like to say two things about that:

These suggestions or implications are untrue.

It suggests that An Garda Síochána have been feeding a line that my motives are selfish.

It seems to me that other members of the force are trying to convince you that the complaints I have made related to personal agendas.

The whole problem with An Garda Síochána is that anybody who in any way steps out of line and queries malpractice, corruption and bad behaviour in the force is regarded as an outsider with a personal agenda. Both the Smithwick and the Morris Tribunals have highlighted this tendency among the Garda establishment. I have to say that I was particularly disappointed to hear that you had not decided whether you were going to make any contact with the victims of these incidents about which I have complained. If you did, you would immediately realise that for their point of view the incidents were very serious life-changing moments in their lives. Far from me being some nit-picking officious crank, they would convince you that the complete failure of An Garda Síochána to respond appropriately to the crimes which they reported is totally unacceptable and very serious in terms of dereliction of duty for a professional police force.

In the end the real reason for what has happened to me and what has happened in relation to the complaints I have made about Garda conduct needs to be investigated. The system grinds down any individual who complains, and pretends there is nothing wrong and does so by rubbishing the complainant, his character and his motives. The reason I am writing this letter is to put on record my deep concerns that other members of the Force are giving you a distorted and wholly untrue picture of me and the complaints that I have raised in the hope that yet again it will all be swept under the carpet. I set out to be truthful in my dealings with you and to bring all of the issues, pleasant or unpleasant, to your attention. In some of the points that you have put to me (and I acknowledge your right to put any point to me) I strongly believe that there are others being untruthful and I reiterate the point that if you were to make contact with the victims and injured parties you would immediately understand where the truth lies.

Yours Sincerely

Maurice McCabe

Guerin read the letter and made no further comment on it. He moved on to the next item on the agenda. Pretty soon, McCabe realised that Guerin had completed his examination of motive at the previous meeting. Still, he had no regrets about putting down on paper how he had felt about the whole matter.

The two men met one last time after that third meeting. Their final engagement was in the Morrison Hotel in Dublin. When they were done, they had completed nineteen hours of interviews. As they were leaving, McCabe turned to the senior counsel.

'Seán, I'm not squeaky clean,' he said. 'I just wanted reasonable standards. People weren't doing their job and I wasn't going to stay there.' They departed on good terms with a handshake. McCabe was aware that this man now held the power to determine whether or not his crusade over the preceding eight years had been worth it.

Guerin had been given six weeks to complete his task and it looked as if he was on track. The report was due to be delivered in the week beginning Sunday, 4 May.

The week got off to a bad start for Alan Shatter. On Monday word began to leak out that the Data Protection Commissioner (DPC) had ruled that the Minister for Justice had broken the law in revealing personal details about fellow TD Mick Wallace on live television.

The incident in question was the appearance of both men on RTÉ's *Prime Time* a year previously, on publication of the O'Mahony report into the ticket-fixing. Shatter had revealed that Wallace had received the benefit of Garda discretion for using a mobile phone behind the wheel some time earlier.

In the ensuing controversy, Shatter revealed that Commissioner Callinan had furnished him with this information in an informal briefing. Wallace complained to the Data Commissioner, and now a ruling was imminent.

RTÉ confirmed on Tuesday that the DPC, Billy Hawkes, had ruled that Shatter had broken the law. Hawkes exonerated Martin Callinan, saying he was entitled to brief the minister. However, the minister was not entitled to inform the nation on television of a private incident involving Wallace that had not resulted in any charge or penalty.

Shatter, who prided himself on both his knowledge of the law and his integrity, kept the head up. He responded to media queries by saying that he acknowledged the role of the Data Commissioner, but pointed out that the Standards in Public Office Commission had received a similar complaint on the incident and had rejected it. He indicated that he would appeal the data ruling.

He also said that his revelation on *Prime Time* had been a mistake and he wouldn't do it again in similar circumstances.

Hours after the ruling was made public, both the Taoiseach and Tánaiste said that the Minister for Justice retained their full backing. Enda Kenny's declaration on that matter came around the time that his office received its copy of the Guerin report. His advisers parsed it through eyes trained to find any incendiary lines. They found one in Chapter 19. Here, the senior counsel stated that there was little documentary evidence in the Department of Justice to suggest that there was any effort to independently investigate McCabe's complaints. Crucially, the report also stated that Shatter had not acted appropriately in dealing with those complaints.

Kenny was informed later that evening that his minister was in the line of fire. The Taoiseach's mind didn't require much making up.

The following morning at around 9.15, Kenny handed Shatter a copy of the report. The Taoiseach told his minister that the contents were very serious, and could have a major effect on the government. Shatter was given three hours to read the report and come to a conclusion on his own future.

Later that morning the minister attended a ceremony at Arbour Hill cemetery to mark the annual tribute to the leaders of 1916. He appeared to be in upbeat form, walking beside the chief justice, Susan Denham.

After the ceremony he returned to Leinster House and read the report once more before coming to what he regarded as the only decision open to him.

He went into the chamber for the last time as a cabinet minister and fielded some questions relating to the defence element of his portfolio. By then he had already written his resignation letter to Kenny. He set out why he felt it would be necessary to resign in order to not deflect from the work of the government. However, even on his cursory reading of Guerin, Shatter had some grave reservations about its conclusions concerning his conduct: 'I would be less than honest if I did not also record my concerns and reservations in relation to his report and in particular certain conclusions reached by him [Guerin],' Shatter wrote. 'I am anxious that any controversy that may arise on publication of the report does not distract from the important work for the government or create any difficulties for the Fine Gael or Labour parties in the period leading up to the European and local elections. It is my judgment that the only way such controversies can be avoided is by my offering you my resignation from cabinet.'

He went on to offer full-hearted praise to his leader: 'I believe you are an extraordinary Taoiseach doing an extraordinary job during what has been a very difficult time for our country and I want to thank you for all the assistance you have given to me.'

A few hours later, Kenny went into the Dáil and announced the resignation. So ended a ministerial career that had promised much, delivered some, but ultimately went down in flames.

The word began to flash across news and social media forums in the early afternoon of 7 May. Lorraine heard about it at the house. She was stunned, but her immediate thought was that the imminent report must be favourable to Maurice if the Minister for Justice was being forced out. She rang him but got no reply. She rang him again. And again.

Maurice was in a meeting in Mullingar about the bullying to which he had been subjected in the station. His phone was on silent but he could feel it vibrating in his pocket. Once outside, he flicked onto his messages. 'Shatter's resigned,' one read. He rang Lorraine immediately.

The Guerin report was published two days later. On the whole it provided a complete vindication for McCabe. Guerin's remit was to examine the complaints to check whether they merited examining by a full commission of investigation, which would have statutory powers. In all but one of the cases examined, Guerin recommended the full monty.

He was also warm in his praise of the sergeant, what he had done and what he had endured. The first few paragraphs of the concluding chapter of the 336-page report summed up best what the senior counsel had uncovered:

> In any organisation whose members face the significant daily challenges and pressures that must be borne by those whose duty it is to ensure the security of the state and the safety of its citizens, a critical voice is in danger of being heard as a contrary voice. The paradigm of the whistleblower is an unattractive one.

The whistleblower, like the referee from whom he gets his name, is seen as someone who is not on the team. The challenge of accommodating and learning from legitimate criticism is always going to be a difficult one, especially in a disciplined force.

But discipline is not merely the absence of insubordination. Discipline is application to the task at hand. The complaints made by Sergeant McCabe all have their origin in what he perceived to be a failure of An Garda Síochána in Bailieboro District to apply itself with discipline and determination to the investigation and prosecution of crime.

Then he touched on how McCabe had been treated since first making complaints.

I have seen extensive documentation ... which gives cause for concern about the personal and professional consequences for Sergeant McCabe of his having made the complaints examined in this report and other similar complaints. It is not for me to express any view of those matters, except to say that Sergeant McCabe's experience calls for examination.

Guerin also mentioned motivation, eliminating any fear harboured by McCabe that his motivation would be called into question.

It should be recorded here that the Byrne/McGinn report found that: 'No malice on the part of Sergeant McCabe is established in the making of his various complaints.'

Guerin went on,

The time I have spent with Sergeant McCabe in the course of extensive interviews has led me to no different conclusion. That said, the better view in any event is likely to be the testimony of the men and women who worked with Sergeant McCabe in the years before he made the complaints that have been examined in this report.

Maurice and Lorraine were on their way home from having lunch in Oldcastle when the details of the publication were announced on the *One O'Clock News*.

Both were ecstatic. They had been confident that some of the cases would be referred to a full commission, but now it turned out that the senior counsel had concurred with McCabe's analysis that nearly all the cases were extremely serious.

Once home, Lorraine ran to the laptop to attempt to download the full document, eager to get the details, while Maurice began fielding calls from family, friends and his legal team.

Later that day he was informed that the interim Garda commissioner Nóirín O'Sullivan was removing the restrictions that had been placed on his access to PULSE in December 2012, some seventeen months previously.

The giddy high soon gave way to a deeper emotion. Had it all been worth it? The isolation, the bullying, the toll taken on the best years of the couple's lives, as their children grew up. There was no conclusive answer to that question. Events had overtaken them. At each juncture, McCabe could have succumbed to the pressures bearing down on him and his family, admitted that he was beaten, accepted that nothing would change, and who was he – a lowly sergeant in a rural outpost taking on a culture that had persisted for decades?

The question wasn't whether or not it was worth it, but would he do it again? To answer that fully would be to wallow in regret, and what would be the point in that at a time when the final instalment of the mortgaged years looked like it had just been paid.

Or so it seemed. In their hour of what felt like their greatest triumph, little did Maurice and Lorraine McCabe realise that things could and would still actually get worse.

Alan Shatter's resignation was a blow to the government and to Enda Kenny in particular. Until a few months prior to May 2014,

Kenny had placed huge store in Shatter's intelligence and political acumen. At the cabinet table the Taoiseach reportedly allowed far more leeway to Shatter than to any other minister. The men were close, particularly since Shatter had backed Kenny in an attempted leadership coup in 2010.

But Kenny's survival instincts were stronger than any loyalty to his Minister for Justice. With each new Garda controversy, as he read each new headline, Kenny inched away from his minister, until finally accepting that he would have to stand down.

As with Martin Callinan, Alan Shatter could legitimately claim that he was effectively sacked in the wrong. Guerin had made an adverse finding against him without ever allowing him to represent himself or defend his actions. As such, Shatter could claim that he was denied natural justice. In time, the Court of Appeal would agree with such a conclusion. That would be over two years later. Shatter's actions in referring on McCabe's complaints would also receive the stamp of approval from the O'Higgins Commission, set up as a result of the Guerin report, which would also complete its work in 2016.

So, retrospectively, the former minister could claim that on the specifics over which he was forced to resign, he had been shafted.

That, however, would be to ignore the wider context in which it was deemed necessary for him to go. By the time Guerin reported, Enda Kenny had lost a lot of confidence in his Minister for Justice. Too much had been handled ineptly. One year previously there was the attempt to tarnish Mick Wallace on live television over benefiting from Garda discretion. Then in October 2013, when the Comptroller and Auditor General's report into the ticket-fixing appeared to dispute the findings of the internal Garda report, Shatter could have taken a step back. Instead, he went into the Dáil and, under privilege, accused McCabe and Wilson of not co-operating with the internal Garda investigation.

Repeatedly, he had refused to apologise for that until finally relenting in the days after the sacking of his kindred spirit in controversy, Martin Callinan. So while the tide of political and public opinion had turned towards the whistleblowers, Shatter appeared to be standing firm beside the commissioner, until the commissioner had to resign.

There was also the GSOC bugging matter. In time, a report from retired judge John Cooke would conclude there was no evidence that the offices of GSOC had been bugged. But Shatter's problem was that he leaped in immediately once the story broke to accuse GSOC of behaving unprofessionally. This was an astonishing reaction to the possibility that the confidentiality of the body overseeing the gardaí may have been compromised.

Each new controversy had further eroded Shatter's political credibility. Eventually the Taoiseach had arrived at a point where it would have taken little to push his erstwhile golden boy overboard. It would have been perfectly plausible for Kenny to stand by Shatter in the wake of Guerin's report. Instead, he acted with the ruthless efficiency of a political leader viewing the bigger picture.

The publication of Guerin, the subsequent departure of Shatter and his replacement by Frances Fitzgerald were also followed by another development. The government announced that an independent review would be established to examine over 200 allegations of malpractice against the gardaí.

These complaints had emerged largely through the work of Mick Wallace and Clare Daly since they initiated the meetings of concerned citizens the previous year. For those involved, it offered the prospect that long-standing grievances would be redressed. Some of these complaints had little substance, notwithstanding the genuine and heartfelt grievance of complainants. Others were serious matters that definitely demanded further scrutiny. Over the following year the number of complaints would swell to over 300. Eventually, the panel of lawyers reviewing the cases would recommend that around seventy of them were worthy of further investigation.

Another initiative announced in the wake of Geurin was a review of the workings of the Department of Justice. The report on the review was delivered on 28 July 2014. It was pretty scathing of some practices within the department and led to the secretary general Brian Purcell stepping aside.

2014 was a transformative year for Maurice McCabe and his family. When the year dawned, he was still an anonymous figure within the force, known as the whistleblower. By the end of January his identity had been revealed and he had appeared before an Oireachtas committee to voice his complaints about ticket-fixing.

Thereafter McCabe's original complaints about criminal investigations and corrupt PULSE records were taken out and dusted down through the parliament. A scoping inquiry vindicated McCabe, prompting the setting up of a full commission of investigation. Finally, the issues he had brought to management in 2008 were to get a full and thorough examination. Two figures whom he had regarded as being hostile to his efforts, Martin Callinan and Alan Shatter, were no longer in office.

But in September 2014 the ticket-fixing issue, which was supposed to have been long resolved, raised its head again. A colleague made representations to McCabe about further abuses and he in turn passed the information on to HQ.

Another examination of the system was set up by Nóirín O'Sullivan and this time McCabe was temporarily seconded to the Professional Standards Unit of the force to root out the malpractice. It was all a long way from not even being contacted by the internal inquiry the previous year.

To top off 2014, it was announced in November that McCabe and John Wilson were to receive People of the Year awards for their work in road safety. The awards were presented at a televised event in Dublin's Citywest Hotel on 6 December.

The citation for the award spoke volumes.

> Maurice McCabe and John Wilson are awarded for their bravery in speaking out to ensure the law was upheld and that the public receive the police service that it requires. Both men jeopardised their professional careers in An Garda Síochána and made many personal sacrifices by speaking out against practices within the force that they believed to be unjust.
>
> McCabe and Wilson's desire to tell the truth was met with resistance on many levels and on many occasions, yet they pursued the issues with integrity and bravery, ultimately leading to increased scrutiny of practices within public bodies, as well as a full review of Ireland's police force.

In a rare interview to mark the occasion, McCabe laid out what his appearance at the Public Accounts Committee and all that flowed from it had meant to him and his family: 'It was an incredible experience, going in and telling somebody what was going on,' he told the *Irish Examiner*. 'I said to them that even though it had been going on for 18 months, that was first time that I'd been interviewed by anybody about what was going on with the penalty points.'

He also reflected on the cost.

'Six years, that's what it took out of our lives. It's shocking when you think about it. But I believe I did my job. I did my duty and that's all that matters.'

So ended 2014. He was entitled to believe all he and his family had been put through was at an end. Within less than six months, however, Maurice McCabe would be abruptly disabused of such a comforting notion.

21

'I don't know what's on the tape, but it's not that shite.
I never said that.' *Maurice McCabe*

McCabe could feel the knot in his stomach tightening. As the lawyers batted back and forth in front of him, he began to feel nauseous. An ugliness he had assumed had been put to sleep was now gearing up to wreak havoc on his life once more.

It was day two of the O'Higgins Commission, Friday, 15 May 2015. There were at least thirty people in the room, an air-conditioned space in the Smithfield Business Centre, a stone's throw from the Four Courts. Lawyers Michael McDowell and Colm Smyth were alternately addressing the chair, retired judge Kevin O'Higgins.

The O'Higgins Commission had been set up on the recommendations of the Guerin report. Kevin O'Higgins was a well-regarded judge, recently retired after a career on the High Court bench and the European Court of First Instance.

Before 2004 a full statutory inquiry would have taken the form of a public tribunal. All evidence would have been heard in public, with everybody lawyered up at great expense. In the 1990s and early 2000s the cost of a number of long-running tribunals had caused public outrage. The only winners appeared to be lawyers.

As a result, a new model of statutory inquiry – the commission of investigation – was introduced in law in 2004 by then Minister for Justice, Michael McDowell.

This allowed for the inquiry to be conducted in private, minimising the legal costs. It also did away with the public airing of allegations in evidence that could be highly damaging yet without foundation.

The format turned out to be a success. A number of commissions, most prominently in relation to clerical sex abuse, used the new model. Costs were greatly reduced and the process expedited.

There was one drawback, however. Just as there were good reasons to hear evidence in private, there was also an argument that such a model went against the instinct that justice had to be seen to be done. That had not become an issue before the setting up of the O'Higgins Commission.

But on 15 May 2015, day two of O'Higgins, Maurice McCabe was getting the impression that what was unravelling behind the closed doors of the commission appeared to be in direct conflict with public positions being taken by the management of An Garda Síochána.

The Garda commissioner, Nóirín O'Sullivan, was telling the world that Maurice McCabe was a valued member of the force to whom she was well disposed, but behind closed doors, her counsel appeared to be putting forward the proposition that he was a man bearing a grudge. And to illustrate the case, the commissioner's counsel was harking back to an allegation that dated from nearly a decade earlier.

The allegation that had been made against McCabe by a colleague's daughter in 2006 has been dealt with in Chapter 3, but its emergence in the O'Higgins Commission requires that it is now revisited in greater detail.

The colleague in question had applied two years previously for the job of sergeant-in-charge at Bailieboro to which McCabe had been appointed. In January 2006 the colleague had been one of three members disciplined after McCabe reported how they had commandeered a squad car after drinking and had driven to attend the scene of a tragic suicide. In early December 2006, McCabe was told by Superintendent Maura Lernihan that the daughter of that colleague had made an allegation against him. The 14-year-old girl – who is now known as Ms D – was claiming that, years earlier, McCabe had touched her in an inappropriate manner.

Both the colleague and his daughter denied that the history between him and McCabe had anything whatsoever to do with the allegation.

McCabe got the news on his day off. After receiving it, he travelled to Dublin to meet Lorraine and the kids as per an arrangement.

For Lorraine, the day in question is burned into her memory.

'We were in Blanchardstown [shopping centre],' she said. 'We had four [children] at that stage and all of them had to wear glasses. So once a year we went for a check-up in the Mater for glasses. Maurice was delayed at work that day so we arranged to meet later.

'We met up and we all went to Eddie Rocket's for the kids. Maurice had nothing to eat. I was up to ninety trying to look after four kids so I didn't notice that he wasn't himself at all. Then Hannah, our eldest, asked what was wrong with Daddy. He was crying. He hadn't told me by then, but then when we got home he did and it was desperate, awful, the most awful feeling you can imagine.'

Prior to making her allegation in December 2006, Ms D had a history of engagement with the child protection services. The previous year she had been referred to the service over behavioural issues, which included alleged sexual behaviour with a young man, and running away from home.

From mid-2005 into 2006, Ms D engaged on a number of occasions with child counsellors and psychiatrists. At no point during these engagements did she ever make an allegation against McCabe. Then, in December 2006, she made the complaint about an alleged historic incident with him.

The divisional officer, Chief Superintendent Colm Rooney, appointed Inspector Noel Cunningham to investigate. Two statements were taken from Ms D, on 6 December and 21 December 2006. They differed in some detail, which is not unusual, but the general tenor was the same. She described being in the McCabes' home in 1998, around Christmas time. Their respective families knew each other.

The girl described the start of a game of hide and seek, in which Maurice had agreed to play with them while the girl's parents and Lorraine were in the kitchen. The girl said she was hiding in the sitting room.

She alleged that Maurice McCabe came in and rubbed up against her inappropriately.

This allegation was being made by Ms D when she was fourteen, about an incident that she said had occurred when she was six. McCabe denied vehemently that the incident, or anything that could even be interpreted as being mistaken for such an incident, ever occurred.

The girl's family had been in his house a few times when he had served as an ordinary guard in the 1990s. Beyond that, as far as he was concerned, the whole thing was in the realm of fantasy.

The investigation was carried out quickly. A file was sent to the DPP in February 2007 recommending that no prosecution was merited.

The report contained the summation, 'Taking all matters into consideration, including the question of whether the event, if it happened, constituted a breach of the criminal law, it is felt that there is no grounds for a criminal prosecution.'

As mentioned in Chapter 3, the local state solicitor Rory Hayden, agreed with Noel Cunningham, noting that the incident, if it occurred, amounted to "horseplay and no more".

The DPP also agreed. The direction, received on 5 April 2007 said no prosecution, and also raised questions about the credibility of the allegation.

"There are no admissions," the DPP letter to Hayden stated. "The incident as described by the injured party is vague. It appears that it was only when she was 11/12 that she decided that whatever occurred was sexual in nature.

"Even if there wasn't a doubt over her credibility the incident that she described does not constitute a sexual assault or indeed and assault. Further, the account given to her cousin differs in a number of respects to that given to her parents and the guards."

Hayden contacted McCabe and related the good news to him. This was not an official notification, but was uncontroversial in the context of the local state solicitor's dealings with the gardai.

Over a month later, on 8 May, McCabe was officially informed of the decision by Inspector Cunningham. The inspector had attempted to contact McCabe on 24 April, but they ultimately didn't manage to get together until the later date.

McCabe had an issue over the fact that he had to wait up to nineteen days – from 5 April to 24 April – before Cunningham contacted him to relay such a huge decision in his life. Given that it was such a serious matter, he felt he should have been informed immediately.

Cunningham has given evidence that the delays were justified. In the first instance, he had been filling in as district officer in Bailieboro for an extended period when the result had been delivered to his office in Monaghan. He says he did not get the result until he returned to Monaghan on 24 April and then acted immediately. Moreover, he says that once he got the result he attempted to meet with McCabe, but McCabe put off the meeting for a number of days.

When they did meet in a hotel in Bailieboro, McCabe was accompanied by a sergeant who was a representative of the Association of Garda Sergeants and Inspectors. By that stage, it would appear that he had developed a grievance over how the matter was being handled. Understandably, the whole affair had brought huge stress on him and Lorraine.

Both McCabe and the girl's father continued to work in the district, albeit in different stations. On at least a couple of occasions they found themselves at the same conference or meeting.

None of that could have been easy on McCabe, because he was of the firm belief that his soured relationship with this other member was behind the accusation. As for the other member, the continuing proximity to McCabe must not have been easy. If this man believed his daughter's version of events, how could he sit easily next to the man whom she had accused?

So it went in Bailieboro's cauldron of policing. The following October, Ms D and her mother travelled to the station looking to speak to McCabe. He was down the town, and was returning when they confronted him outside the station. A colleague arrived and ushered him inside. The whole thing was highly unsettling for McCabe. He thought the matter had been dealt with.

By then the merry-go-round of superintendents at Bailieboro had moved on to the next transient occupant. In August 2007 Maura Lernihan was replaced by Superintendent Michael Clancy.

McCabe suggested to the new superintendent that Ms D's family must not have received the full details of the DPP's direction. A course of action that emerged from discussions between them was to see if the girl's family could receive the full direction from the DPP. This, McCabe felt, would finally clear the air, as he believed the direction had shown in the clearest terms that the allegation had absolutely no foundation.

As it would turn out, that wasn't possible. There were strict rules in place about who can view directions from the DPP (which have since been relaxed). If the guards were seen to be bending the rules for two of their own in that regard, it could create major problems. In any event, McCabe didn't want any rules broken. He accepted that it wasn't possible and tried to put the whole episode behind him.

Within the HSE and its child protection services, a trail of poor management was to ensure that it would be ten years before McCabe's name was fully cleared and the allegation deemed to lack credibility.

McCabe's complaints of malpractice surfaced over a year after the December 2006 allegation. Despite the consequent change of attitude towards him among many members in Cavan/Monaghan, the allegation was not revisited in any form. The Byrne/McGinn report made no mention of it and clearly stated that McCabe's motive for his complaint was entirely pure.

Then, nearly seven years after the matter had concluded, a series of newspaper articles began referencing an incident involving a garda. The articles started in April 2014, after the Guerin inquiry had been set up. They were written in the *Irish Independent* under the byline of Paul Williams, the country's leading crime reporter who was known to have excellent Garda contacts.

They quoted a young woman who claimed she had been sexually assaulted by a garda. She had made the allegation to gardaí in 2006, relating to an incident some years previously. She said she was unhappy with how it had been handled. No names were mentioned. To have named McCabe in the story would have been libellous.

The woman quoted said that she wanted her case included in the Guerin Investigation along with the other matters about which McCabe had complained. She also said she wanted to meet Micheál Martin to that effect.

Martin agreed to meet her in Leinster House in April 2014. He listened to her and passed on her concerns to Enda Kenny. Kenny in turn passed the matter on to the Department of Justice, which had set up a review group to examine around 200 complaints of Garda conduct that had come to light in the wake of the McCabe controversy. The review group would ultimately rule that the Garda investigation into the woman's allegation had been handled correctly.

Micheál Martin did not insist that the woman's allegation be included in Guerin, as she had reportedly wanted.

Further articles appeared in the *Irish Independent* in the weeks following the meeting with Martin. In one, the woman said the incident, alleged to have occurred in 1998 when she was six, had sent her into a 'downward spiral'. She also stated that she was considering taking legal action against the guard whom she alleged had assaulted her. No legal action was ever initiated.

The last of the articles appeared on 19 June 2014. On the same day, Alan Shatter, who had resigned as Minister for Justice a month earlier, made a contribution in the Dáil related to the Garda controversies. In the course of his speech, he said the following about the forthcoming O'Higgins Commission that was being set up in the wake of Guerin: 'If the statutory inquiry is to be comprehensive, it should include all cases dealt with in Bailieborough Garda Station which have given rise to complaint. There is a matter which has been the subject of articles in the *Irish Independent*, which included a report of Deputy Micheál Martin meeting an individual who alleges she was the victim of a sexual assault and her complaint was not recorded on the PULSE system and did not result in a prosecution.

'I understand from the newspaper report that Deputy Martin was to provide information on this matter to the Taoiseach and I presume he has done so. This case should clearly form part of any statutory inquiry.'

Some years later it was to emerge that Shatter had met with the girl two days before making that speech. The meeting had been arranged by Paul Williams.

In any event, the McCabes must have believed that that was the end of the matter. There was no question of Garda malpractice in the investigation. The DPP's ruling had been emphatic. No media outlet had dared mention Maurice McCabe by name, which ensured that the vast majority of the public had no idea it related to him. The tenor of the articles, and quotes from the woman in question, suggested an allegation that was far more serious than had actually been the case. Still, the matter appeared to be closed.

As far as the McCabes were concerned, it had been an effort to resurrect an eight-year-old allegation, dating from an alleged incident a further eight years before that, in order to discredit McCabe. If that was the motivation for it, then it hadn't worked.

Then, in May 2015, on day two of the O'Higgins Commission hearings, the past was once more dragged out as Exhibit A in the case against Maurice McCabe.

The commission was hearing evidence in relation to the first criminal case to be examined when the issue of McCabe's motivation came up.

Counsel for the Garda commissioner, Colm Smyth, indicated that it would be his client's case that McCabe had borne a grudge against the gardaí and this motivated him to make the complaints of malpractice. There followed a series of exchanges between Smyth, McCabe's lawyer Michael McDowell, and the chairman, Judge Kevin O'Higgins.

McDowell reacted angrily to the suggestion that McCabe's motivation would be under the microscope.

> **Michael McDowell:** I am shocked that it is coming from counsel instructed by the Commissioner for a variety of reasons, very, very deeply shocked that this line of questioning is coming in this way, but so be it, we can deal with that. But if now his

[Maurice McCabe's] character and his motivation is about to be impugned, I am entitled as a matter of simple constitutional and natural justice, firstly, to have full notice of the attack that is going to be made on his character or his credibility or his motivation and I must be in a position to know what is coming.

After further exchanges, the judge set out what was unfolding as he saw it.

Judge O'Higgins: The question of credibility of witnesses can be probed in the normal fashion in relation to clearly the accuracy of somebody's memory bears on the credibility of their evidence and so forth but if it goes beyond that, if it is the Commissioner's case that she wishes to impugn the motivation and the integrity of Sergeant McCabe, if those are the instructions that you have, Mr Smyth, I think you should say so in so many words.

Colm Smyth: Do you want me to respond?

Judge O'Higgins: Please.

Smyth: I have instructions from the Commissioner, Judge. This is an inquiry dealing with the allegations of malpractice and corruption on a grand scale by members of An Garda Síochána.

Judge O'Higgins: No, this part of the Inquiry—

Smyth: I appreciate that but my instructions are to challenge the integrity certainly of Sergeant McCabe and his motivation.

Judge O'Higgins: The integrity?

Smyth: His motivation and his credibility in mounting these allegations of corruption and malpractice.

Judge O'Higgins: There is a difference. In relation to the question of credibility, as I have already indicated, that is an everyday matter. One can suggest to a witness that his evidence shouldn't be believed because of something but an attack on somebody's credibility, on his motivation or integrity is something that really doesn't form part of this Inquiry. It would be necessary I think for you to go further and say that the complaints and the actions of Sergeant McCabe on your instructions were motivated by . . . his motivation was dishonest or wrong. In other words that he made these allegations not in good faith but because he was motivated by malice or some such motive and that impinges on his integrity. If those are your instructions from the Commissioner, so be it.

Smyth: So be it. That is the position, Judge.

Judge O'Higgins: Those are your—

Smyth: Yes, as the evidence will demonstrate, Judge.

Judge O'Higgins: Okay, those are your—

Smyth: If we are allowed to proceed.

Judge O'Higgins: Those are your instructions from the Commissioner.

Smyth: Those are my instructions, Judge.

Judge O'Higgins: Very good.

Smyth: I mean this isn't something that I am pulling out of the sky, Judge, and I mean I can only act on instructions.

Judge O'Higgins: If those are your instructions, so be it, we will have to deal with them then.

McDowell: If that is the case, I must have advance knowledge of the so-called evidence.

Some minutes later, the judge brought up the issue again.

Judge O'Higgins: But you are attacking his motivation and you are attacking his integrity.

Smyth: Right the way through.

Judge O'Higgins: Full stop.

Smyth: Yes, full stop.

Judge O'Higgins: So be it.

Then, later again, the judge wanted further clarification. He suggested adjourning so that Smyth could go and check his instructions, to be sure that it was to be the case that McCabe's motivation and integrity should be attacked. The repeated efforts of the judge to seek clarity show how important this point was. The commission was set up to examine the alleged malpractice, but now it seemed that the Garda commissioner was instructing her barrister that the allegations themselves were tainted by McCabe's personal grudge.

Following the brief adjournment, Smyth reappeared.

Smyth: My instructions are reconfirmed.

Judge O'Higgins: Very good. Your instructions, as I understand them, are that Sergeant McCabe acted as he did for improper motives.

Smyth: Yeah.

Judge O'Higgins: And that his integrity is being challenge in that respect.

Smyth: In that respect.

Judge O'Higgins: Okay, fine, so be it.

It couldn't have been clearer, or emphasised any more. The lawyer acting for the Garda commissioner was instructed to attack McCabe's motivation in bringing his complaints. O'Higgins had been told there would be evidence to inform the attack. McCabe's lawyer, McDowell, had demanded sight of the evidence and that was to be provided the following day.

McCabe could hardly believe what he saw unfolding. He thought he was past all this. Out in public, Commissioner Nóirín O'Sullivan had praised him. She had temporarily appointed him to the Professional Standards Unit to help sort out the problems over ticket-fixing. She had advocated strongly that members who see wrong-doing should speak out.

Behind closed doors, however, hidden from public view, it appeared to McCabe that the Commissioner was gunning for him.

He felt sick to his stomach. After seven years, this was a new departure. At no point during the investigations into his complaints in Bailieboro had it ever been suggested that he was motivated by a grudge.

Now they were attempting to drag up the allegation from nearly a decade before and using it as a stick to beat him with.

There had been nothing about his motive or the allegation in the Byrne/McGinn investigation. That inquiry ran between 2008 and 2010. The inquiry interviewed a huge number of members in the division, including those whom McCabe had implicated in his complaints. The report of the inquiry explicitly stated that there was no issue over McCabe's motivation. Whatever problems McCabe had with Byrne/McGinn, the report never for a second attempted to suggest that he was going after members because of a personal grudge.

Now this. McCabe spoke with McDowell and his solicitor Kathryn Ward at the end of the day, but as he got into his car he felt dazed.

He drove to the station in Mullingar, where he met the local superintendent. There had been an earlier discussion that McCabe might take control of the traffic unit in Mullingar. Now, he told his superintendent, he couldn't do it. To his mind, he had just heard that the Garda commissioner was questioning his motives, attacking his character. How could he accept a form of promotion under those circumstances? How could he trust anything to do with the force after that? He still loved being a guard, but he was coming to hate being in the Guards.

The weekend that followed saw him plunge the depths of despair. On the Sunday night he curled up on the couch in front of the television, wishing above all else that he wouldn't have to go back into the Smithfield Business Centre the following day to face this ordeal.

The hearing resumed on Monday. Before it commenced, McCabe's lawyers were handed a document that had been prepared in the Chief State Solicitor's Office, which was acting for the commissioner. This laid out the case that the Garda commissioner's counsel would be making that McCabe bore a grudge against elements of the force.

The five-page document was divided into 20 paragraphs. It set out the background to McCabe's arrival in Bailieboro, and how the girl's father had applied unsuccessfully for the sergeant-in-charge job.

Then it dealt with the allegation and investigation, including the fact that the DPP 'communicated the decision not to initiate any form of action against Sergeant McCabe and the observation was made that it was doubtful that the allegation could constitute a crime at all.

Later, though, the document dealt with McCabe's request to Superintendent Clancy that the colleague's family be given the full direction from the DPP, because of both parties having to work in close proximity to each other.

Clancy was unable to accommodate that request, the document pointed out. Later, McCabe made his complaints of malpractice at Bailieboro. The officer initially appointed to examine some of his complaints was Superintendent Noel Cunningham, the same man who had investigated the allegation by the girl against McCabe.

Then, crucially, the document suggested that McCabe had disclosed to Cunningham that he bore a grudge.

The penultimate paragraph in the Chief State Solicitor's document laid out the details of a meeting in Mullingar station between McCabe, Cunningham and a Sergeant Yvonne Martin in August 2008.

'Notes were taken at the meeting and countersigned by Sergeant Martin and a detailed report of the meeting was prepared by Superintendent Cunningham and its contents agreed by Sergeant Martin, and forwarded to Chief Superintendent Rooney. In the course of this meeting Sergeant McCabe advised Superintendent Cunningham that the only reason he made the complaint against Superintendent Clancy was to force him to allow Sergeant McCabe to have the full details of the DPP directions conveyed to him.'

The document was the basis for the case against McCabe's motivation and, O'Higgins had been told, was a guide to evidence that would be heard. If there was to be evidence, the crucial aspect would be what transpired at the Mullingar meeting. If, as the document stated, McCabe had expressed a grudge against Superintendent Clancy, then evidence to that effect would have to be heard.

It never got that far. Once McCabe read the document, he looked up at his legal team and said, 'I taped that meeting.'

The lawyer and solicitors regarded him as if he had just arrived from Pluto. You taped the meeting? Why didn't you say so? What's on it?

'I don't know what's on the tape, but it's not that shite. I never said that. It's not true.'

McCabe told his team that he had never thought the meeting was relevant. Nothing had come of it and it didn't have an impact on any element of his case. That was, not until now.

If McCabe could produce the tape, it would not only back up his story, but would expose the case being made against him as, to put it at its mildest, wildly inaccurate.

The hearing resumed and before long the matter of McCabe's motivation arose again. McDowell took the opportunity to provide his opinion on the document that he had been handed in, which purported to cast serious aspersions on his client.

> **McDowell:** I have to say, Judge, and I hope that this does get back to the Commissioner because it is utterly and completely inexplicable, bearing in mind the things she has said and done in public in relation to my client, including appointing him to the professional standards unit of An Garda Síochána on a limited basis in recent times. I find this a despicable document, I have to say.

Once McCabe was able to confirm the existence of the tape, his counsel contacted Judge Higgins' counsel, Sean Gillane. The element of the hearings related to McCabe's motivation was suspended.

McCabe provided the recording and transcript to the commission, which in turn confirmed its veracity. Two days later Judge O'Higgins told the hearing that he had now heard the recording and was satisfied of its veracity. He pointed out that the recording was in conflict with the document prepared by the Chief State Solicitor's Office. All the evidence confirmed that McCabe had not expressed any grudge against any member of An Garda Síochána as the reason for highlighting malpractice.

And there the matter lay. There was no further exploration of an issue that on the face of it was of vital importance. Judge O'Higgins had been informed – and had himself repeatedly requested clarification on the issue – that a case would be made that the substance of his inquiry, the complaints of malpractice, was contaminated by McCabe's nefarious motive.

This case was being made by the head of the police force through her lawyer. The judge had received a document purporting to be the basis for the case against McCabe from the state's law agency, the Chief State Solicitor's Office. The document implied that there would be sworn evidence from other police officers to back up the case. Now it all appeared to be a bottle of smoke.

Despite the seriousness of what had been unfolding, the commission did not re-examine the matter. There was no exploration of how the state's law agency could have produced a document that was potentially hugely damaging to a citizen, who was also a serving garda, yet which was shown to be false.

There was no more than a cursory exploration of what had transpired at the contentious meeting in Mullingar in 2008. There was no evidence called from the Garda commissioner as to why she might have believed that McCabe was motivated by a grudge. It was as if the whole affair had not occurred, or was something not relevant to the Maurice McCabe story.

In November 2015, on the day before Garda commissioner Nóirín O'Sullivan was to give brief evidence relating to her peripheral role in McCabe's complaints in 2008, her lawyer addressed the commission. Judge O'Higgins had asked him to clarify anything that had occurred earlier, referring to the exchanges on day two the previous May.

Smyth pointed out that he had not been the one to describe McCabe's motivation as involving 'malice'.

> **Smyth:** As far as the commissioner was concerned, at all stages I had instructions to challenge Sergeant McCabe in relation to motivation and credibility.

> **Judge O'Higgins:** And integrity?

Smyth: No, there was no mention of integrity.

Later the lawyer said any mention of integrity 'was an error on my part'.

Judge O'Higgins: Well, that is the clarification I sought. So the position now is that his motive is under attack, credibility is under attack from the commissioner but not his integrity.

Smyth: Just to be clear about it. The credibility in so far as he made these allegations of corruption and malpractice. There is no question about that.

Later in the exchange Smyth gave a fuller explanation. 'Judge, the Commissioner has a duty of care to all members. She wasn't acquiescing. She has to hold the balance between, on the one part she has Sergeant McCabe who she has a concern for and his welfare and on the other hand she has a concern for the Superintendents who are under her control. She has to hold the balance. She cannot come down on the side of Sergeant McCabe and say I agree with everything he says without challenge.'

The clarification didn't clarify an awful lot. There was nothing in it about the conflict uncovered by McCabe's recording. Nothing about whether or not a mistake had been made or how one could have been made. Nothing about an apology to McCabe if there was a misunderstanding at issue.

The lawyer's instructions about the commissioner being obliged to strike a balance between McCabe and the superintendents who could have been implicated in the alleged malpractice was also curious.

Smyth was acting not just for Commissioner O'Sullivan, but also for some of the senior officers whom McCabe had complaints against, including Superintendents Cunningham and Clancy and retired Chief Superintendent Rooney.

O'Sullivan represented the force from a corporate and organisational perspective. There were conflicts between some of her senior officers and one of her sergeants. How could she strike a balance if she was sharing counsel with the senior officers? She couldn't, for instance, have the senior officers cross-examined. The optics, if nothing else, pointed to the commissioner lining up beside her senior officers who were in conflict with McCabe.

From McCabe's perspective, that is precisely what was unfolding at the O'Higgins Commission. The exchanges on day two of the commission, and all that flowed from it, were not referenced in the final report.

Legal sources consulted in the research for this book have suggested that there may be a credible explanation for the exclusion of the matter. If Judge O'Higgins had referenced it, he would have been obliged to provide the full background, including details of the allegation against McCabe dating from 2006. That would have been unfair. At the time the whole affair was not in the public domain and there was no reason to believe that it might end up there. To give public airing in an official report to a historic allegation, found to be without legal substance, would be to give the whole affair unwarranted oxygen.

But the outcome did leave some disturbing questions hanging in the air. What if McCabe didn't have that recording? Would evidence have been heard alleging that he held a grudge? Would the evidence have been believed? Would the evidence have affected the content and tenor of the final report? What impact would it have had on McCabe's credibility? What impact would it have had on his life?

22

'Sergeant McCabe has shown courage and performed a genuine public service at considerable personal cost. For this he is due the gratitude, not only of the general public, but also of An Garda Síochána.'
Judge Kevin O'Higgins

The events of the first few days of the O'Higgins Commission set the tenor for McCabe's involvement thereafter. He was alert at every juncture, waiting for the next ambush, as he saw it.

This increased the pressure during his frequent appearances in the witness box, and even his daily attendance. Pretty soon, he was being medicated for the stress.

Each day could bring a new attack or ambush, and many did. There were attempts to implicate him in a number of his own complaints, according to three different sources who were present at the hearings.

The commission was set up to examine the manner in which criminal investigations were handled in the Cavan/Monaghan division. Yet at times, over the eight months of hearings, McCabe saw that much of the focus was directed at attacking him, rather than on the substantive issue. None of this emanated from the commission itself. In fact, in any cases where there were attempts to blame McCabe, O'Higgins ultimately ruled that he bore no culpability.

One tactic that was constantly deployed was to suggest that because McCabe was sergeant-in-charge at Bailieboro, he had ultimate responsibility for the crimes being investigated. This was erroneous. The sergeant-in-charge is not responsible for investigations carried out by particular units at a station. The role is more administrative and represents a link to senior management.

In a submission at the end of the hearings, McCabe's legal team put it as follows: 'It is important to state in these submissions that when Sergeant McCabe reported the various matters to the authorities in An Garda Síochána, in particular the reports that he made to the Byrne/McGinn investigation, no case was ever made by any member of An Garda Síochána or any member in a position of authority that the matters as reported by Sergeant McCabe were in fact his responsibility, in fact his fault.

'This concept lately came or was brought into existence at the hearing …. In any event, when Sergeant McCabe departed from his post on the 19th March [2008] the malpractice and wrong-doing continued.'

Other attempts to divert blame onto McCabe also surfaced at the commission. It was suggested that he had exaggerated the alleged offences in the Lorraine Browne case. This was the woman who complained that three males on her minibus had abused other passengers and had assaulted at least one of them. McCabe categorised the alleged assault as a sexual assault, since it had involved grabbing a woman's bottom.

The attempts to portray the categorisation as exaggerated came to naught when another sergeant gave evidence that he too had categorised it as a sexual assault, based on Ms Browne's statement.

The Lakeside Manor endangerment case also saw McCabe targeted. This was the case in which a driver reversed recklessly towards patrons and security personnel who were standing at the door of a nightclub.

McCabe had assisted one of the investigating officers by accompanying him to Dublin to check out a possible lead. At the commission there were attempts to portray McCabe as having been in charge of the investigation. O'Higgins rejected those efforts.

Then there was the urine in the vinegar bottle in Cafolla's restaurant. There was an attempt to suggest that McCabe knew the details of this case six weeks after it had occurred, yet did nothing for another six months. He was able to show through contemporaneous records, however, that this claim was entirely false. In her evidence, Majella Cafolla was reported to be effusive in her praise of how McCabe had handled the complaint once it came to his attention.

There were further efforts to blame McCabe in the handling of the Mary Lynch case, where Ms Lynch, a taxi driver, was assaulted by Jerry McGrath, who went on to murder Sylvia Roche Kelly. Again, the judge rejected all these attempted accusations.

However, despite repeated efforts of this nature, there was little in the final report to reflect that there appeared to be a pattern at work.

A number of factors relating to how the commission was constituted also impinged on McCabe. The issue of representation has been touched on in the previous chapter. Colm Smyth was counsel for both the Garda commissioner and for senior gardaí in Cavan/Monaghan against whom McCabe had made allegations. This ensured that Smyth was not in a position to cross-examine the senior officers on behalf of the commissioner, who is the nominal guardian of the force. In the legal arena of the inquiry, Nóirín O'Sullivan was thus standing shoulder to shoulder with the senior officers and against McCabe.

The prominent role of the commissioner at the inquiry was questionable in any event because she was required only as a minor witness in relation to a peripheral matter that had occurred back in 2008.

Prior to the setting up of the O'Higgins Commission, most if not all commissions of inquiry involved individuals coming in with representation to give evidence before the chair. This usually resulted in there being about half a dozen individuals with direct interest being present.

In the O'Higgins Commission the room was full of various parties and their legal representatives, including up to forty individuals at a time. Crucially, the Garda commissioner was allowed to have a representative present at all times, a senior officer who reported directly to her.

This created a situation in which all serving officers in a disciplined force who gave evidence did so in front of the commissioner's eyes and ears. If any of them had something negative to say about senior officers, or the corporate approach of the force, this scenario must surely have given them pause for thought, particularly given the fate of the sergeant who was the centre of attention at the commission.

McDowell objected to this arrangement early on but to no avail. He made the point that the prevailing situation would have been akin to the Archbishop of Dublin having a representative present to hear the testimony of the victims of clerical abuse at the Murphy Commission of Inquiry into clerical abuse.

In one submission to the judge, McDowell said, 'It is a most unusual step, bearing in mind what is happening, because members of a disciplined force subject to discipline are being required to give evidence here knowing that everything they say is reported back to the commissioner. That is most unusual and in my view not a private hearing at all in concept and I am just making this point.'

O'Higgins, however, had determined that the arrangement he had constituted was the most appropriate for this particular inquiry.

The act under which commissions of investigation are conducted provides for a draft report to be sent to all concerned parties. This gives everybody the opportunity to read the report and make further submissions if they believe they have been unfairly treated. It is then up to the judge to review the report and decide whether or not adjustments are warranted.

McCabe received the draft report of the O'Higgins Commission in February 2016. He and his legal team were taken aback. Most of the modules involving the criminal cases were fully examined and appropriate conclusions reached. The commission had spotted and dismissed the various attempts to implicate McCabe in any of the complaints. There were, however, other conclusions that McCabe and his team found inexplicable. In particular, the judge had criticised him in a number of instances, and failed to take account, McCabe felt, of transgressions by some senior officers. Most glaring of all, there was no mention of the attempted ambush on day two of the inquiry.

McCabe and his legal team were minded to take legal action to prevent publication of the report in its current form. There is precedent for this kind of reaction to a major inquiry. In 2010 a draft report of the Moriarty Tribunal into the awarding of the second mobile phone licence in 1995 criticised some senior public servants. The individuals felt that the report did not reflect the evidence. Moves were made to have the matter rectified, including a threat to take legal action against the tribunal. The matter was satisfactorily resolved.

Now McCabe and his legal team felt compelled to go down the same route on the basis of the draft O'Higgins report. A draft affidavit was prepared, laying out where McCabe felt he had been unfairly dealt with by the inquiry.

'If this report were to enter the public domain, no witness could give a bona fide account without risk of personal and professional ruination,' he stated. 'I say that many of the participants were given carte blanche to levy accusations against me. I say that the report conceals from the reader the fact that I was, in effect, placed on trial and I was pilloried.'

McCabe touched on the events at the outset where the commission was informed that his motivation would be attacked based on a disputed meeting. After he produced the recording from the meeting, he pointed out, nobody 'was ever called to give evidence [on the matter]. I say that this involved an outrageous manoeuvre and attracted no sanction or condemnation whatsoever.'

Following further contact between the inquiry and McCabe's legal team, a number of adjustments were made to the draft report. The threat of legal action was dropped.

The O'Higgins report was sent to the Department of Justice on 26 April 2016. There followed a period during which the attorney general was obliged to check that the report did not present any legal difficulties. Occasionally, a report like this might have to include some redacted passages if a legal issue arises.

Word got around quickly that the report was with the department. Media speculation filled the vacuum.

On Monday, 9 May, RTÉ radio's *Morning Ireland* programme announced that it had possession of a leaked copy of the O'Higgins report. The station's crime correspondent, Paul Reynolds, went through detailed sections of the report, quoting directly from passages of the 350-page document.

In detailing many of the various cases, Reynolds stated what the judge had ruled about the shoddy work or malpractices, and then what he had said about McCabe. In some of the cases, Judge

O'Higgins had made mildly negative comments about McCabe, particularly that he had exaggerated details in some instances.

Arguably, the comments about McCabe were relatively sparse, and the import minor, compared to the malpractice that he had highlighted. Yet the impression that might have been received by listeners to Reynolds' report was that O'Higgins was consistently critical of the sergeant who had reported the malpractice. Reynolds made little or no mention of the shortcomings of the internal Garda Byrne/McGinn investigation which O'Higgins had highlighted. These comments were at least as prominent as anything the judge had to say about McCabe, yet escaped mention in the broadcast.

In the media and public relations realms, it is received wisdom that the first version of a story is the one that sticks. In the case of the coverage of the O'Higgins report, RTÉ's reporting on 9 May was the first version. Typically, only a very tiny cohort of the public would ever read O'Higgins. The impression of its contents is largely gleaned from the media, and the broadcast on 9 May looked at the time to be delivering the definitive interpretation.

Lorraine McCabe was driving to Granard, Co. Longford that morning to supervise a state exam, a form of work she engaged in annually. She couldn't believe what she was hearing on the radio. 'I was inside in the exam hall after that and my mind was full of it. I just didn't want to have to leave that room. I didn't want to have to face going back out there again with all this stuff coming out over the airwaves. I knew that wasn't the real story, or any true reflection of what had gone on behind closed doors, but that's what everybody was hearing.'

McCabe was at work in Mullingar. He heard the broadcast and also listened with a sense of despair. He recognised some of the phrases used from the draft report. But the presentation of the material was not how he would have interpreted what was written.

Some of those who were familiar with the details of the story were also shocked at the broadcast. Clare Daly, the TD whom McCabe had approached four years previously, rang him that morning. McCabe told her that what was being heard was not a true reflection of the thrust and detail of the report. Daly went on the RTÉ *One O'Clock News* to urge people to await publication of the report before forming any sort of an opinion.

The final report did state that McCabe had exaggerated some claims. One example was the Cafolla's incident. McCabe first reported this incident to the Byrne/McGinn inquiry. Nearly four years after it occurred, years during which McCabe felt he was being intimidated and stonewalled, he reported it to the confidential recipient, Oliver Connolly. By then McCabe was classifying the incident as an 'attempted poisoning'.

O'Higgins ruled correctly that this was an exaggeration. No reference, however, was made to context. By 2012, when he passed it on to Connolly, McCabe was highly disillusioned by the way his complaints had been received and dealt with by Byrne/McGinn. Emotionally and psychologically he had received a battering from the institution he had aspired to serve since childhood.

There were a few other instances in a similar vein. But in each one, any embellishment or overstatement of the facts faded dramatically in light of the malpractice the sergeant was highlighting.

It was also the case that his complaint of corruption against the former commissioner Martin Callinan in 2012 was misplaced. McCabe had claimed that Callinan was instrumental in the promotion of Superintendent Michael Clancy, who, in McCabe's view, had overseen shoddy work and malpractice. (O'Higgins exonerated Superintendent Clancy.)

The allegation of corruption against Callinan in this instance was unfair, and what some might term reckless. But again, by 2012, McCabe was of the view that his complaints were being buried. He saw his allegation of corruption as a tactic to attempt to have an outside body investigate his complaints.

And if such a move was unfair on Callinan, McCabe was operating in a vicious milieu. He had been treated appallingly. Would anybody argue that Mr Callinan had, to put it as its most benign, sought to protect McCabe from any form of retribution within the ranks of the force?

Expecting McCabe to conduct himself through the years in a hostile wilderness as somebody determined to be fair to those he saw as lined up against him would be to regard him as some class of a saint. He was not a saint, nor ever claimed to be.

In time, the origins and content of the 9 May broadcast would form a term of reference in a tribunal set up to examine the treatment of Maurice McCabe by An Garda Síochána.

The O'Higgins report was published on 11 May, two days after the *Morning Ireland* broadcast. A more nuanced, and arguably more balanced, version of the contents began to make its way into the media. Even within RTÉ, versions at great variance with the 9 May broadcast began to be disseminated.

The commission upheld most of McCabe's complaints, making numerous findings of shoddy work and malpractice in the investigations of criminal cases. O'Higgins also made a number of remarks in the report about McCabe, noting that 'the events leading up to and including this commission of investigation have been extremely stressful for him and for his family over a long period of time'. O'Higgins mentioned the Father Molloy computer case where a disciplinary action was pursued, albeit unsuccessfully, against McCabe. 'This was especially upsetting for him because he had no part in that investigation. He also had reason to believe that he was being 'set up' and wrongly implicated in relation to important aspects of the Jerry McGrath investigation. His understandable beliefs in that regard remain unproven.'

McCabe had 'impressed the commission as being never less than truthful in his evidence, even if prone to exaggeration at times'.

Then the report touched on those who 'cast aspersions on Sergeant McCabe's motives': 'Sergeant McCabe acted out of genuine and legitimate concerns, and the commission unreservedly accepts his bona fides. Sergeant McCabe has shown courage and performed a genuine public service at considerable personal cost. For this he is due the gratitude, not only of the general public, but also of An Garda Síochána.

'While some of his complaints have not been upheld by this commission, Sergeant McCabe is a man of integrity, whom the public can trust in exercise of his duties. Assistant Commissioner [Derek] Byrne told the commission that, "Sergeant McCabe is regarded as a highly efficient sergeant, competent". This assessment is shared by the commission.'

The report detailed the shortcomings in the various investigations. Supervision emerged as a major problem. In particular, a number of the cases involved probationary gardaí leading the investigation, with little in the way of supervision. There was some mild criticism of senior officers.

The shortcomings of Byrne/McGinn were also touched on: 'The commission is critical of aspects of the Byrne/McGinn findings, and in particular for failing to address certain specific complaints of Sergeant McCabe regarding the incidents that are the subject matter of this inquiry.'

O'Higgins noted that Byrne/McGinn, in particular, didn't address complaints directed at senior officers. In this, 'the commission considers there was a corporate closing of ranks. The commission does not consider that this was done consciously or deliberately. There was no question of bad faith.'

(The question that does arise is how there can be a corporate closing of ranks not done deliberately.)

Overall, the report was a major vindication of McCabe's complaints and his persistence in attempting to have them rectified. To friends and family, he professed himself perfectly happy with the final outcome after all these years.

Two days after the publication, on Friday, 13 May, the *Irish Examiner* published a front-page story detailing what had occurred on day two of the inquiry. Under the headline 'Garda Commissioner claimed Maurice McCabe was motivated by "malice"', the story related what had occurred, culminating in McCabe's production of the recording of the disputed meeting.

The story took off over the following days, generating extensive political and media comment. On Monday the commissioner felt it necessary to issue a statement:

> Like every member of An Garda Síochána, Sgt Maurice McCabe's contribution is valued and the service has changed for the better in response to the issues about which he complained.
>
> I want to make it clear that I do not – and have never regarded – Sergeant McCabe as malicious.
>
> Any member of An Garda Síochána who raises issues will be fully supported. Each and every one of them must know they have the right and responsibility to raise their concerns and be confident that they will be listened to and addressed.
>
> They won't always be right and we in management won't always be right either.
>
> But we are on a journey towards a markedly better policing service and we will learn from every mistake we make.

The controversy rumbled on. Two days after that statement, RTÉ News – through its crime correspondent, Paul Reynolds – revealed the later exchanges at the commission where Colm Smyth SC said he had erred in his instructions.

Nóirín O'Sullivan announced that she was referencing aspects of the matter to GSOC. This was interpreted classically as kicking the can down the road. Owing to the nature of its work, and stretched resources, any GSOC investigation could take years.

At no point during the controversy did the commissioner contact Maurice McCabe to express concern for his welfare, or regret that there had been a misunderstanding, or to inform him that the story in the media was erroneous. She simply did not pick up the phone to somebody she had described as a valued member of the force.

Ultimately, Ms O'Sullivan emerged from the affair damaged. While an investigation would determine the facts, the perception was that her credibility had suffered a major blow. Since being promoted, she had constantly referred to the force being on 'a journey' of reform, in which it must listen to criticism from within the ranks.

Now there appeared to be something else at play. It didn't look good for Nóirín O'Sullivan, and pretty soon it was going to look a lot worse.

23

'We wanted to destroy you.'
Superintendent David Taylor to Maurice McCabe

McCabe sat in his car for a few seconds. He had found the estate, off Griffith Avenue on the north side of Dublin, with little difficulty. He looked across at the house he was about to visit, wondering what awaited him there. It was a few minutes before 4pm on 20 September 2016. McCabe found an old familiar nervousness making itself known to his senses.

Another meeting with another senior garda. For the best part of ten years he had been attending these meetings, usually to discuss his future, or his claims of malpractice, or an inquiry into his conduct.

This was different, no question about that. But just how different he was about to find out.

He rang the doorbell. Within seconds Michelle Taylor appeared. They had already met twice and now greeted each other with smiles. Once inside, McCabe encountered Michelle's husband, David, the man he had come to meet. They shook hands, both tentative, circling each other. Both knew the other by reputation but they had never met.

Pleasantries were exchanged, and Michelle ducked back to the kitchen. She reappeared with some red wine and cheese and biscuits. All three sat down, Dave and Michelle beside each other. And then Taylor emitted a deep breath, like a man winding up to unburden himself. None of it was going to be easy, this business of confronting his own past and his role in attempting to destroy the man who was sitting before him.

Anybody reading Dave Taylor's CV would have had him down as a man destined for big things. A native of County Tipperary, he joined An Garda Síochána in 1982. After a spell in Dublin he was transferred to Special Branch where he was involved in operations against republican subversives.

In 1997 he was promoted to sergeant, and later inspector. After leaving Special Branch, he moved to Internal Affairs and then went on to Crime and Security.

That particular posting included accompanying the president of Ireland on overseas trips. Photographs of him in the company of both Michael D. Higgins and Mary McAleese adorn the wall of his living room.

Along the way he married Michelle, their family in time expanding to include two daughters. With a varied and well-regarded career, he was an obvious choice for promotion to superintendent in 2012, assigned to head up the Garda Press Office.

This was a plum posting. It guaranteed close access to the commissioner. The elevation of media relations right across public and corporate bodies ensured that the head of the press office in An Garda Síochána would be a valued adviser in headquarters. All the most recent occupants of the office did their few years and left with a promotion to chief super.

Taylor got stuck in to the brief, familiarising himself with the media world, cultivating contacts among the print and broadcasting corps, particularly the crime correspondents.

Among the media he was regarded as a breath of fresh air. His approach was more open than that of his predecessors. It was a demanding and rewarding brief in which the press officer was rarely off the job. From getting a briefing on the early editions of the Sunday papers on a Saturday night to being prepared to respond to anything breaking, to attending impromptu meetings at any time when a story had to be dealt with.

Through it all one figure kept popping up on the agenda of the press office. As far as Taylor could observe, HQ was preoccupied with the whistleblowing sergeant, Maurice McCabe.

This was at a time when McCabe's claims about the ticket-fixing were making serious waves in the Dáil and beyond. The force's dirty linen was getting an airing in the public square and management was entirely discommoded at the spectacle.

An Garda Síochána is a disciplined force, yet here was one of its members effectively defying HQ, making contact with outside agencies and making some of the most serious allegations ever laid against senior management as a collective. Added to that was the sense of impotence that there was little that could be done to put this upstart sergeant back in his box.

Taylor accompanied Callinan to the Public Accounts Committee meeting in January 2014. As press officer, he found himself at the centre of the storm kicked up by the commissioner's 'disgusting' comment.

In terms of the quasi propaganda battle that was developing between headquarters and McCabe, Taylor was at the heart of operations. His role therein would in time come back to haunt him, but as far as he was concerned, he was following orders.

His hectic work schedule continued apace until Callinan's tenure came to an end in March 2014.

On the evening Callinan retired, Taylor passed to an RTÉ reporter a letter that had become a focus of controversy. It showed that, contrary to media speculation, the commissioner had informed the Department of Justice about the recordings in Garda stations, the item that had prompted Callinan's retirement. By then, Taylor's boss had changed. Nóirín O'Sullivan wasn't happy about Taylor performing a task for her predecessor, even though the man had vacated the office only hours earlier. Some within the force saw that gesture as souring relations between Taylor and his new boss.

Worse was to come. Within weeks, Taylor was moved out of the press office. He wasn't totally surprised, but he was disappointed that the move wasn't accompanied by what he had regarded as the requisite promotion. Instead, he was shifted to traffic management.

Meanwhile, in the background, another controversy was brewing. The previous year there had been an erroneous but near hysterical reaction to a story involving children being allegedly kidnapped by Roma families. In the course of a few days, the gardaí briefly took away two children from two Roma families.

The names of the two children were leaked to the media. The outcome was an investigation conducted by the Ombudsman for Children, Emily Logan. Her report was published on 1 July 2014, over two months after Callinan's resignation: 'Sensitive information regarding Child T entered the media inappropriately on the morning of October 22 [2013]. On the balance of probabilities the information in question came from someone within the gardaí,' she wrote.

On foot of that, the commissioner launched an investigation to determine whether somebody in the force was responsible for the leak. She appointed her husband, Detective Superintendent Jim McGowan, to head up the investigation. Pretty soon, focus came onto the former head of the press office.

Taylor was suspended from duty in April 2015 and his phones

and laptop were confiscated. This move ensured that any information retained on the devices was now in the possession of headquarters.

On 28 May 2015, Taylor was arrested at 7.30am when he attended, by appointment, a garda station in north county Dublin. He was held under the Garda Síochána Act, which includes a provision about the release of confidential information. As per procedure, Taylor was held in a cell, and had various personal effects removed from him for the period of his detention. He was the most senior garda ever to be arrested in a criminal investigation. After the twenty-four-hour period was up, Taylor was released without charge and a file was sent to the DPP. In time the Director's office would rule that no criminal charge would be pursued.

Apart from being investigated for the specific offence, Taylor was also subjected to an internal disciplinary investigation. This was headed up by a chief superintendent appointed by the commissioner. Taylor had an exemplary discipline record. Why exactly it was felt that such an inquiry was necessary, particularly since he was already under investigation on a criminal matter, is not known.

The investigation into the leaking of the Roma child's name was entirely appropriate. The information was sensitive, and the child and his family had as much right to privacy as the family of any government minister or captain of industry. However, context is required. Taylor has always denied being the source of the leak. He was not interviewed in the Ombudsman's inquiry. But on the assumption that he was the prime suspect, there are mitigating factors. The culture at the Garda/media interface, developed over decades, ensured that informal contacts between the press office and certain crime correspondents were routine.

Within the force, many felt uneasy at the vigour applied to the pursuit of Taylor. A consensus evolved that if Taylor was to be subjected to inquiry, it should be disciplinary rather than criminal.

Equally, the manner in which Taylor was arrested left many

members uneasy. Yes, he was the subject of a criminal investigation and the investigation team were perfectly entitled to treat him as they would the subject of any other investigation. As Martin Callinan had pointed out in a different context, members of the force did not shirk when it came to investigating colleagues on serious criminal charges.

This was different. Those other other instances involved personal crimes like theft, fraud, assault or sexual crimes. Taylor was accused of leaking the name of a child to a reporter in his capacity as a senior Garda officer. An offence, yes, but not one that portrayed him as a rogue cop or possessing personal flaws of character.

That was the context in which many in the force viewed Taylor's treatment in the investigation. Some had sympathy for him, others were angry at what they regarded as unfair treatment, and even more were just puzzled. 'Proportionality is the big problem,' one former senior garda said in an interview for this book. 'If he did something wrong, so be it, but the scale of the operation that was mounted against him bears no relation to the business of passing names to the media, whether or not he was involved in that.'

By June 2016 Taylor's life had been completely transformed. He was on reduced pay, and his family's standard of living suffered as a result, at a time when his two daughters were going through second- and third-level education.

Since he had entered the force, his working life had been extremely busy. Now the clock crawled as he spent endless hours at home. He enrolled in education courses, but all the time he was battling against what had become of his life. One minute a well-regarded senior garda, working in close proximity to commissioners and presidents, the next something of an outcast, with whom even former colleagues were wary of associating. Those colleagues who were investigating him with what Taylor considered excessive zeal were, as he had once been himself, only following orders.

That was Dave Taylor's station when he came into contact with Maurice McCabe. In early June 2016 an acquaintance of McCabe's had been in touch with Taylor on a separate matter. In the course of a conversation, Taylor expressed regret for what had been visited on McCabe by senior management over the years.

Some weeks later this was conveyed to McCabe in a casual manner, but the sergeant found it interesting. Where was this guy coming from? McCabe had known Taylor only by reputation and by sight from television on the numerous occasions he was seen on the shoulder of Martin Callinan. Now he was sounding as if he was on McCabe's side. He asked the acquaintance for Taylor's phone number.

One evening a few days after receiving the number, McCabe was sitting at home when he decided to take the plunge. He dialled and got an answer.

'Dave?'

'Who's this?'

'Maurice McCabe.'

There was a pause.

'Hello, Maurice.'

'Can you talk there a minute?'

'Not just now. I'll ring you in the morning.'

The call took Taylor by surprise. He felt agitated when the call ended. What did this fella want? Did he know that Dave was in a vulnerable place? What did he know? What the hell did he want?

Taylor couldn't face into a conversation with McCabe unprepared.

He didn't ring the following morning, but his wife did. Michelle told McCabe that Dave was a in bad place and not really up to meeting. It was true that he was feeling emotionally fragile, but it was also the case that he had great trepidation about facing McCabe.

Instead, Michelle suggested to McCabe that she meet him. A few days later, they met in the Skylon Hotel on the Swords Road, near the Taylors' home. Michelle reiterated that Dave was in a bad place, and sent his apologies.

She poured out to McCabe all that her family had had to endure since Dave's ejection from the inner sanctum of the Guards and his subsequent suspension. It soon became obvious to McCabe that she was sussing him out, checking whether he might harbour any animosity towards Dave Taylor. Through it all, she displayed a burning sense of grievance at what had befallen her husband.

They parted, resolving to meet again, next time perhaps with Dave. Another meeting was subsequently arranged, but once again Michelle Taylor came alone to the Skylon. After that, the summer intervened. McCabe had organised an extended family holiday in France where his daughter was studying.

Once he returned, contact resumed and the meeting for 20 September was arranged, to take place in the Taylors' home.

'We wanted to destroy you,' Taylor told him. Over the course of four and a half hours, as the sun went down and the night drew in, David Taylor unburdened himself to Maurice McCabe in the Taylors' front room. He went into detail of how he had been involved in a campaign of black propaganda against McCabe in his role as head of the Garda Press Office. The objective was to destroy McCabe's credibility by any means available, and in particular to spread false and scurrilous rumours about his character.

It should be noted that the senior officers whom Taylor claimed were either privy to or directing such an operation deny any knowledge whatsoever of its existence. Yet Taylor is adamant that he is speaking the truth.

There were a number of strands to the campaign, he told the incredulous McCabe. The most basic was the conveyance of hundreds if not thousands of text messages to media and Garda personnel casting McCabe in a bad light.

Journalists were briefed that McCabe was a person against whom an allegation of sexual abuse had been made. 'I did always clarify to the journalists that a file had gone to the DPP and that there was no prosecution,' Taylor later revealed in a statement. 'However, this was the narrative. It was put in such a way that there was no smoke without fire.' Taylor was prepared to believe anything that was passed to him in relation to McCabe. He didn't question its origins or veracity. Many within his circle believed the worst of this Cavan-based guard who would not leave them alone.

He told McCabe that an intelligence file had been created on him in Garda HQ. The file was kept under a Christian name, which correlated with the name of the offspring of a senior officer.

An intelligence file is created only if the subject is suspected of a serious crime, usually involving violence. Yet HQ, according to Taylor, saw fit to place McCabe in such company.

Twice, as he poured out his confession, Taylor broke down. He was in a highly emotional state confronting his past. When he was doing his job, following orders as he saw it, McCabe was simply regarded as the enemy.

McCabe's head was spinning. He knew that management had been discommoded by his complaints, knew that he'd had to battle along the way, but this was off the scale. At one point he told Taylor that there was a lot of information coming at him, and he'd like to take notes if that was okay. Taylor said had had no problem with that.

One incident that Taylor related was the meeting between Martin Callinan and John McGuinness in January 2014, ahead of McCabe's appearance at the Public Accounts Committee. In May 2016, following controversy after the publication of the O'Higgins report, McGuinness had told the Dáil about the meeting with the commissioner in a hotel car park.

Now, four months later, Taylor added further context. He told

McCabe that, Callinan had been in Dundalk, about to give a press conference on the first anniversary of the murder of Garda Adrian Donohoe. Such was his eagerness to meet McGuinness that he postponed the media event and drove down to Dublin. All this to convey to John McGuinness that McCabe was not to be trusted.

Sitting there, taking all this in, McCabe found himself having to suppress a rising anger. The man seated before him was telling him of a conspiracy at the upper echelons of the force which he, McCabe, was serving, designed to destroy him. Everybody else at HQ would deny that there was any such conspiracy that they were aware of, but McCabe accepted Taylor's bona fides.

The confession went on until 8.30pm, some four and a half hours after McCabe had arrived at the house.

Once back in his car, he texted his solicitor Kathryn Ward, who was working with Seán Costello and had been by his side through the darkest days at the O'Higgins Commission. Something major had come up. Following further communication, he travelled to the home of his barrister, Michael McDowell, to inform his legal team of what had just unfolded.

At the house, the gathering quickly came to the conclusion that this was a major development. It was also soon agreed that there was only one way to deal with it. McCabe had come into possession of information that alleged some serious wrong-doing at the highest level of the force. The fact that he was the target of the wrong-doing was secondary to possession of the information itself. Therefore, his only course of action was to make a protected disclosure about the allegations. (A protected disclosure is a new form of whistleblowing introduced in legislation in 2014. It provides for somebody to report malpractice or illegality and to be protected in law from any retribution at work.)

It was close to midnight when he got back on the road to Cavan.

As Maurice drove up the M3, the anger that he had suppressed during the meeting kept rising to the surface.

Here, alone with his thoughts, the effects of what he had heard began to settle in his consciousness. They had tried to destroy him. He believed he knew what they were capable of after what had happened at the O'Higgins Commission, but this was on a different plane altogether. And the 'they' who were doing it were not some aliens, not some hardened criminals, or anonymous beings with an agenda against An Garda Síochána. 'They' were An Garda Síochána, his own people, the force he had aspired to join, sworn to serve, and served faithfully. They had tried to destroy him.

The following day McCabe rang Taylor and arranged to meet him again. There were a couple of things he wanted to clarify.

They met at Taylor's home the day after that. McCabe asked him again about some of the details relating to the text messages. Then he informed Taylor that he was obliged to make a protected disclosure on the matter: 'You've told me this stuff and if I don't pass it on, I could be accused of being complicit,' he told Taylor.

Taylor shrugged. He hadn't objected to the note-taking at their first meeting. He knew that once he had agreed to meet with McCabe, nothing would be held back. He knew that through McCabe's travails, the sergeant had managed to keep his head above water by ensuring that he always acted according to the law.

Having accepted that McCabe was going to make a protected disclosure, Taylor then concluded that he also would make one in order to protect himself.

Over the following days, both men separately put together disclosures. Taylor's was largely based on what he knew, McCabe's on what Taylor had told him. McCabe also included what he believed had transpired at the O'Higgins Commission which, in his opinion, amounted to another example of elements in the force setting out to destroy him.

The two disclosures were handed in to the Department of Justice on 29 September 2016. The story broke in the *Irish Examiner* the following Tuesday, 4 October, although the identities of the gardaí involved were not made known in the initial report.

That afternoon, Fianna Fáil leader Micheál Martin raised the matter in the Dáil: 'I do not know if the Taoiseach has read the report in today's *Irish Examiner* in relation to whistleblowers being strategically undermined and under attack, both their personal and professional reputations, at the instigation of senior Garda management,' he said. 'It demands a fairly dramatic response from the government. It cannot just be allowed to drift into a process.'

The Taoiseach expressed himself suitably concerned. The following day Clare Daly called in the Dáil for the Garda commissioner to resign. Within hours the Garda Press Office released a statement on behalf of the commissioner: 'Commissioner O'Sullivan would like to make it clear that she was not privy to nor approved of any action designed to target any Garda employee who may have made a protected disclosure and would condemn any such action,' said the statement. 'It would be inappropriate for An Garda Síochána to comment on the specifics of any protected disclosure.

'In order to maintain public confidence in An Garda Síochána, we are anxious that the full content of the disclosures giving rise to the commentary be comprehensively examined at the earliest opportunity.'

By the end of the week the Minister for Justice, Frances Fitzgerald, had appointed a retired judge to examine the disclosures to see whether or not they warranted a full statutory inquiry.

Judge Iarfhlaith O'Neill got stuck into his task, and once more the heat was temporarily released from a Garda controversy. Some thought the whole affair would be shunted off into a sideline where controversies often go to die.

Not this time. For over the horizon, on the far side of Christmas, there awaited the biggest shock of all in relation to the Maurice McCabe story, one that would chill many citizens to the bone.

24

'Our personal lives and our family life, and the lives of our five children, have been systematically attacked in a number of ways by agencies of the Irish state and by people working for the state in those agencies.'
Maurice and Lorraine McCabe

Maurice and Lorraine McCabe had one overriding concern about the review into Superintendent David Taylor's claims. One of the allegations about the scurrilous rumours spread about Maurice was that he had sexually abused his own children.

Processing the fact that this stuff was actual currency among some elements of the force was difficult enough. Even more worrying was the prospect that it could find its way into the public domain. By late 2016 the couple's five children now ranged from the early twenties down to eight. Throughout the turbulent and traumatic years, Maurice and Lorraine did everything possible to protect their offspring. Now this had come along like something designed to thrust them into a deeper hole of despair than any already experienced.

O'Neill completed his report and passed it to the Department of Justice on 6 December 2016.

It wasn't until late January that word began to seep out from government buildings that a decision was imminent. On Tuesday, 7 February 2017, the cabinet approved the setting up of a commission of investigation into the claims that there was a campaign to smear Maurice McCabe from within the Garda Síochána. Supreme Court judge Peter Charlton was announced as the chair of the new commission.

The commission would centre on David Taylor's claims that such a campaign existed. Included in this were allegations that Commissioner Nóirín O'Sullivan was involved in the smear campaign.

When asked whether the government would request the commissioner to stand aside for the duration of the inquiry, Justice Minister Frances Fitzgerald replied that what was being examined were only allegations: 'There is no prima facia case against anybody,' she said.

The following day in the Dáil, matters took a different turn. Brendan Howlin, the leader of the Labour Party, told the House that he had been given information from a journalist that Garda commissioner Nóirín O'Sullivan had in the past forwarded information to journalists alleging that Maurice McCabe was guilty of 'sexual crimes'.

This was the first time that it had been stated in public that the attempts to smear McCabe had included the spreading of rumours of sexual crimes. Howlin was protected from any defamation because the utterances were made in the House. And, to be fair to him, his motivation was obviously to highlight the wrong done to Maurice McCabe, rather than to add to the man's woes.

Later that day, the Garda Press Office issued a press release on behalf of Nóirín O'Sullivan denying that she had engaged in what Howling had alleged. In the statement she denied 'in the strongest possible terms the suggestion that she had engaged in the conduct alleged against a serving member of An Garda Síochána'.

Issuing denials was becoming a habit for the commissioner. The previous May she had to deny that she had been involved in an attempt to smear McCabe at the O'Higgins Commission. In October 2016 she had denied any knowledge of what Dave Taylor had alleged was a campaign in HQ to smear McCabe. And now she had to come out again to set the record straight as she saw it.

All that, though, was about to fade into the background. For within twenty-four hours of Howlin's utterances, a bombshell was about to land that would dwarf any other strands of the public narrative concerning the smearing of Maurice McCabe.

The most bizarre and disturbing aspect of the scurrilous rumours propagated about McCabe had its origins in a visit by Ms D to a counsellor on 24 July 2013. This was the woman who had made the allegation in 2006 about an incident she alleged had happened in the McCabe home around 1998. As seen in previous chapters, this had been dealt with and revisited by various parties in the media and in the O'Higgins Commission in 2015. Now though it was about to emerge that there was yet another strand to this narrative.

Ms D attended for counselling on 24 July 2013 over issues she was having. One, she later said, was that she was hearing Maurice McCabe's name and it was bringing up old feelings for her.

By July 2013 McCabe's name had not featured in the print or broadcast media, but his name may have been prominent locally over the ticket fixing controversy. At the session, she revealed the 2006 allegation again and said it had been dealt with.

The counsellor contacted Tusla to inquire whether this disclosure was on file and was erroneously told that it was not. As a result she compiled a retrospective disclosure form as she was obliged to do.

Then the major mistake. In compiling the form she used a template that mixed up the actual allegation – catagorised as horseplay when it was first made – with another case involving child rape.

The allegation now was that Ms D was alleging that at the hands of McCabe she had 'suffered sexual abuse in childhood that this abuse involved digital penetration, both vaginal and anal'.

It also included a line that 'the alleged perpetrator of this abuse threatened her father if she said anything'. These statements were utterly false, and involved a completely separate allegation in the counsellor's files with a different alleged perpetrator and victim.

That error, as it was classed, would not be discovered for nine months.

In the interim, there was a catalogue of errors and omissions around the whole issue. In August 2013, a few weeks after the counselling disclosure, a social worker wrote to Superintendent Noel Cunningham, who had investigated the original allegation in 2006-7. She wrote that she wanted to meet him to discuss that allegation in light of the Ms D bringing up the allegation again.

Cunningham received the letter after returning to work after extended leave. He set it aside to be dealt with but, he would later explain, it slipped his mind due to a heavy workload.

The following April, a social worker got around to examining the erroneous alleagation. She prepared intake records on the four McCabe children which had been on file since 2007. (Their fifth was born in 2008). This was done on the basis that the allegation of child rape suggested their father may pose a danger to them. By April 2014, two of the McCabe children were over eighteen, but their names still recorded as if they were minors. The children's names in the file were prefixed with the word 'suspect', and were referenced as being 'in contact with alleged perpetrator of sexual abuse'.

The social worker also prepared a notification for the garda, as is standard in instances of allegations of child abuse.

The notification was sent to Bailieboro station, and opened by

Superintendent Leo McGinn. He was surprised at what he saw and called in Ms D's father, Mr D, who worked in the station. Mr D said he would check it out.

When he contacted his daughter she reacted in horror, telling him that she made no allegation of child rape. She then rang the counsellor, and put in train attempts to have the error rectified.

The counsellor compiled a report on what had gone wrong. (In her original report, she referenced the woman who is now knowns as Ms D as Ms X).

'On page one of the original "Retrospective Disclosure of Abuse Report" I sent on behalf of Ms D, under the title "Description of Abuse" the subsequent three sentences contain incorrect information. The information erroneously placed in this report pertains to a different client of mine whom I shall refer to as Ms Y to maintain confidentiality ... in this one section where I was to describe the nature of the abuse suffered by Ms D, I had mistakenly described the alleged abuse suffered by Ms Y.'

It would also emerge that within the gardai the erroneous allegation was sent first to the divisional officer for Cavan/Monaghan and then onto the Assistant Commissioner for the region. He in turn submitted a report to Garda HQ on the matter. Thus, by June 2014, there was a report in HQ that the garda whistleblower, the man who had been a thorn in the side of management, had been accused of child rape. So a series of errors had blown up an allegation of "horseplay" – as catagorised by the local state solicitor – from the daughter of a colleague with whom McCabe had some history – to one of abusing a child in the most grievous manner.

The McCabes were totally unaware of these issues. Nobody informed Maurice McCabe that a file had been created that had effectively branded him as a suspected child rapist. Neither the HSE nor Tusla considered it their duty to inform a citizen that this had occurred. McCabe's employer, An Garda Síochána, was also aware that this had, to a greater or lesser extent, been in circulation between August 2013 and May 2014. Nobody told McCabe. Nobody felt it necessary and proper that he be informed. All this would come to light when he eventually got access to the file.

It may well be a coincidence, but the timeframe in question – August 2013 to May 2014 – was a significant one in Maurice McCabe's story.

In August 2013 his concerns about corruption in fixing tickets were alive, but appeared to have been dealt with and largely dismissed by an internal Garda investigation.

Over the following months, he became a major thorn in the side of the force and the government as he pursued his concerns all the way to the Public Accounts Committee in January 2014. Around this time he lost his anonymity. He was no longer a faceless whistleblower but Maurice McCabe, whom the PAC had regarded as highly credible.

Soon after, articles began appearing in the Irish Independent about a garda whom, it was alleged, had sexually abused and grievously affected on the physical and psychological wellbeing of a young girl.

In February 2014 McCabe's dormant complaints about malpractice in criminal investigations were reactivated through the intervention of Mick Wallace and Micheál Martin. In March the Garda commissioner resigned.

Then in May the spurious allegations were suddenly discovered to be erroneous.

There the matter may have rested. Maurice and Lorraine may never have known what had gone on, but for another startling mistake.

On 29 December 2015, some eighteen months after the spurious allegation was discovered and corrected, another social worker wrote to McCabe, telling him he might be a risk to children. It outlined an allegation of 'abuse allegedly involving digital penetration' when 'the victim was 6/7 years old'. The social worker requested a meeting to assess whether further investigation of his character was required.

'If the assessment outcome is that you may pose a risk to children, I will have to bring this view to the attention of any relevant third party. This may include your employer or your family.'

On reading the letter, McCabe felt an old familiar tightening in his stomach, except this was worse than anything that had gone before. At the time, the hearings for the O'Higgins Commission had just been completed, bringing to an end eight months of high stress during which McCabe had been on medication. The O'Higgins draft report was due within weeks. And now this.

His solicitor, Seán Costello, wrote back, pointing out that the allegation was 'wholly untrue', and relating the history of the other allegation that had been investigated: 'What you may not know is that our client, when originally informed of the complaint, insisted that [the girl] be interviewed again in the presence of an independent social worker and that her allegation be carefully recorded. Both her accounts were sent to the DPP in the file.

'The DPP not merely directed that no prosecution take place, but you should know that the DPP clearly stated that no criminal offence had been described or disclosed in the complaint.'

It was six months before Tusla finally got back to Costello with an apology, pointing out that the letter had been sent in error without reference to the discovery in May 2014 of the 'administrative error' about the serious sexual abuse.

The McCabes wanted to know the full story, so they applied under the Freedom of Information Act for the file on the whole affair as pertaining to Maurice McCabe. Another six months elapsed before they got the full reply. Only then, in January 2017, did what had been perpetrated against them become apparent. The most wounding aspect was the opening of files on their children, deemed to be at risk.

The weeks after receiving the file were among the darkest that the McCabes had experienced since Maurice first reported malpractice in Bailieboro in 2008, about the management and investigation of criminal cases. One scenario that kept emerging from the darker recesses of their imagination involved leaping decades into the future. What if they had not discovered all this through the error of the social worker who had written to them a year previously?

What if decades down the line one of their children had found themselves thrust innocently into a scenario where a routine background check was made on them. And there on file would be an allegation that they may possibly have been abused as children on the basis of a serious allegation of sexual abuse against their father. The potential for the damage to reach down through the generations did not bear thinking about.

And all through what? An 'administrative error'? Of all the administrative errors, of all the allegations, concerning all the people in the country, this one has to involve the whistleblower, the man who had been a giant pain in the neck to An Garda Síochána. .

Once the black mood lifted, Lorraine felt anger and rang the Minister for Health to demand an explanation for how her family had been treated. She was well received but directed to the Minister for Children, Katherine Zappone.

On 25 January Maurice and Lorraine met Zappone in her ministerial office. They found her both receptive and horrified at the detail of what had unfolded. Her concern for their plight was such that Maurice found himself apologising for impinging on her busy schedule, but she waved away any concerns. She said she would get back to them, but events were to overtake any plans.

The commission of investigation was announced on Tuesday, 7 February 2017 and Howlin's intervention came the following day. Then on the Thursday the story about Tusla broke on the *Irish*

Examiner website, and that evening was followed by a major report on RTÉ's *Prime Time* by Katie Hannon.

The reaction was immediate, with political, media and public opinion reeling in shock over the details of how the McCabe family had suffered.

The revelation in the *Irish Examiner* that the McCabes had met Katherine Zappone kicked off a political furore. When two days previously the cabinet had set up a commission of investigation, Ms Zappone was at that cabinet table in possession of information which suggested that the investigation should be much wider than envisaged. Why did she not tell her colleagues? Or did she?

The political furore developed to a point where Enda Kenny revealed he had had a conversation with Zappone ahead of her meeting with the McCabes. Zappone denied this and Kenny was forced to apologise in the Dáil for his faulty recollection of a conversation that had never taken place. The incident was badly received within his party, ending with a resolution that he set a particular timetable to step down as Taoiseach, as he had already pledged to do.

Meanwhile, the McCabes were not letting the matter rest. On 13 February solicitor Seán Costello released a statement on behalf of Maurice and Lorraine.

> We have endured eight years of great suffering, private nightmare, public defamation, and state vilification arising solely out from the determination of Maurice to ensure that the Garda Síochána adheres to decent and appropriate standards of policing in its dealings with the Irish people.
>
> Our personal lives and our family life, and the lives of our five children, have been systematically attacked in a number of ways by agencies of the Irish state and by

people working for the state in those agencies.

These events have, one way or another, given rise to a long series of state investigations, ranging from internal Garda investigations (disciplinary and administrative), the Fennelly Commission, the O'Higgins Commission, several GSOC investigations (some of them targeted indirectly at Maurice), and investigations within HSE and Tusla (some of them targeted at both of us and some of them concerning what those agencies have done to us) and the reports of Seán Guerin SC and former Judge Iarfhlaith O'Neill. All of these have taken place in private.

We have also been the subject of a long and sustained campaign to destroy our characters in the eyes of the public, and public representatives and in the eyes of the media.

Today, we have heard one Minister, Simon Harris, state that we are entitled to 'truth and justice'.

We wish to make it clear that we are definitely not agreeable to that entitlement being wholly postponed so that another Commission of Inquiry can conduct a secret investigation behind closed doors and make a report, into which we have no input as of right, in nine or eighteen months' time.

We are entitled to the truth today – justice can follow in its wake.

The Need For A Public Inquiry

Our experience of the O'Higgins Commission of Investigation is too fresh in our minds to allow for a repetition. Although that Commission investigated a number of serious instances of malpractice in the policing function in Bailieboro and upheld Maurice's complaints in respect of all of them, the public has never been made aware that, throughout the proceedings before that Commission, Maurice, at the hands of the legal team representing the current Commissioner, was cast in the role of culprit and/or defendant, and as a person making those complaints in bad faith and without cause.

When challenged in that respect, that legal team sought and obtained confirmation from the present Commissioner that they did so on her personal instructions.

Because the 2004 Act prohibits under pain of criminal law the publication of the actual evidence tendered to such Commissions, the public has little or no appreciation of what was done, and attempted to be done, to Maurice in the course of its hearings.

For example, against the background of the current Tusla controversy, the entirely false allegation made of sexual abuse in 2006 against Maurice was repeatedly the subject of attempts at introduction in the proceedings for the purpose of discrediting his motives and testimony.

The entire transcript of that Commission (to which we still have access) is also in the possession of the Minister for Justice and Equality and the foregoing comments can easily be verified by inspecting same.

For these reasons, we have consistently submitted that any further inquiry into these matters must be a public inquiry.

Now that the truth has emerged of the false and shocking campaign to vilify us and discredit us, there is no reason to have any secret or private inquiry under the 2004 Act.

The statement went on to detail all the questions that has arisen from what was emerging about how Maurice McCabe had been badly wronged by the entirely false allegation generated within the child protection services.

The request for a public tribunal, as opposed to a commission of investigation behind closed doors, met with universal approval. Later in the week the government announced that the original commission of investigation, which had been announced the previous week, would now be replaced by a tribunal to include the Tusla allegations. Judge Peter Charlton agreed to chair the tribunal. The McCabes' allegations of what had transpired at the O'Higgins Commission were also to be included in this new tribunal.

The following month an *Irish Times* Ipsos MRBI poll found that more than 70% of respondents felt that the Garda commissioner should step aside for the duration of the tribunal or resign. Half of all respondents felt that confidence in the force had been damaged as a result of the revelations about Garda whistleblower Maurice McCabe.

25

'Ultimately the gradual erosion of discipline within An Garda Síochána
is a developing situation that will, sooner or later, lead to disaster.'
Retired Judge Frederick Morris

By early 2017, the McCabes had been through nearly a decade of living on the wrong side of An Garda Síochána. These were the years through which their children grew and matured, taking formative steps towards the future, while their parents grappled fiercely with the present. Years that were to a certain extent lost in stress and worry.

Once the shock of the Tusla revelations died down, Maurice and Lorraine were able to take a step back. Another inquiry, this time a public one, was due, but Maurice would not be the main focus.

The substance of the inquiry concerned the treatment of Maurice McCabe, but now it was for others to answer as to how they had conducted themselves through this long, unwinding story.

The personal toll has been huge. But what of the actions of Maurice McCabe? It is safe to say that what he did and what he endured has resulted in the biggest upheaval in a force that was badly in need of substantial reform.

Until the early years of the twenty-first century, An Garda Síochána had been largely untouched by changes that swept across policing in the western world since the mid-to late twentieth century. In places such as the USA, the UK and Australia, various scandals and investigations uncovered police practices that were corrupt in one form or another.

In some cases this involved officers on the take. In others it was the treatment in custody of suspects, often people from minority groups. Yet elsewhere it was police practices in pursuing convictions by illegal means. All this was unfolding at a time of greater awareness of human rights and the requirement for accountability in the police.

The fallout included inquiries and reform in places like New York, New South Wales, Queensland, and within a number of police forces in the UK. Irish observers were particularly aware of corrupt and illegal practices in the UK as Irish citizens such as the Birmingham Six and Guildford Four were wrongly convicted and served long prison sentences.

There were rumblings in Ireland about police practices from the 1970s on. In particular, there was copious evidence that suspects associated with republican groups were ill-treated in custody in attempts to extract confessions. Stories were legion about one particular loose group of gardaí, known as 'the heavy gang'. (One of those associated with the alleged heavy gang told a court years later that the gang never existed, but was an invention of the media.)

Two government ministers at the time would later relate that they had been informed by gardaí that others in the force were abusing suspects. Garret FitzGerald would say that he was shocked and intended to deal with it but the matter slipped away through the blizzard of issues with which his government was dealing.

Conor Cruise O'Brien later related that a garda had told him of others 'beating the shit' out of a suspect in a particular case. O'Brien related that he hadn't been too concerned at the news.

To a large extent the failure of the body politic to address garda malpractice could be attributable to the conflict in Northern Ireland. The great fear was that the violence might spill across the border. As a result, the gardaí's role in the security of the state insulated the force from scrutiny. For some politicians, the Guards were all that stood between the Republic and anarchy.

This ensured that few questions were ever asked of the force and the methods deployed by some of its members. There was precious little accountability. One might even conclude that to a large extent An Garda Síochána was a law unto itself.

Scandals persisted right through the 1980s, including the Kerry Babies Tribunal, which examined why members of a family could have been charged with murder, when no murder had occurred. Then in 1997 another scandal, this time in County Donegal. Following the death of a cattle dealer named Richie Barron, a family in the town of Raphoe, the McBreartys, came under intense scrutiny from the gardaí. Wrongful arrests, intimidation and harassment all followed. Eventually, the persistence of Frank McBrearty and that of a private detective he retained, Billy Flynn, uncovered what was afoot. A tribunal chaired by retired judge Frederick Morris was set up to investigate police practices in the county. Eight reports were published, the final one in 2008.

There was much breast-beating about the shocking revelations from the tribunal, most principally on the matter of discipline: 'An Garda Síochána is losing its character as a disciplined force .... Ultimately the gradual erosion of discipline within An Garda Síochána is a developing situation that will, sooner or later, lead to disaster,' Morris reported.

Some reforms were enacted. The Garda Síochána Act 2005

introduced a Garda ombudsman for the first time. There was also provision to set up a Garda Inspectorate to oversee standards and process in the force.

These measures and others met with resistance in a force that had no interest in oversight or outside interference. The effectiveness of GSOC was blunted by the resistance, and the body politic showed little interest in beefing up the powers of GSOC.

The Garda Inspectorate produced – and continues to produce – some fine reports detailing what is not being done properly and how it should be done.

Change, however, came dropping very slowly. The 2005 Act was a good start in instilling accountability, but even more so than other vested interests, the gardaí were well capable of undermining any attempts at outside agencies looking in.

In the same year that Morris delivered his final report, across the state in another border county, a sergeant's frustration was about to initiate a journey that would both endorse Morris's view and bring reform onto a whole new plane.

The issues that Maurice McCabe highlighted have had a major impact on the force. In October 2014 the Garda Inspectorate published a report into crime investigation. Included were the issues that McCabe had highlighted in Bailieboro. The Inspectorate found that what had transpired in Bailieboro was more the rule than the exception.

Among the report's conclusions was the following: 'While the Guerin Report identified issues in the investigation and prosecution of crimes in one district, extending to a division, the Inspectorate's report found these same issues across seven divisions in all regions. The findings of the Crime Investigation Inspection has resulted in a significant number of recommendations, designed to improve the initial actions taken during the investigation of a crime, to ensure accurate recording of incidents and to ensure that crimes are investigated properly and to a good standard.'

The Inspectorate and the state's chief accountant, the Comptroller and Auditor General, also endorsed McCabe's complaints about abuse of the fixed charge notice system of sanctions for road traffic offences. (In this McCabe was assisted by former guard John Wilson.)

The issues that McCabe brought to the fore led to a major increase in the powers of the Garda ombudsman, GSOC. Before 2014 the ombudsman had experienced major obstructions to investigations into members of the force at every turn. Following the controversy about the ticket-fixing, new powers of investigation were provided to the Garda ombudsman.

The Policing Authority was also established in the wake of McCabe's actions. The impetus for the authority was the political fallout over how the sergeant's complaints had been handled. The authority has the potential to be the biggest transformative instrument in policing.

In 2017 it emerged that there had been nearly one million false breath tests recorded at mandatory alcohol-testing checkpoints. In April of that year the Public Accounts Committee began examining financial irregularities at the Garda training college in Templemore. The details of how public funds were used and even diverted in one case to a private entity were shocking. It also emerged how senior management within the force had appeared for years to be reluctant to do anything about the irregularities.

The impetus for the matter to be finally redressed came from the civilian members of management who had been drafted in to the force in recent years. The head of Human Resources, John Barrett, summed up in a letter what he had discovered about the affair, and could well be applied to the travails of Maurice McCabe: 'The ugly truth tends to recur if it is not properly root-caused and appropriate lessons genuinely learned,' he wrote.

Maurice McCabe was not the first garda to challenge from within the ranks the ways that things were done. Down through the years there have been others who felt that they couldn't simply turn a blind eye to a culture that fell well short of what was required of a law-enforcement agency. Others raised the problems and attempted to have them examined. They were all, to a greater or lesser extent, stymied. The power of the force to silence contrary voices, as demonstrated in this book, can be overwhelming to anybody against whom it is directed.

At various times elements within the force made an issue of his motivation. Some claimed that everything changed for McCabe following the allegation in 2006 from his colleague's daughter, Ms D. This school of thought has it that his disillusion with the force was directly attributable to his belief that colleagues did not rally to assist him at a time when he was highly vulnerable.

The allegation was roundly dismissed by both the local state solicitor and the DPP's office. But McCabe did have an issue with the investigating member around how long it took to inform him of the outcome. Later, a problem arose over a failure to ensure that the D family were informed of how emphatic was the rejection of the allegation. In an organisation known for circling the wagons when something goes wrong, there was no circling for McCabe, as he saw it, when he had done nothing wrong and would have appreciated more support.

The fall-out from the allegation certainly shook him. It may well have dented his confidence in the organisation he served with dedication. But any notion that his later complaints were motivated by malcontent on the back of this experience falls well short of a credible explanation. There is copious evidence that things were pretty shaky in the Bailieboro district for some time, and the fact that practically all his complaints were upheld speaks for itself. What stands out about Maurice McCabe's story is his persistence in pursuing the complaints once he embarked on that road.

He succeeded where others failed. His success was achieved against awesome odds. He did not just have to face down powerful internal pressures within the force, he also found himself up against powerful elements in both politics and the media.

One thing that worked in his favour through it all was the tendency of many to underestimate him. For some, this upstart Garda sergeant from a rural outpost in the north-east had to be put back in his box, lest he discommode those who ran the country and shaped opinion. Many of those who dismissed him would eventually come to regret their initial assessment that Maurice McCabe couldn't be the sharpest tool in the shed.

He was, to some extent, lucky. He was lucky in his family, in those he met along the way, in the stupid moves of some who opposed him. He was also astute. In at least four instances his efforts to highlight malpractice could have come a cropper had he not recorded conversations with other members of the force.

Most of all, though, he was persistent, bolstered by a number of strong character traits at various points on the journey. He was propelled by a sense of righteousness early on, just as he was by a sense of grievance in the later stages. He also has a reservoir of stubbornness that ensured that there was to be no turning back. As his wife Lorraine declared of a stage in 2011 when it looked like his endeavours had come to the end of the road, 'It was never over with Maurice. He was like a dog with a bone. They weren't going to get the better of him.'

Two others who travelled the hard road with him also referenced his character as key.

'It took a serious amount of mental strength to keep going through several years,' Mick Wallace said. 'He was able to keep that up. He stayed in control of himself and I'm sure it wasn't easy at home. But the Guards will never be the same again and nobody has done more to change things than Maurice McCabe because of the risks he took with his career, his family, his life. He laid everything on the line.'

Clare Daly has grappled with the juxtaposition between the 'mild-mannered man' she encountered back in 2012 and the impact that same individual has had: 'It's unprecedented. Never before did somebody from the inside come out and show how it all happened. He's a very untypical hero but there is no doubt that Maurice is a catalyst that will change policing for the better but it also showed up the way that they reacted to him and how it came out and was laid out for everybody to see.'

As Judge Kevin O'Higgins noted, McCabe did the state some service. Of that there is now little doubt. But one overriding question overhangs his odyssey. At what cost?

In early 2017 Lorraine McCabe was asked to put down on paper her version of what the preceding nine years had been like. The exercise was required in preparation for a legal action to be taken by the family against An Garda Síochána. She did so, and here is an edited version of what she compiled.

In 1993 I married a decent, honourable and, above all, an honest man. For the last 9 years, because of these admirable traits and his decision to challenge the system for all of the right reasons, his life has intentionally, relentlessly and systematically been rendered intolerable for him at every turn. This has had a profound and very destructive effect on me, my children, my marriage and on our life as a family.

The events of the last 9 years have taken a very heavy toll on Maurice's psychological health and general wellbeing. Needless to say, whilst the difficulties that we have had to deal with all stem from work-related matters, it has been utterly impossible for Maurice to leave these difficulties 'at work', particularly as the systemic campaign against Maurice and attempts to vilify and discredit him were largely conducted outside the work environment. Accordingly what happened and how it was handled by 'the system' has permeated every aspect of our home life.

It is usual in a marriage to be able to turn to your partner for support. In my case, given the pressure that Maurice has been under, I have not felt able to burden him further at times when I would have ordinarily needed support. I have largely had to cope with other trials and difficulties in our lives, including the death of both of my parents, alone. I have also had to shield Maurice from many of the day to day family concerns, regarding the children and otherwise, what would ordinarily be dealt with together. As such, at times in the past 9 years, I have parented alone.

Maurice will testify to the direct effects that the events had on his psychological and physical wellbeing. I can corroborate all that he attests to. As a wife, the manner in which he was treated and the effect that it had on him has been a source of immense and ongoing distress to me. I have witnesses first-hand on a daily basis his tremendous angst at what has happened to him; his utter devastation on foot of the vile rumours, innuendos and the accusation that he has been forced to defend, and his/our immense fear at what may come to pass.

Worry has been my constant companion for the last 9 years. Given the systematic/constant bullying and isolation to which he has been subject at work, I have been continually concerned for Maurice's welfare while at work. I have been equally fearful at times that he may never come home. No wife should ever have to live from day to day with such stress, taking comfort only when her husband walks through the door. Now when all of this is over, I worry about the future and will we ever recover from the trauma of it all.

I am very angry now when I think of how close they were to destroying us, it's frightening and I can't get it out of my mind, and for what?

Maurice was the most dedicated of guards, he lived for his job, he never set out with the intention of things developing as they did. Had they only met him halfway, we would be in a different place today. But no they hammered him at every opportunity, it was relentless.

One of the most difficult episodes for me was when Maurice was so low that he was admitted into St John of Gods for help. I will never forget the desperation I felt that night after leaving him and driving home alone and wondering how I could shield the children from this.

We have five children, the eldest of whom is now 21. Tom was only a baby when all of this began. Given the length of time over which this has endured, despite my best efforts their entire childhoods have been marred. All of the usual family events and celebrations since this began have been impacted on one way or another by the situation in which Maurice has been placed. In addition to the general pall cast over any celebration by virtue of what has been going on in Maurice's work life, simple things, like choice of venues for family events, were also influenced by what was happening.

Furthermore, the run-up to any events that had a public dimension (e.g. First Holy Communion) was filled with dread in case another story would 'hit the press' and ruin the occasion. I have also had to constantly worry about the next item of publicity, to figure out how to shield our children from its effect and to worry about what they might have heard in the school yard. Many times I have simply chosen to abandon plans and to stay at home rather than face the world in the wake of yet another story.

We live in a small community where we have deep roots but

where anonymity is impossible. I am deeply concerned about the impact that this has had on how we are perceived as a result of which I now limit my activities within the community. I have also suffered the embarrassment and ignominy of being publicly shunned by garda colleagues of Maurice (and their spouses). This has not only been extremely demeaning but has also caused me to limit my activities and has taken a toll on my confidence.

I am very concerned of the psychological damage that Maurice has suffered over the last 9 years and particularly through the O'Higgins commission. I feel he is severely damaged by the false evidence that was being introduced, in a very sinister attempt to destroy him, and I believe in my heart that this was orchestrated by the most senior of garda officers.

The period of the O'Higgins commission was very difficult and I am only discovering now exactly how torturous it was for Maurice, he was put on trial and used up every ounce of energy he had in defending himself, days, nights, weekends going through piles of paperwork and recordings.

And then we had the leaking of the report. I can't describe the hurt this caused and the damage it has done to Maurice. Robert heard this on the bus going to school and phoned me quite distressed as to what it was about. How can you tell an 18-year-old not to worry about this, how can you explain to him how rotten the system is.

Our lives have been destroyed, for years we lived in fear and now that fear has turned into extreme anger at what they tried to do and how things could have ended but for the relentless fight we had to endure and the tireless work of our legal team.

I am still married to a decent, honourable and above all an honest man. However, he, I and our children have paid a very high price for his honesty and his decision to challenge the system in the interest of others.

And yet, through it all, chinks of light, little reminders of what he has done, who has been affected.

The function room in the Bloomfield House Hotel was full. Ordinarily, this is where weddings, club events, annual dinners are held, all offering the chance to meet and be merry.

On 20 November 2016 a very different emotion permeated the room. The occasion was World Day of Remembrance for Road Traffic Victims, which falls each year on the third Sunday of November.

The function is organised by the Irish Road Victims' Association. Gathered were around 400 relatives and some friends of those whose lives had been lost on Irish roads. Many carried framed photographs of their deceased loved ones. For some, this has turned into an annual pilgrimage, a chance to remember in a structured environment the lives cut short.

Strangers who find themselves seated beside one another quickly fall into conversation, as if reaching out to mine shared experience for some small helping of solace. Few who attend ever regret doing so, while most head for the hills with at least a small measure of comfort.

The growing significance of the event is reflected in the presence most years of those who work in the field of road safety, through government departments and agencies such as the Road Safety Authority. In 2016 members of An Garda Síochána were also present, most prominently from the traffic unit of Mullingar.

Also present at a separate table was Maurice McCabe, who had been specifically invited to attend.

On the day in question, the families gathered in the function room for some remembrance around 2pm, a few songs and stories and a light snack. Afterwards the gathering filed out of the hotel and down to a lake that nestles in the accompanying grounds. There, balloons were released into the winter sky, each representing a lost life.

Then it's back inside for dinner and a brief ceremony to present awards.

One of the awards presented on the day was that of Ambassador of the Year for Road Safety and Road Victims. The association's chairperson, Donna Price, introduced the award with an address about the recipient.

'The road traffic legislation is there to protect all road users and to keep our roads safe for everybody,' she said. 'When that law is not seen to apply even-handedly or when an investigation is not thoroughly conducted, the integrity of the whole justice system is called into question and our bereaved families are left to live with the consequences.

'In 2012 Sergeant Maurice McCabe had concerns in relation to fines and penalty points being wiped from drivers who had numerous penalty points wiped already. He shared his concerns with colleagues and reported his concerns to the Confidential Recipient. He also went to An Taoiseach, the Department of Justice, Department of Transport, the RSA, the Comptroller and Auditor General.

'These steps taken by Maurice resulted in a number of reports, audits and inquiries being commissioned, each of which Maurice engaged with fully and where the vast majority of his complaints were upheld.

'It's fair to say that Maurice had an uphill battle trying to stop the culture. He was ridiculed, sanctioned and not believed until he finally met Noel Brett of the RSA who believed him and who started the ball rolling with the then Minister for Transport to stop this abuse of the penalty points system.

'The internal report in An Garda Síochána concluded there was a small problem in what Sergeant McCabe was alleging. Three independent reports done by the Comptroller and Auditor General, the Garda Inspectorate and the Public Accounts Committee into the penalty points allegations concluded there was widespread abuse of the system by senior officers which was impacting on road safety and resulting in serious loss of revenue.

'For his very courageous endeavours at great personal cost, for the good of all of us, we have great pleasure in presenting Maurice with our Ambassador of the Year Award for Road Safety and Road Victims.'

The announcement was met with applause. McCabe rose from his seat near the back of the room and walked to the stage. Within seconds people began getting to their feet. By the time he shook the hand of Donna Price as she handed him the award, the whole room was standing, including those at the table hosting the gardaí.

The applause fell off and he stepped up to the microphone. 'I tried to make a difference,' he said, 'and I think I have.'

Afterwards, when proceedings were brought to a close, a stream of people made their way across the room to his table to shake his hand. Among those who did so were most of the gardaí in attendance.

ACKNOWLEDGEMENTS

Many thanks are due to those who contributed along the way. I am very grateful to everybody who gave of their time and, in particular, to Lorraine, Maurice and the McCabe family. Thanks are due to Kieran Williams, John Wilson, Mary Lynch, Clare Daly, Mick Wallace, John McGuinness, and Noel Brett. There are many others, including retired and serving members of An Garda Síochána who prefer not be identified, who provided valuable information and insight.

Tim Vaughan, the former editor of the *Irish Examiner*, was totally supportive of the pursuit of this story from its earliest stages. Many thanks are due to him and to the rest of the editorial management at the newspaper, including John O'Mahony and Allan Prosser.

Maureen Gillespie waded through the early chapters in their rawest form and offered valuable advice. My mother Aideen supplied the bread and water when I was locked away in Cork breaking the back on this project. She also provided helpful suggestions with her reader's eye.

John Burke and Shane Coleman were generous with their time and insight.

Thanks to all at Hachette, particularly Ciara Considine, who was a diligent and supportive editor.

Luke and Tom Clifford survived the weekends and kickabouts foregone.

The biggest debt of gratitude, as always, goes to Pauline, for everything.

This book is dedicated to the memory of my father, John Clifford, who died in 2016. John never met Maurice McCabe but, in researching this book, I discovered that he had once stayed at the Sheelin Shamrock while on a fishing trip. Maybe a teenage Maurice McCabe served him his breakfast on that occasion, before a day out on the lake.

John often voiced particular admiration for individuals who had the courage to stand apart from the herd. I like to think he would have got a kick out of this story of one man's fight for justice.

The publishers and author would also like to thank *The Irish Times/* Miriam Lord and the *Anglo-Celt* for permission to reproduce excerpts from published articles.